N'

Money and Exchange in Canada to 1900

by A.B. McCullough

Published by Dundurn Press
in co-operation with
Parks Canada and
the Canadian Government
Publishing Centre
Supply and Services Canada

Dundurn Press Limited
Toronto and Charlottetown
1984

Acknowledgements

The preparation of this manuscript and the publication of this book were made possible because of assistance from several sources. The author and publisher are particularly grateful to Parks Canada, and to the Publishing Group, Canadian Publishing Centre, Supply and Services Canada. The publisher acknowledges the ongoing generous financial support of the Canada Council and the Ontario Arts Council.

J. Kirk Howard, Publisher

Copyright© Minister of Supply and Services Canada
Catalogue No. R64-158/1984E
ISBN 0-919670 86 5

Editor: Blaine R. Beemer
Design and Production: Ron and Ron Design Photography
Typesetting: Small Faces Typography Inc.
Printing and Binding: Les Editions Marquis, Canada

Dundurn Press Limited
P.O. Box 245, Station F
Toronto, Ontario
M4Y 2L5

Canadian Cataloguing in Publication Data

McCullough, A. B. (Alan Bruce), 1945 –
  Money and exchange in Canada to 1900

Published in collaboration with Parks Canada.
Bibliography: p.
Includes index.
ISBN 0-919670-86-5

1. Money - Canada - History. I. Parks Canada.
II. Title.

HG652.M22 1984   332.4'971   C84-099218-1

Money and Exchange in Canada to 1900

by A.B. McCullough

Contents

Illustrations..8

Tables..11

Preface..14

Introduction and Definitions.......................................17

1. New France..25
2. The Province of Quebec, Lower Canada,
    Upper Canada, the Province of Canada,
    and the Dominion of Canada, 1760 – 1900..............55
3. Acadia, Ile Royale and Nova Scotia.....................119
4. New Brunswick..161
5. Prince Edward Island...185
6. Newfoundland...205
7. Western Canada..225
8. Common Threads...245

Appendix A: Commercial Exchange Rates...................251

Appendix B: Intrinsic Value of the Silver Dollar...........282

Appendix C: Army Sterling and Customs Currency........286

Appendix D: Currency Conversion Table.....................289

Appendix E: Monetary Weights...................................293

Appendix F: Conversion of Shillings and Pence to
    Decimal Currency...294

Notes...295

Bibliography 311

Index...321

Illustrations

Sample of coins in New France, 1660 – 1700

    Louis d'or, 1670..26

    Louis d'argent, 1653..26

    Douzaine..26

Sample of currency in New France, 1730 – 1750

    Louis d'argent, 1709 and 1718.............................27

    Sol, 1739...27

    Double sol, 1739...27

    24-livre card, 1742...28

    3-livre card, 1749...28

Sample of currency in Lower Canada, 1780 – 1800

    Guinea, 1787...56

    Moidore, 1723...56

    Johannes, 1759...56

    Spanish (Peruvian) dollar, 1790...........................56

    Louis d'argent, 1753...57

    Pistareen 1722..57

    Bon 1788...57

Bills of exchange
Bill of exchange drawn on
    Harley and Drummond......................................58
Bill of exchange drawn on
    The Hudson's Bay Company.............................59

Sample of coins and tokens in Upper Canada, 1830 – 1840

    U.S. eagle, 1803..60

    Mexican dollar, 1834..60

    U.S half-dollar, 1806...60

    Shilling, 1834..60

    Bank of Montreal 1d. token, 1842.........................61

8

Brock token 1816 61

Wellington token..61

Sample of paper money in Upper and Lower Canada, 1810 – 1840

$10.00 army bill, 1815...62

$1.00 Bank of Montreal note, 1819...........................62

25s./$5.00 Bank of Upper Canada note, 1826..............63

10s./$2.00 City of Toronto note, 1838.......................63

Sample of central Canadian circulation, 1867

U.S. eagle, 1847..64

Sovereign, 1829..64

U.S. half-dollar, 1861...64

Canadian 20¢ piece 1858 64

U.S. dime, 1857..65

Canadian 10¢ piece, 1858.......................................65

U.S. half-dime, 1853...65

Canadian 5¢ piece, 1858...65

$1.00 note, Province of Canada..............................66

$2.00 note, Gore Bank, 1852..................................66

Sample of coins in Nova Scotia, 1830

Chilean doubloon, 1819...120

Spanish (Mexican) doubloon, 1804..........................120

U.S. dollar, 1799..120

British half-crown, 1820...121

Province of Nova Scotia halfpenny token, 1823.......121

Commercial Change halfpenny token, 1815..............121

Paper money in Nova Scotia

£1 treasury note, Province of Nova Scotia, 1854.......122

Paper money in New Brunswick

5s. note, Bank of New Brunswick, 1820...................162

£5 note, Bank of New Brunswick, 1838...................162

Sample of coins in Prince Edward Island, c.1815
    Guinea, 1798..186

    Bank of England dollar, 1804................................186

    Bank of England 3s. piece, 1814............................186

    "Holey" dollar..187

    Plug from "holey" dollar....................................187

    British penny, 1807...187

$10.00 Union Bank of Newfoundland note, counter-
    stamped by the Government of Newfoundland.......206

Hudson's Bay Company notes for 1s. and £1 sterling.......226

Tables

1. Revaluations of French Coins, 1602 - 1726...................43
2. Card Money and Treasury Notes Used in Purchasing Bills of Exchange.....................................47
3. Coins Found in the Wreck of the *Auguste*.................53
4. Ratings of Coins under Military Rule.......................68
5. Ratings of Coins Established by the Ordinance of 14 September 1764...............................70
6. Ratings Established by 17 George III, An Ordinance for Regulating the Currency of the Province of Quebec, 1777..76
7. Ratings Established by 36 George III, C.5 1796, Lower Canada and 36 George III, C.1, 1796, Upper Canada......80
8. Revised Rating for Doubloons, Louis d'or and French Pistoles, Established by 48 George III, C.8, 1808, Lower Canada, and 49 George III, C.9, 1809, Upper Canada...81
9. Ratings of Postrevolutionary French Coins Made Legal Tender in Lower Canada by 59 George III, C.1, 1819, Lower Canada................................90
10. Ratings Established for British Silver by 7 George IV, C.4, 1827, Upper Canada..................................94
11. Ratings Established by 6 William IV, C.27, 1836, Upper Canada...97
12. Ratings Established by 4 - 5 Victoria, C.93, 1841, Province of Canada....................................104
13. Average Weight of Principal Coins in Circulation In Lower Canada c.1830 and 1840 Compared to their Mint Weight...105
14. Ratings Established by 16 Victoria C.158, 1853, Province of Canada....................................109

15. Customary and Legal Ratings in Canada, 1860..........111

16. Paper Currency in Circulation in Upper and Lower Canada and the Province of Canada, 1812 - 1855
....115

17. Ratings Established by 28 George III, C.9, 1787 Nova Scotia..136

18. Customary and Legal Ratings of Coins in Nova Scotia, c.1805..137

19. Treasury Notes Authorized in Nova Scotia, 1812 - 1862 140

20. Customary and Legal Ratings of Coins in Nova Scotia,1822..144

21. Customary and Legal Ratings of Coins in Nova Scotia,1836 and 1842...150

22. Ratings Established by 23 Victoria, C.3, 1860, Nova Scotia 157

23. Paper Money in Circulation in Nova Scotia, 1812 - 1867 158

24. Ratings Established by 26 George III, C.16, 1786, New Brunswick...165

25. Treasury Notes Issued in New Brunswick, 1805 - 1818
....167

26. Ratings in New Brunswick in 1821 as a result of 26 George III, C.16; 58 George III, C.22; and 60 George III C.25...169

27. Ratings in New Brunswick in 1844 under 26 George III, C.16; 58 George III, C.22, s.3; 5 William IV, C.7; and 7 Victoria, C.29.......................................176

28. Ratings Established by 15 Victoria, C.85, 1852, New Brunswick...180

29. Bank-Notes in Circulation in New Brunswick, 1820 - 1867 182

30. Ratings Established by Order in Council of 22 September 1813, Prince Edward Island....................190

31. Ratings Established by 12 Victoria, C.24, 1849, Prince Edward Island...196

32. Ratings Established by 34 Victoria, C.5, 1871, Prince Edward Island...202

33. Treasury Notes, Treasury Warrants, Bank-Notes and Coin in Circulation in Prince Edward Island, 1825 – 1871 202

34. Proposed Ratings in Draft Legislation, Newfoundland, 1845 212

35. Ratings Established by 19 Victoria, C.11, 1856, Newfoundland 217

36. Ratings Established by 26 Victoria, C.18, 1863, Newfoundland 221

37. Newfoundland Coinage Issued after 1863 222

38. Ratings Established by 58 Victoria, C.4, 1895, Newfoundland 224

39. Estimates of Money in Circulation in British Columbia and Vancouver Island, 1860 – 1870 244

40. Quebec and Montreal Prices of Sterling Exchange on London, 1760 – 1899 266

41. Halifax Prices of Sterling Exchange on London 1757 – 1879 274

42. Sterling Value of Silver Dollars, 1700 – 1848 285

43. Currency Conversion in British North America 292

Preface

The history of money and exchange in Canada provides an excellent introduction to the history of money in the western world. During the period 1600 – 1900 Canada, in common with other nations facing the Atlantic, experienced major changes in its monetary system. Beginning the period with a bimetallic system which was dominated by Spanish-American silver, Canada ended the period with a monometallic, gold standard, system. Canada was among the first of the western nations to experience government issued paper money; at first it was viewed with suspicion but by 1900 government and bank issued paper money had replaced both gold and silver coins as the common circulating medium throughout Canada and most of the western world.

This study of the money which circulated in Canada before 1900 and the rates at which it was valued in Canadian currency was originally prepared as a guide to interpreters at National Historic Parks and as an aid to Parks Canada's historians, archaeologists and material culture researchers working with seventeenth, eighteenth and nineteeth-century documents and accounts. It is now published as an accessible and comprehensive treatment of the history of money and exchange in Canada, of value to historians, economists and numismatists.

Readers are forewarned that this is a study of money and exchange; it does not attempt to deal with prices or relative values.

I wish to thank Irene Spry for reading and commenting on the chapter "Western Canada"; T.J. O. Dick, University of Lethbridge; Douglas McCalla, Trent University; Angela Redish, University of British Columbia; and Gordon Bennett, Parks Canada, for reading and commenting on the manuscript. Graham Esler, Chief Curator and Head of the Currency Museum of the Bank of Canada, provided invaluable advice on numismatic matters. Kenneth Donovan, Historian at the Fortress of Louisbourg, provided advice on the currency of Ile

14

Royale. I alone, of course, am responsible for the opinions expressed in the paper and for any errors which it contains.

The standard bibliographic references cannot adequately acknowledge the debt which this volume owes to the late Dr. Adam Shortt. His published works, and more particularly the notes on monetary history in his papers in the Public Archives of Canada, have illuminated the more obscure corners of Canadian monetary history.

I also wish to thank the Bank of Montreal and the Hudson's Bay Company for permission to consult copies of their records in the Public Archives of Canada and the Canadian Historical Association for permission to incorporate exchange rate data from Julian Gwyn's "The Impact of British Military Spending on the Colonial American Money Markets, 1760 - 1783" in the tables of commercial exchange rates. Photographs are reproduced with the permission of the Public Archives of Canada, the Archives of the Hudson's Bay Company and the National Currency Collection, Bank of Canada, photographer, James Zagon.

Introduction and Definitions

Money, broadly speaking, is a commodity which can be conveniently divided into units of a standard value and used as a medium of exchange. Traditionally the commodities used as money have been gold, silver and copper. For ease in calculation these metals were generally divided into coins of a standard weight and purity. Pure gold and silver were too soft to be used alone in making coins and were alloyed with a harder metal. From the seventeenth to the nineteenth century a typical gold or silver coin was about 90% precious metal and 10% alloy.

Gold or silver which has not been coined or worked is called "bullion" and is not generally considered to be money, but a commodity; coins themselves may be converted to bullion by melting or may, if valued merely for their precious metal content, be considered bullion. If their face or "nominal" value is less than their value as bullion, they may be melted down (although this is often illegal) and sold as bullion. If their face value is substantially more than their value as bullion they may be described as debased or "token" coinage, and individuals will not willingly receive them at their face value but will take them at a discount equal to the difference between their face value and their market value as bullion.

"Specie" is either gold or silver coin or bullion but the term is usually applied only to coins; this book will use that narrower definition.

I will also make use of two archaic terms, "real" money and "ideal" money. Seventeenth and eighteenth-century writers referred to coins as real (that is, physical) money to distinguish them from money of account, which they called imaginary or ideal money. I have adopted the terms because they emphasize the distinction between what we now refer to as cash, and the bookkeeping credits and debits which are our money of account. The distinction is an important one in understanding the development of the monetary systems in seventeenth, eighteenth and nineteenth-century Canada, because the units of real money often did not correspond to the units of ideal money.

The development of paper money as a substitute for coin is a relatively recent phenomenon. Basically, any written promise by one party to pay money to a second party which can be transferred to a third party is a form of paper money. In practice, paper money is more narrowly defined as a promise to pay which can be transferred to a third party without endorsement, which does not bear interest, and which is issued in standard denominations. Originally, paper money was not considered to be real money; it was a promise to pay in real money, in coin. During most of the period of this study it was not legal tender: it did not have to be accepted in payment of a debt, and creditors could demand to be paid in gold or silver coin instead. So long as holders of paper money were confident that their paper money could be exchanged for coin, paper money was accepted at its face value; insofar as this confidence was impaired, paper money lost its value. Sometimes governments decreed that paper money had to be accepted at face value whether or not it could be redeemed in coin – but such decrees could often be evaded. During the nineteenth century, paper money gradually came to be regarded more and more as real money and less as a promise to pay in coin. Today in most economies paper is the principal form of real money and coin has taken a secondary role as fractional currency or change.

In addition to real money, coins, and more recently paper money, there are moneys of account, which are imaginary or ideal moneys used for accounting. Today the units used in moneys of account usually correspond with units of real money. Thus the pound sterling is represented by a coin, the sovereign, or by a £1 bank note, and the shilling and penny are represented by coins of the same names. However for about 100 years prior to 1817 there was no British coin which was equal to the £1 sterling, the largest unit of the money of account. Prior to the adoption of decimal currency in British North America, accounts were kept in Halifax *currency* which used the pound, shilling and pence as units of account; but there was no £1 Halifax currency *coin*.

There are two types of exchange: exchange of coins (*cambium mintum*) and exchange of bills (*cambium per litteras*). *Cambium mintum* is the giving or receiving of one type of money for an equal value of another type of money. Typically it involves the relationship between moneys of different states (foreign exchange) but it may also involve the exchange of coin for bullion, or paper money, or the exchange of coins for other types of coins of the same state, particularly of gold for silver or vice versa. In a sense which is particularly relevant to colonial America, it may involve converting real money to a money of account.

In exchange of coins the rate of exchange is determined by the precious metal content of the coins involved. In transactions involving exchange of gold for silver, the difference in value of gold and silver must also be considered. From the seventeenth to the nineteenth century the silver-to-gold price ratio in western countries ranged from about 14:1 to 16:1. (Today with gold at $350 per ounce and silver at $7.60 per ounce, the ratio is about 46:1.)

The statement of the exact value of one coin in terms of another coin is the "true par" between the coins. For example, the U.S. gold eagle, worth $10.00, contained 232.2 grains of pure gold and the British sovereign, worth £1 sterling, contained 113 grains of pure gold. The true par between the eagle and the sovereign was $113 \div 232.2 = .4866$. Since the two coins were the principal coins in the American and British currency systems, the true par between them was taken as the true par between the currency systems, so that $4.866 was equal to £1 sterling.

Because it was impractical to determine the exact pure metal content of every coin in every transaction, calculations were usually made on the basis of a par established by law or custom, the nominal or "customary" par. The nominal par was not always the same as the true par. For example in 1703, British tests established that the average Spanish dollar was worth about 4s. 6d. sterling. Through custom and law this remained the nominal par until at least the 1820s although as the silver content of the dollar declined the true par fell to 4s. 4d. and then 4s. 2d. sterling.

When coins are rated in terms of money of account or when two monies of account are compared, it is usually in terms of a customary or nominal par. For example, Halifax currency was based on the Spanish dollar which was rated at 5s. currency, an increase of one-ninth over its customary sterling value of 4s. 6d. Other coins were also rated at one-ninth over their sterling value and sterling money of account was converted to currency by the addition of this amount. This ratio, £111.11 Halifax currency to £100 sterling,[1] remained the accepted or nominal par into the 1840s and 1850s even though, as a result of the decline in value of the silver dollar and other factors, the true par was about £121 currency to £100 sterling as early as 1825.

Cambium per litteras or exchange of bills is a transaction by which debts of individuals residing at a distance from their creditors are cancelled without the transmission of real money. Typically the debtor (the payer) purchases a bill of exchange which is an order by one party (the drawer) to a second party (the drawee) to make a payment to a third party, the creditor (the payee). Having purchased his bill of exchange, which was usually issued in triplicate or quadruplicate, the payer sends it to the payee who then presents it to the drawee. After a specified period of time (usually 30, 60 or 90 days), the drawee pays the payee the face value of the bill. "Sight bills" are paid immediately upon presentation although 3 days of grace may be allowed.

The price which a payer pays for a bill of exchange compared to its face value is the commercial rate of exchange. If the payer has to pay more than the face value of the bill to obtain it, the bill is said to be at a "premium". If he pays less, the bill is at a "discount". If the payer pays only the face value, the bill is at "par". The price paid for bills is determined by several factors. First, since the payee does not get his money for some time after the bill is presented to the drawee, the payer is in effect making a loan to the drawer and his interest is deducted from the face value of the bill. Also the reliability of the drawee affects the price paid: bills on reliable drawees fetch higher prices than bills on unreliable drawees. Supply and demand also play a major role in the price of bills. Finally, the cost of shipping coin affects the price of bills of exchange, for if the cost of bills rises too high the payer can ship coin to his creditor and avoid buying a bill of exchange.

Bills of exchange involve moneys of account, not real moneys. If a bill is purchased in one money of account and paid in another, the exchange between moneys of account has to be considered in the price although in reality it does not affect it. The value of one money of account in terms of another money of account is the "nominal par of exchange". For

20

example, if a payer in Quebec City purchased a £100 sterling bill on London at par and paid for it in sterling he would pay £100 sterling, but if he paid for it in Halifax currency he would pay £111.11. £111.11 Halifax currency was the nominal par of exchange; in this case it was also the commercial exchange rate. If sterling bills were at a 3% premium the payer would pay £103 sterling or £114.44 Halifax currency. If they were at 3% discount he would pay £97 sterling or £107.77 Halifax currency.

In the above examples the commercial exchange rate has been compared to the nominal par; in fact the commercial rate is more closely related to the true par and is usually a good indicator of the true par. If the commercial exchange rate is consistently and substantially (say 5 – 10%) above or below the nominal par, it is a good indication that the true par and the nominal par are different.

This book describes the various aspects of money and exchange as they apply to Canada before 1900. It details what money, both coin and paper, was in common use, the relative importance of the various types of coins, and the values assigned to different coins by custom and law. It also describes the money of account which was used at various times and places and the relationship of this money of account to sterling, that is, the nominal par of exchange. Finally, it deals with bills of exchange, principally sterling bills drawn on London, and the commercial or market rate of exchange. Appendix A contains a series of commercial exchange rates for Montreal/Quebec and Halifax bills drawn on London from 1760 to 1900.

Although I have organized material on a colony-by-colony basis there is a common thread which runs through the monetary history of Canada: the search for a sufficient and reliable circulating medium. In the seventeenth, eighteenth and early nineteenth centuries both British and French colonists in North America complained that the coinage in circulation was inadequate for the needs of the colonial economies. Because they had neither mines nor mints to produce more coins, North American colonial governments regularly overvalued foreign coins (in effect devaluing their own moneys of account) in hopes that foreign coins would be attracted to the colonies.

The complaints of a shortage of specie have been treated with scepticism by some historians and economists. For example, A. Redish notes that the idea of a scarcity of specie "is directly contradictory to a fundamental tenet of the theory of international trade and finance. Since at last the mid-eighteenth century, economists have argued that, in the long run the world's supply of specie metals will automatically distribute itself among nations so that each will be in monetary equilibrium."[2] Redish argues that Canada suffered the effects of Gresham's law ("bad money drives out good") and that when colonists complained of a shortage of coin, the complaint should be taken to mean a shortage of *good quality* coin. In fact there is evidence that only poorer quality coin circulated in Canada and that better quality coin reposed in strongboxes. Whether there was an "adequate" amount of either bad or good coin cannot be known because prior to the 1820s there are no satisfactory estimates of the amount of money in the colonies. It does seem important that colonists believed the supply was inadequate. Redish also notes that colonists' views of coinage were coloured by mercantilism, a school of thought which tended to equate coin with wealth, and which saw the export of coin as sapping national wealth. She suggests that "monetary historians have too readily accepted the mercantilist fears" embodied in colonists' statements about shortages of coin.[3] It is true that historians should consider this context in their interpretations of colonists' statements. On the other hand, they cannot disregard the context in explaining the colonists' actions, particularly as they relate to currency legislation.

When devaluation failed to attract an adequate supply of coin, most of the colonial governments experimented with the issue of government paper money. Paper money provided a quick and cheap solution, but its reliability was another matter. Unlike coins, paper money has no intrinsic value and is subject to depreciation if it is overissued. Colonial governments' motives in issuing paper money were mixed: in addition to supplying a circulating medium, paper money served as a cheap alternative to taxation or borrowing in government finance. As a result there was a temptation to issue more notes than the goverment's credit or the economy's needs would support. There was always danger that an overissue of notes would lead to depreciation of the currency. In fact there was massive depreciation in New France and New England but in most jurisdictions this government-caused inflation remained a manageable problem.

Similar dangers attended the issue of private bank-notes. Nevertheless in the 1820s and 1830s the colonies witnessed the rapid growth of private banks and in the century after 1830 private bank-notes dominated the Canadian circulating medium. Bank-notes were not totally reliable: banks occasionally failed, causing losses to noteholders, and bank-notes were often at a slight discount to coin; nevertheless they provided a generally satisfactory currency until the mid-twentieth century when the last private bank-notes were withdrawn from circulation.

Chapter One

New France

Sample of coins in New France, 1660–1700

louis d'or, 1670

louis d'argent, 1653

douzaine, counterstamped with a fleur de lis

Sample of currency in New France, 1730–1750

louis d'argent, 1709

louis d'argent, 1718

sol, 1739

double sol, 1739

24-livre card, 1742

3-livre card, 1749

Little is known for certain of money or exchange during the early years of the colony at Quebec. From 1608 to 1660, when the affairs of the colony were in the hands of various trading companies, it is unlikely that much money circulated. Internal trade was probably carried on by barter and accounts kept with the company.

What money did find its way to the colony would have been French, or possibly Spanish, since Spanish *pistolles* and their fractions were legal tender in France. The French monetary system was similar in concept to the English system; both could trace their antecedents to the Carolingian, and perhaps to the Roman system. In both the English and the French systems the original unit of account had been a pound (English "pound", French "livre", Roman "libra") weight of silver which was divided into 20 units (English "shilling", French "sou" or "sol", Roman "solidus"), each of which was further divided into 12 units (English "penny", French "denier", Roman "denarius"). Both the English pound and the French livre were primarily monies of account and were not necessarily represented by coins; during the entire period under discussion there was no French coin equal to one livre and during the eighteenth century there was no English coin equal to one pound. Moreover, by the seventeenth century both the pound and the livre had been greatly devalued: in 1640 the pound represented only .2984 pounds troy of pure silver and the livre only .0225 pounds troy of pure silver.

Although both the English and French systems had originally been based on a silver standard, by the seventeenth century both had a bimetallic standard. In France the principal gold coin at the beginning of the seventeenth century was the *écu d'or*, valued at 3 livres 5 sols in 1602, and 5 livres 4 sols in 1636 (see Table 1). The principal silver coin was the *quart d'écu*, valued at 16 sols in 1602.[1] Fluctuation in value of the coins in terms of money of account was typical of French coinage throughout the seventeenth and eighteenth centuries. Some changes in the rating of coins were made in an effort to keep the relative values of gold and silver coins equal to the relative market values of the two metals and so keep both types of coins in circulation. More often, increases in the ratings of coins were made in an effort to attract gold and silver to France or to remedy the inadequate finances of the French government. As well as changing the ratings, the French government, particularly in the years 1709-26, made frequent changes in the gold and silver content of the coins.

The first major French recoinage which affected Canada was that of 1640 – 41. The écu d'or was replaced by the *louis d'or*, containing 116.53 French grains (see Appendix E) of pure gold and the quart d'ecu was replaced by the *louis d'argent* (also known as the *éscu blanc*) containing 473.74 grains of silver. The louis d'or was also issued in doubles and halves and the louis d'argent in halves, thirds, quarters, fifths, sixths, twelfths and twentieths. The older coins continued to be minted (the quart d'écu until 1646 and the écu d'or until 1656) and remained in circulation for many years. A few half-écu and quart-d'écu were found in the treasury at Quebec in 1725.[2] However, the louis d'or, the louis d'argent, their subsidiary coins, and various copper coins were probably the first coins to appear in the colony in quantity.

The copper coinage consisted of *deniers*, double deniers, and, after 1649, *liards*. The denier was a coin of so little value that it did not circulate in Paris and after 1664 was not current in Canada. Liards were valued at 3 deniers in France until 1658 when they were revalued at 2 deniers. In 1658, 15- and 30 – denier silver pieces called *sols* and double sols were minted.[3] These coins were among the first small French coins to be minted by machine rather than by hand. In Canada, where they were quite common, they were dubbed *sols marqués* to distinguish them from handmade sols. Unfortunately for our understanding of coinage in Canada, the sobriquet was transferred to several later issues of varying denominations.[4]

The louis d'or had originally been valued at 10 livres and the louis d'argent at 3 livres, but by 1652 the ratings were increased to 12 livres and 3 livres 6 sols. This increase was evidently followed in Canada for in 1654 when the coins in France were reduced to their original value, the council in Quebec ordered that all coins in Canada should be reduced by a similar amount except that one-eighth should be added "pour les risques de la mer".[5]

Measures to Attract Coin

This reference to increasing the value of coins circulating in Canada is the first official notice of the practice, but as early as 1636, coins had been rated at 25% above their value in France.[6] The practice was not unique to Canada: virtually all of the English colonies to the south followed similar policies. The overvaluation of coin in Canada was ended by the French government in 1717 but was reintroduced under British rule and continued until the adoption of decimal coinage. The reason given for the overvaluation of coin in 1654 was that it was to cover the risks of the sea – but a more common reason was that it would attract coin to the colony and keep it there.[7] Another, often unstated rationale for overvaluing coinage, was that at least in the short term, the resulting inflation could benefit both colonial governments and colonial debtors. Significantly, the home governments and creditors in the home country usually opposed overvaluation of coin.

The preoccupation of the colonists with attracting coins may be difficult for the modern reader to appreciate. Today, coins are used almost exclusively for small transactions and for making change. This was an important function in earlier periods and shortages of small coins led to inconvenience in small day-to-day transactions, but the importance of coins in the seventeenth, eighteenth and nineteenth centuries went far beyond small change. Coins were the only legal tender, the only form of payment which could not legally be refused. They were the basic and most reliable form of money. Paper money was a recent innovation, subject to forgery by individuals, to overissue with resulting depreciation, and to repudiation by the issuing agency. The precious metals from which coins were produced had an intrinsic and remarkably stable value which made the coin a secure store for surplus wealth. Coins were also given importance by the leading economic theory of the seventeenth and early eighteenth centuries, mercantilism. Mercantilism identified precious metals, or coined money, with wealth. Because there was a finite amount of precious metals, wealth was acquired, not created. Nations became wealthy by acquiring coin from other nations. The colonists, in seeking to attract coins to their jurisdiction, were simply copying the policies of the home governments.

Evidently the increase of one-eighth in 1654 was not sufficient to attract coin or to cover the risks of the sea, for in 1661 the colonial council ordered that the quart d'écu should pass at 24 sols in New France and others in proportion. Assuming that the quart d'écu was in fact a *lis d'argent* valued at 20 sols, this represents an increase of 20% in the valuation of coins in Canada. Only a year later the colonial council revalued the coins again, rating the louis d'or at 14 livres 13 sols 4 deniers, the louis d'argent or silver écu at 4 livres, and the lis d'argent or quarter écu at 26 sols 8 deniers. There is some confusion as to whether this represented an increase of one-quarter or one-third on rating in France. Ten years later the increase was definitely established at one-third and remained at that level until 1717. As a result, from 1672 to 1717, 133 livres 6 sols 8 deniers money of Canada was equal to 100 livres money of France.

Although an ordinance of 1662 mentions 17 different coins (six of them Spanish) there was evidently very little coin in circulation prior to 1662. The first large infusion of coin into the colony's economy resulted from the introduction of royal government, particularly from the arrival of regular troops in the colony in 1662 – 63, who were paid in coin and purchased their supplies with coin.[8] In addition, government expenditures on fortifications, Indian presents, and industrial development brought hard money to the colony.

It is doubtful that much of this coin remained in circulation for long. With the exception of a few years in the eighteenth century, Canada had a deficit in its external trade, and the payment of the deficit absorbed most of the coin shipped to the colony by France. Equally important, the French government normally did not send out large quantities of cash to meet its expenses as it had in 1662 – 63. The shipment of coin always involved the loss of interest on money in transit and on several occasions involved the loss of the cash itself through shipwreck or capture during wartime. To reduce the risk of shipping coin across the ocean, the government usually sent out some coin to cover immediate needs and sent the rest of the colonial budget in trade goods which could be sold to finance the colonial government through the year. The French government also sold bills of exchange payable in France and, in some cases, drew bills on merchants in Quebec, to reduce the amount of coin which it had to forward to the colony.

In an effort to supplement the supply of coin, the colonial government made certain commodities legal tender. Wheat was made legal tender at the rate of 100 sols per *minot* about 1647. A 1665 ordinance provided that wheat would only be accepted in payment for debts at a price established by experts in grain, not at a flat rate. A provisional edict of 1669 set the rate at 4 livres per minot, but this decree was in force for only three months. In 1682 wheat, peas, Indian corn and salt pork were received at set rates for the purchase of arms to be used by the militia. In 1674 moose skins were made current at the *prix ordinaire* and at one point wild cat skins were given currency, on an informal basis, at Niagara.

Mintings for the Colonies

In a more orthodox attempt to solve the currency problem, the king in 1670 ordered the minting of 100,000 livres of 15 – and 5 – sol silver pieces, and 2 – denier copper pieces specifically for circulation in the North American colonies. Their export was forbidden on pain of confiscation. Circulation was intended for both the island and continental colonies but few if any of the coins came to Canada.[9] However, a royal decree of 1672 which provided that these coins and all coins of France which circulated in North America should be rated at one-third above their face value evidently did apply to Canada. This decree put the king's *imprimatur* on the increase which had been ordered by the colonial council in 1662.

The shortage of coins in the colony did not extend to the smaller copper coins. Liards and deniers, which passed for 2 deniers and 1 denier respectively in France, passed for 6 deniers and 2 deniers in Canada. As a result, French merchants shipped quantities to Canada, flooding the market. To prevent this the Superior Council reduced the rating on liards to 3 deniers and then to 2 in 1664. Deniers were reduced to their face value of 1 denier and what were known as *petits deniers* were denied currency. A similar problem arose with sols marqués, which had been increased in 1662 to one-third above their face value of 15 deniers and then had been increased to 24 deniers. As a result, quantities were imported and drove other coins out of the market. In 1667 they were reduced to 20 deniers in an attempt to stem the influx. In 1680, having learned that the sols marqués had been reduced to 12 deniers in France, the council reduced them to 16 deniers in Canada. At the same time a coin first issued in 1674, the 4-sol piece, was reduced in value so that it was "in proportion" to the louis d'or and louis d'argent. In France it passed for 3 sols 6 deniers.

New France also obtained some coin in illicit trade with the English and Dutch to the south. To avoid restrictions and taxes placed on the fur trade in Canada many French traders took their furs to New York where furs were either bartered for trade goods or sold for hard money, usually Spanish dollars. A small amount of Spanish coin may have entered the colony legitimately as a result of trade with the West Indies or directly from France, where certain Spanish coins were legal tender. There were evidently Spanish coins in Canada as early as 1662, since the colonial council established a rating for Spanish *pistolles*, dollars and *patagons* in that year.

In 1664 the French West Indies Company had been granted the monopoly of the beaver trade in Canada and its interests were damaged by the clandestine trade with New York. When the Superior Council declared in 1681 that all foreign coins in the colony should have currency by weight, the company demanded that the colony assist it in controlling the illegal trade in furs by banning the circulation of dollars. The company also pointed out that the king had forbidden the circulation of foreign coin in France. The council responded that if the company could replace the dollars with French coin it would accede to the request. The company could not, so the council allowed the circulation of the dollars to continue and even strengthened their position by providing for the identification of "light dollars". Dollars of full weight were to be stamped with an identifying *fleur de lis* and were to pass for four livres. Light dollars were to be stamped with a fleur de lis and a Roman numeral which indicated a weight category into which they were to fall. Halves, quarters and eighths were to be rated in proportion.

In spite of these measures the coin supply of the colony remained low. The problem was not confined to Canada – there was a shortage of coin in the British colonies, in Britain and in France itself. The shortage in France was as acute as in Canada and economic conditions were worse. It is not surprising that the French government attempted to reduce expenses as much as possible by financing the Canadian administration by the sale of trade goods and on occasion had to refuse to forward the coin requested by the colonial government. By 1684 and possibly before, the French government had hit upon the expedient of sending bills of exchange drawn on Canadian merchants. By this means the government hoped to raise coin in Canada and thereby save itself the risk and expense of transporting it to the colony. The problem of course was that with the shortage of coin in Canada it was very difficult for the merchants on whom the bills were drawn to pay them. In 1684 the merchants were unable to meet the bills in their entirety.[10]

Card Money

As a result by January of 1685 the Intendant, Jacques de Meulles, had run out of money. During the next six months he managed to operate the government and support the troops on the basis of his own credit and that of his friends and by such means as having the soldiers hire themselves out as labourers. By June 1685 these sources of funds were exhausted and de Meulles was forced to issue what were in effect promissory notes. These were issued in three denominations: 15 sols, 40 sols and 4 livres. Their circulation as money was guaranteed by a penalty of 50 livres for anyone who refused them in any payment or who sold goods for higher prices if they were paid for in the notes. The proclamation introducing the notes specified that they would be redeemed as soon as funds arrived from France. Because the notes were written on playing cards cut in different sizes according to denomination, they were referred to as "card money".[11]

The cards were a success. They circulated freely and evidently at face value and were redeemed in September 1685. However, by February 1686 the colonial treasury was again without funds and was forced to issue a new series of cards in 40 - sol and 4 - livre denominations. These were issued on the same terms as those of 1685 and were redeemed in September 1686.

When the king heard of the issue of card money in 1685, and before he had heard of the issue of 1686, he promptly condemned it on the grounds that the cards could easily be counterfeited. In fact there were some forgeries of subsequent issues of card money and in the 1730s several forgers were condemned to death. Nevertheless forgery does not seem to have been a major problem. In later years it became clear that a more serious objection was that the issue of cards weakened the king's fiscal control over Canada. The French government suspected the colonial government of extravagance, if not corruption, and hoped to limit its spending by tying spending to coin, bills of exchange, or trade goods forwarded from France. If the colonial government could issue card money without prior authorization it could present the home government with a fait accompli.

From the point of view of the colonial administration the cards doubtless seemed a very useful innovation. Although it was probably not averse to raising money in the colony through the sale of bills of exchange on France (a course approved by the French government), the shortage of coin in the colony frequently made this impossible. The colonial administration would also have been satisfied with supplies of coin shipped from France, but such shipments were unreliable due to the hazards of navigation or war or, increasingly, the weakness of French finances. Even if supplies of coin did arrive from France they did not reach Canada until August or September, two-thirds of the way through the fiscal year. This should merely have been a bookkeeping problem, but the home government was seldom able to send out sufficient coin to carry the colony through to the next year. Instead shipments of coin were usually employed in paying off past debts.

In spite of the king's condemnation of card money the temptation to use it was great, and new issues were made in 1690, 1691 and 1692. These were justified on the grounds of losses suffered at sea, delays in converting the king's supplies to cash, and budget overruns. Unlike the issues for 1685 – 86 these were not retired immediately. Some of the issue of 1690 were redeemed by notes on the colonial treasurer in Quebec City rather than by payment in coin or with bills of exchange on the French government. These notes may have circulated as money, as they did in the 1720s; it is known that cards, either of the original or subsequent issues, were in use in trade in 1696 and continued until 1700.

In 1699 the king ordered an accounting of all issues of card money since the original issues, directed that all that remained in circulation be withdrawn and forbade further issues. A year later the intendant reported that he had withdrawn all the cards, but only two years later the colonial government began to issue them again. In 1702 at least 5000 livres were issued followed by 160,000 livres in 1703 and 1704. In 1704 the king once again ordered the withdrawal of all cards in circulation. This was attempted but it was found that there were 100,000 more livres of cards in circulation than there were coin or bills of exchange to redeem them. The evident surprise with which this fact was reported suggests that the colonial government had lost track of how many cards it had issued. The inability of the government to redeem all of the cards evidently hurt their credit, since the Intendant, Raudot, issued an ordinance *de faire valider encore* ("to make valid once more") all the cards issued up to 1705 and to enforce their circulation with a penalty of 100 livres. (This is not the first evidence that the cards' credit had been impaired. In 1691 Intendant J. Bochart de Champigny had mentioned that the troops, who were paid in cards, had to purchase supplies at much higher rates than if they had paid for them in coin.)

By 1706 the cards had been accepted by the French government. The governor and intendant promised not to increase the number in circulation. At the same time they admitted that, under pressure from the Canadians, they had issued some small notes of 2 livres and 10 sols but had withdrawn an equal value of cards issued by Champigny and François de Beauharnois. They also noted that those issued by Champigny and Louis-Hector de Callières (prior to 1702 – 03) were badly worn and in need of replacement.

The home government rather grudgingly accepted the necessity of replacing the worn cards but insisted that all cards had to be retired as soon as possible. Perhaps the concession was granted because the French government itself had begun to issue paper money. By 1706 this money was evidently more discredited than the colonial paper money. The Raudots, father and son, complained that their salaries were being paid in paper money in France and that they lost 40 to 50% in converting it to cash. More important for the colony, the home government began to redeem bills of exchange on the treasurer of the marine in depreciated paper money. The bills of exchange were purchased by Quebec merchants to pay their bills in France, and their creditors covered their losses by raising their prices to the Canadian merchants, who passed their costs on to Canadian consumers.

At about the same time, the small amount of coin which had circulated in the colony disappeared either into hoards or back to France. This may initially have been prompted by an ordinance of 1699 which prohibited the export of coin to America. Although the prohibition did not necessarily apply to government shipments, it did reduce the possibility of coin reaching Canada. The losses suffered on bills of exchange must also have led many merchants to pay their bills in France by shipping coin if at all possible. Even the small coins disappeared and the colonial government continued to issue small-denomination cards to supply the need for change. As well, the government began to have the colonial treasurer of the marine issue notes against one-half the funds which he expected to receive each year. Pontchartrain, the Minister of Marine, viewed this as merely an expedient to get around the prohibition on the further issue of card money; although he disapproved, he did not forbid it. To what extent these notes circulated is not known although several decades later similar notes were to form a major part of the circulation.

The delays and losses involved in the payment of bills of exchange in France made it increasingly difficult to sell the bills in Canada. After 1708 few of the bills were paid at all, and in 1709 and 1710 the colonial government was unable to raise sufficient funds to finance the colony, and resorted to a new issue of cards. It is not known how many were issued in 1709 but 244,092 livres, money of Canada, were issued in 1710 in denominations of 32, 16, 9 and 2 livres. In 1711 a further issue of 450,000 livres in 50 – and 100 – livre notes was made.

The rapid increase in the volume of cards in circulation plus the almost complete collapse of the credit of the bills of exchange combined to quadruple prices in Canada by 1711 – 1712. The French government was aware of the problem and of its causes but as long as the war with Britain continued it could do nothing and the colonial merchants continued to accept card money because they knew that bills of exchange were even more unsound.

Retiring the Card Money

With the approach of peace in 1713 various schemes were put forward to restore French finances and retire the card money. Most of the proposals for retiring the card money involved reducing it in value and issuing interest-bearing bonds in its place. In 1714 the French government announced a five-year plan to retire the money. Each year 160,000 livres of bills of exchange on the treasurer of the marine would be sold in the colony on the basis of 1 livre of bills of exchange for 2 livres of cards. To ease the loss the bills of exchange would be payable not in bonds as previously proposed but in coin. The card money which remained in circulation would not, in theory, be reduced in value; it would only be reduced for the purpose of buying bills of exchange.

It is a measure of the lack of confidence in the card money that this scheme was very favourably received in the colony. In the first year not only was the intendant able to dispose of 160,000 livres of bills of exchange payable in March 1715, he was able to sell a further 158,055 payable in March 1716, thereby retiring 636,110 of the estimated 1,600,000 livres of cards in circulation. Unfortunately, when the time came for the payment of the first bills of exchange in March 1715, the treasurer of the marine was unable to meet them. As the Canadian merchants were counting on the income from these bills to purchase their supplies for 1715, the failure threw the whole policy of retiring the card money in doubt. In addition, the French government was unable to supply coin for the current expenses of the colony, and the colonial government began to issue more card money.

Instead of issuing new cards, the officials reissued old ones. The cards had been redeemed at half their face value but were reissued at their full face value. Even the officials of the Ministry of the Marine were startled by this expedient and wrote

il paroit dailleurs bizarre qu'une monnoye que le Commis du Tresorier recoit pour la moitié de sa premiere valeur que ce meme Commis la donne en meme tems sur le pied de cette premiere Valeur pour les Depenses que Sa Ma té fait.[12]

In 1715, as a result of the failure to pay the bills of exchange due in March of 1715, the intendant was only able to retire cards to a value of 61,000 livres of bills of exchange due in March 1717. However, the French government was slowly getting its finances in order. By June 1716 it had been able to pay off about three-quarters of the bills of exchange due in March 1715 and was confident of paying off those due in March 1716 during the course of the year.

In spite of its efforts, the government had not made much of a dent in the total volume of card money in circulation. By 1717, about 1,150,000 of the 1,600,000 livres of cards had been traded for bills of exchange. However, with the reissued cards, the net reduction was only about 300,000 livres. Because the cards continued to circulate by law at their face value in Canada but were only redeemable in bills of exchange at half their value, the merchants had protected themselves against the loss by doubling their prices on imported goods. Goods produced in the colony also rose to compensate for the losses caused.

In 1717 the government made a final attempt to deal with the problem of card money. After a final issue for the fiscal year 1716 – 17 all card money was to be converted into bills of exchange on France payable in three annual installments, and after the departure of the vessels in 1718 any remaining card money would be valueless. Card money was to be reduced to half its face value, and in addition, the distinction between *monnoye du pays* and *monnoye de france* was to be abolished, representing a further reduction of 25% on top of the original reduction of 50%. The reduction of circulating card money to half its face value was delayed until 1718 with the provision that debts contracted since 1714 could also be paid at half the rate specified. When it became clear that the French treasury could not meet the payments on the bills of exchange for 1718 and that the ship with the supply of coin for 1718 – 19 would not arrive, the period during which cards could circulate was extended to the departure of the ships in 1719. That year the king was able to send about 355,000 livres in coin in payment of the expenditures of 1718 and 1719 and in partial payment of the anticipated expenditures of the following year. This money made the final retirement of the cards possible and they ceased to circulate in the autumn of 1719.

Revaluations and recoinages

From 1700, when the French government made a shipment of coin to Canada to retire the card money, to 1719 when the card money was again retired, little if any coin was shipped to Canada and it is doubtful if much was in circulation. Nevertheless, one cannot ignore coin in considering card money, for coin was the standard against which card money was measured.

From their first mintings in 1640 – 41 until 1709 all louis d'or and louis d'argent and their fractions contained a constant amount of pure gold or silver. However, their rating in terms of the money of account, the livre, varied greatly. In general the tendency was inflationary. The louis d'or, valued at 10 livres in 1640 was increased to 12 livres in 1652, decreased to 10 livres in 1654 and then gradually increased again to 13 livres 5 sols in 1700. This devaluation reduced the pure gold content of the livre from 11.65 grains (French measure) to 8.79 grains. However, fluctuations in the period 1640 – 1700, only some of which are shown in Table 1, were modest compared to those of the period 1708 – 26. During this period the French government was virtually bankrupt. Its desperate attempts to stay afloat involved at least six recoinages, and even more changes in the ratings of coins.

To what extent the detailed changes in French coinage filtered down to Canada is unclear. Canada was insulated by distance and poor communications. Proof that a change in France did not automatically result in a change in Canada is found in a letter dated 5 November 1694 in which the governor and intendant explained that they had decided not to follow a recent reduction of the rates of coins in France because to do so would have denuded Canada of all money. Particularly in the years 1709 – 26 it is probable that many changes in ratings were obsolete before news of their existence reached Canada.

In spite of these moderating factors some of the changes in France were given legal effect in Canada. The louis d'or, established at 14 livres 13 sols 4 deniers monnoye du pays in 1662 was raised to 15 livres 6 sols 8 deniers in 1687 and 15 livres 9 sols 4 deniers in 1690. Other coins were normally raised in proportion. Strangely there is no mention of an increase in the rating of silver money in 1687, although an increase would have been necessary to keep it circulating alongside the enhanced louis d'or. In 1690 the louis d'argent, at 4 livres monnoye du pays in 1662, was raised to 4 livres 2 sols 8 deniers.

In September 1700, in response to a change in ratings in France, louis d'or in Canada were reduced to 17 livres 13 sols 4 deniers and silver écu to 4 livres 12 sols. Since this reduction was to a level above that of the last known rating of 1690, there had obviously been some changes in the interim. Although there had been no recoinages during the 1690s, coins had been recalled several times during the decade and overstruck, thus changing their design but not their weight, and these changes probably occasioned changes in ratings.

In 1709, 1716, 1718, 1723, and 1726 there were recoinages which involved changes in the weight, design, and value of the gold and silver coins. In 1715 and 1720 recoinages resulted in changes in the design and value of the major coins. In addition, there were at least 10 changes in the rate at which coins were received. The general tendency of the changes was to devalue the livre: in 1708 it contained 9.14 French grains of gold; at its nadir in September 1720 it contained only 3.13 grains.

Although each of the recoinages included a recall of previous issues, the recalls were not complete and it was necessary for the government to establish ratings for each type of coin in circulation. By 1726 there were eight separate types and six different weights of louis d'or in circulation in Canada: depending on the issue the louis d'or might be rated at 16 livres 16 sols, 21 livres, 24 livres, 25 livres 4 sols, 27 livres 6 sols or 31 livres 10 sols. When it is remembered that the recoinages and adjusted ratings also involved the half and double louis d'or and the louis d'argent and its halves, thirds, quarters, fifths, twelfths and twentieths the confusion in the coinage can hardly be underestimated. Fortunately by 1726 France had restored some order to its finances, and the recoinage of 1726, along with the rating of the louis d'or at 24 livres and the silver écu at 6 livres, remained in effect until 1785.

42

Table 1   Revaluations of French Coins, 1602–1726
Gold content of the livre, money of France, 1602–1726[13],
Based on the écu d'or to 1636 and the louis d'or from 1640

Date	Weight (grains*)	Rating (Livre/ Sol)	Purity	Gold Content (grains)	Grains per Livre
1602	63.56	3/5	.9583	60.91	18.74
1636	–	5/4	–	–	11.71
1640	127.12	10/0	.9167	116.53	11.65
1652	–	12/0	–	–	9.71
1654	–	10/0	–	–	11.65
1656	–	11/0	–	–	10.59
1666 Jan	–	10/15	–	–	10.84
Sept	–	11/0	–	–	10.59
1686	–	11/10	–	–	10.13
1687	–	11/5	–	–	10.36
1689	–	11/12	–	–	10.05
1700	–	13/5	–	–	8.79
1708	–	12/15	–	–	9.14
1709 Apr	153.6	16/10	.9167	140.81	8.53
May	–	20/0	–	–	7.04
1713 to 1715	–	14/0	–	–	10.06
1715 Dec	153.6	20/0	.9167	140.81	7.04
1716	230.4	30/0	.9167	211.21	7.04
1718	184.32	–	.9167	168.97	–
1719	–	35/0	–	–	4.82
1720 Aug	–	36/0	–	–	4.69
Sept	184.32	54/0	.9167	168.97	3.13
Dec	–	45/0	–	–	3.75
1723	124.54	27/0	.9167	114.17	4.23
1724 Feb	–	24/0	–	–	4.75
Mar	–	20/0	–	–	5.71
Sept	–	16/0	–	–	7.14
1726 Jan	153.6	20/0	.9167	140.81	7.04
May	–	24/0	–	–	5.87

( ) = Statute weight

*French measure. 1 grain French measure = .053115 grams = .8196898 grains troy weight

Table 1 (Continued)   Revaluations of French Coins, 1602–1726
Silver Content of the livre, money of France 1602–1726
(Based on quart d'écu, 1602, and on the louis d'argent (escu blanc, écu) from 1641)

Date	Weight (Grains*)	Rating (Livre/Sol)	Purity	Silver Content (grains)	Grains per livre	Silver to Gold ratio
1602	182.86	0/16	.9167	167.63	209.54	11.18
1641	516.79	3/0	.9167	473.74	157.91	–
1652	–	3/6	–	–	143.56	14.78
1653	–	3/10	–	–	135.35	–
1654	–	3/0	–	–	157.91	13.55
1666 Jan	–	2/18	–	–	163.36	15.07
Sept	–	3/0	–	–	157.91	14.91
1689	–	3/2	–	–	152.82	15.21
1700	–	3/9	–	–	137.32	15.62
1708	–	3/8	–	–	139.34	15.24
1709 Feb	–	3/7	–	–	141.41	–
April	576.0	4/8	.9167	528.02	120.00	14.06
May	–	5/0	–	–	105.60	15.00
1713	–	3/10	–	–	150.86	15.00
1715	576.0	5/0	.9167	528.02	105.60	15.00
1718	460.8	–	.9167	422.42	–	–
1720 Sept	460.8	9/0	.9167	422.42	46.94	15.00
Dec	–	7/10	–	–	56.32	15.02
1723 Aug	–	6/18	–	–	61.22	14.47
1724 Feb	–	6/3	–	–	68.69	14.46
Mar	–	5/0	–	–	84.48	14.80
Sept	–	4/0	–	–	105.60	14.79
Nov	444.14	4/0	.9167	407.14	101.79	–
1726 Jan	555.18	5/0	.9167	508.93	101.78	14.46
May	–	6/0	–	–	84.82	14.45

*French measure: 1 grain French measure = .053115 grams = .8196898 grains troy weight

Colonial finance and more card money

With the retirement of card money in 1719 the French government attempted to run the colony on a "sound" basis, paying
expenses entirely with coin shipped out each year, with the
receipts from the sale of merchandise forwarded by the crown,
and on the receipts of the colony. However, France's finances
were still not strong and she could not always forward the

necessary money: in 1727 the colony received only 5,000 livres in specie to apply to a budget of 308,156 livres, and in 1728 and 1729 no specie at all was received. Accidents also upset the plans: in 1725 the year's supply of coin, 83,000 livres, was lost with the sinking of the *Chameau*.[14]What specie did arrive in Canada was usually quickly shipped back to France by the merchants to pay their bills.

In spite of attempts at budgetary control the colonial government still managed to exceed its budget. In 1726, 1727 and 1728 it overspent by about 170,000 livres, or 50% each year. The excesses were covered by notes drawn on the provincial treasurer (as had been done in the 1690s) or by dipping into funds advanced for the succeeding year.[15] To what extent these treasury notes or *ordinances de paiment* circulated as money in the 1720s is not known, but they were to become one of the principal forms of circulating money in the 1730s.

As a result of the difficulties the French government had in supplying the colony with coin, and the underlying problem of Canada's imbalance of trade, there was a shortage of circulating money in Canada throughout the 1720s: Vaudreuil and Bégon estimated that there was only 100,000 livres of real money in the colony in 1720 after the cards had been withdrawn.[16] Towards the end of the decade the Canadian merchants began to agitate for a return to card money to solve the problem. The king, doubtless made more receptive to this appeal by his own financial problems, agreed in 1729 to an issue of 400,000 livres of card money. The money was to pass current in the colony and would be the sole means of purchasing bills of exchange on the treasurer-general of the marine. In this way it was hoped that their credit would be maintained and the merchants would be provided with a safe means of remitting money to France. Two hundred and fifty thousand livres of bills of exchange were to be sold each year. The cards received from the sale were not withdrawn but were reissued or replaced. The returned cards formed a major part of the colony's budget and reduced the amount of coin which had to be sent out.

The authorized issue, in denominations of 24 livres, 12 livres, 6 livres, 3 livres, 1 livre 10 sols, 15 sols and 7 sols 6 deniers, was completed by October 1730; an additional 60,000 livres, authorized by the intendant and the governor, was issued in 1731. Issues beyond the original amount had been expressly forbidden by the king, and the action brought prompt rebuke and orders that the issue be withdrawn. The governor and intendant promised that this would be done as soon as the cards came in from the purchase of bills of exchange in 1733.

In 1730 when the bills of exchange on the treasurer-general of the marine were put on sale, only 167,791 livres worth of cards were brought in, although 250,000 livres of bills were available (see Table 2). However, 108,557 livres of *acquits de depense* (certificates or notes on the colonial treasurer) were submitted in payment for bills of exchange. Although the bills of exchange were supposed to be sold only for card money, the intendant received both card money and *acquits* up to a total of 250,000 livres. When a similar course was followed in 1734, the intendant pointed out that to have refused the acquits would have damaged their credit. The excess, about 26,000 livres, evidently all acquits, was converted to card money and returned to the holders.

The bills of exchange sold in 1730 were paid promptly. Fewer cards were returned in 1731 and fewer still in 1732. The governor and intendant attributed this phenomena to the confidence which the population had in the cards and to the need for the cards in domestic trade. It may also be that the bills of exchange were not needed in 1731 and 1732 because the colony was unusually prosperous as a result of wheat exports and had little need of exchange. A third possibility is that Canadians had less confidence in the acquits than they had in the cards and consequently returned the acquits first; with the exception of the year 1731 the value of acquits submitted for redemption increased steadily from 1730 to 1734.

The reports of large number of acquits being used in payment of bills of exchange indicate the extent to which this secondary paper money had developed. The practice of issuing acquits had begun in the 1720s, when officials in the more remote districts (and Montreal counted as one of these), made payments by writing orders for payment on the treasurer of the marine at Quebec and later on his deputy at Montreal. Often these notes circulated from person to person as money before being sent to Quebec where they were exchanged for coin or, after 1730, bills of exchange. From the number submitted for bills of exchange in 1730 it is obvious that they already formed a substantial part of the circulation. By 1734, according to one estimate there were 300,000 livres worth of acquits in circulation compared to 450,000 livres of cards.[17] Although they were issued by the government they had no legal standing until 1733. In that year the colonial government, finding that some merchants were refusing the notes or were giving preference to card money, ordered that the notes should be treated exactly the same as the card money. In 1734 when receipts of cards and notes totalled far more than the supply of bills of exchange provided, the loss fell equally on holders of cards and notes alike.

Table 2   Card Money and Treasury Notes Used in Purchasing Bills of Exchange[18]

Year	Card Money (livres)	Notes on Treasurer (livres)	Total Bills of Exchange Sold (livres)	Excess (livres)
1730	167,791	108,557	250,000	26,348
1731	136,489	94,459	230,948	Nil
1732	63,000	162,000	225,000	Nil
1733	–	209,000	–	–
1734	82,000	300,000	267,252	114,747
1735	–	–	–	–
1736	–	–	–	–
1737	–	–	–	–
1738	–	–	–	–
1739	–	–	–	–
1740	–	–	–	–
1741	176,000	464,000	–	–
1742	142,000	491,000	–	–
1743	213,000	438,100	–	–
1744	–	–	–	–
1745	–	–	–	–
1746	–	–	–	–
1747	55,392	2,669,358	–	–
1748	65,984	2,104,435	–	–
1749	–	–	–	–
1750	–	–	–	–

Although the policy of accepting cards and notes equally was necessary to preserve the credit of the notes, the fact that all of the cards and notes returned to the colonial treasury could not be exchanged for bills of exchange must have damaged the credit of both. Hocquart estimated that the failure to redeem all of the cards in 1734 had cost the holders from 10% to 12% loss, presumably by reason of their funds being kept idle in Canada for a season or by having to buy bills of exchange on a secondary market. This had caused murmurs on the part of many merchants and he feared that if the king did not provide for more bills of exchange in 1735 there would be "another and more dangerous reverse".[19]

Although the initial credit which the card money enjoyed must have been gratifying, its success posed some problems. The annual sale of bills of exchange was intended to provide roughly one-half the colony's budget. When the cards did not come in, the government was left short of money. On the other hand, when receipts of cards and notes exceeded the allotment of bills of exchange, the excess had to be redeemed with coins, cards or notes from the government's meagre supply. It was this second type of problem which led to the colonial government's unauthorized issue of 60,000 livres of card money in 1731. The issue of additional cards was quickly condemned by the home government, but it said nothing about the acquits. Their proliferation over the years suggests that the colonial government came to rely on them to cover its deficits.

The success which the card money enjoyed combined with the growth of trade in the 1730s persuaded the king to authorize the issue of another 200,000 livres of card money in 1733.[20] No further issues of cards were made until 1742 but the volume of notes in circulation grew with the continuing deficits of the colonial government. Guy Frégault estimates that from 1730 to 1741 the average annual deficit was 40,456 livres.[21] Presumably the deficit was financed by the issue of notes on the treasury: the total deficit for the 11 years, 445,016 livres, was roughly equal to the value of notes which were submitted for redemption in 1741.

Growth of paper money

It is not clear to what extent the growth in the supply of paper money affected its credit. The 1730s were a prosperous period for Canada and the growth in the money supply may have matched the growth in the economy. On the other hand the rationale for declaring acquits as legal tender in 1733 indicates that they were suffering in comparison with the cards. Frégault suggests that as early as 1730 merchants made distinctions

48

between payments in coin and payments in cards. Writing in 1735, the governor of Montreal complained that there was no coined money in his district and that prices were higher when payment was made in cards. In 1740 Governor Beauharnois complained that the unrestricted issue of notes was causing the troops and public very much suffering.[22]

In spite of detractors the intendant remained confident of the strength of the cards, and even the governor joined him in urging a further issue. They argued that of the 600,000 livres of cards already issued, only one-third actually circulated; the rest were held in hoards or in government coffers. The small circulation was insufficient for the needs of the country, which was prospering. The official request for a further issue of cards was supported by the merchants of Quebec who argued that although orders on the treasurer did circulate as money, they were not as readily accepted as the cards.

In response to these appeals the king authorized a further issue of 120,000 livres of card money in 1742. The cards, in denominations of 24 livres, 12 livres, 6 livres, 3 livres, 1 livre 10 sols, 15 sols, and 7 sols 6 deniers, were issued under the same conditions as earlier issues and were all in circulation by the fall of 1742.

The new issue of cards was far from sufficient to finance the colonial government, and its deficits continued to mount. In the short term the deficits were met by orders and notes on the treasurer. However, as the home government's finances became increasingly strained, it had more and more difficulty redeeming the whole issue at the end of the year. In 1747 over 2.6 million livres of notes, and 55,000 livres of cards were presented for redemption; in order to redeem them it was necessary to extend the date for payment of the bills of exchange well into 1748. As the colonial merchants were quick to point out, the delays in payment of the bills of exchange damaged their credit and made it difficult and expensive for them to arrange for the shipment of supplies for 1749. The delays also caused increases in colonial prices which were eventually passed on to the colonial government.

In spite of these problems, or perhaps in an effort to regularize what could not be prevented, the king agreed to a further issue of 280,000 livres of card money in 1749, bringing the total issued to one million livres. The new issue was justified on the grounds that it was required by trade but it seems

49

probable that the credit of the card money was better than that of the notes. As early as 1748 Intendant Bigot had reported that illiterate habitants would refuse to accept the handwritten notes but would accept printed card money. Partly as a result of this preference and partly to save labour, the government began issuing its notes, as well as the card money, in printed form in 1752.

The return of peace in 1748 brought little abatement in expenditurees in the colony and the excess of expenditures continued to be financed with short-term notes on the treasurer: in 1750 – 51, almost 2.4 million livres were issued. In order to redeem them the French government was forced to extend the period of payment on its bills of exchange further and further into the future. After 1753, bills of exchange were normally paid off in three annual installments. While this put off the day of reckoning for the French treasury, it also meant that the bills of exchange could only be negotiated at a discount. One report suggests that by 1757, 12% was deducted from the second installment and 18% from the third.

War and inflation

Throughout the 1750s, prices in Canada rose alarmingly. The French government attributed the inflation to excessive expenditures of the colonial government and the large issues of paper money which the expenditures entailed. It believed that if expenditures could be made in coin, inflation could be controlled, and in 1755 and 1756 it supplied coin for the pay of the regular army in Canada. This coin, about 1 million livres in 1755 and a similar amount in 1756, was the first large supply of specie to appear in the colony since the 1730s.[23] It did little to curb inflation but it did undermine the paper money. Goods which were available for 100 livres of card money could be had for 80 livres of coin. To support the paper, Bigot refused to accept coin in payment of bills of exchange and only accepted card money or orders. In any event the coin did not stay in circulation for long. The risks of war and the threat which coin posed to the paper money persuaded the French government not to send out coin after 1756. The same risks of loss prevented Canadian merchants from using coin for remittances to France. Most of the coin was bought up, often at the rate

50

of 7 livres of paper for 6 livres of specie, and disappeared into hoards, not to appear again until after the fall of Canada.

During the Seven Years' War, expenditures mounted relentlessly. The French military commander, Montcalm, estimated that the colony's expenses, which had been considered very high at four million livres in 1755, would be thirty-six million livres in 1759. Virtually all of this was financed by orders or notes, thirty million livres of which were in circulation in early 1759. As the amount of paper in circulation increased its credit fell, and in April 1759 Montcalm noted that people were offering 36 livres and even 48 livres of paper for 25 livres of coin. Later in the year Bigot was reduced to begging army officers for any coined money they had in order to purchase wheat; the habitants refused to accept paper money of any sort. What little credit the paper money had was lost in June 1760 when it was announced that the king had suspended payment on bills of exchange drawn on the treasurer-general of the colonies.

The commander of the British forces at Quebec, General Murray had already forbidden the circulation of the money in the portion of the colony which he controlled and he heaped scorn on this announcement:

> It is to be presumed that the circular letter speaks more truly when it says, that the notes or ordinances will be retired and duly paid as soon as circumstances will permit, because circumstances will never permit.[24]

Murray's prohibition of the circulation of paper money was followed by one in the government of Three Rivers. Although no prohibition was issued in the government of Montreal, the paper ceased to have value as money by mid-1760.[25]

Although the paper ceased to circulate as money it still retained some value as a speculative commodity. Merchants who believed that ultimately the French government would redeem the money bought it up or took it in trade at a discount estimated at about 85%. This trade became very active after the French king included a declaration of his intention to redeem the bills and letters of exchange in the Treaty of Paris. In spite of the efforts of the military government to check speculation, most of the paper, which had not been carried back to France by departing officials and merchants in 1760, passed

51

into the hands of British merchants. From the point of view of Canada this was just as well, for very little was ever realized on most of the paper.

Postscript

A tragic postscript to the conquest provides a final look at the coinage of New France and a preview of the types of coins which were to form the specie for the British colony of Quebec. Following the surrender of Montreal in 1760 most of the professional soldiers and civil servants and some of the leading merchants of the colony returned to France. Many of them travelled aboard a captured French vessel, the *Auguste,* which had been chartered for the purpose.

On 15 November 1760 the vessel ran aground off the northeastern coast of Cape Breton and broke up several hours later, with the loss of all but 7 passengers and crew.[26] In 1976 this wreck site was discovered and in 1977–78 was excavated by divers. Among the artifacts recovered were 1,236 coins, presumably the property of the passengers (see Table 3). Because of the conditions in the colony very few of the coins found in the wreck of the *Auguste* would have been in regular circulation but the treasure trove does provide a sample of the higher denomination coins which found their way to the colony.

Not surprisingly, most of the coins were French: silver écus were particularly numerous. Spanish-American coins, particularly dollars minted in Mexico, were also common. Their prominence is something of a surprise, for there is little mention of them in eighteenth century records, although they had been common in the seventeenth century. It is conceivable that they had been introduced into the colony by the British Army.

Table 3   Coins Found in the Wreck of the *Auguste*[27]

French Coins

Double louis d'or	1
Louis d'or	23
Ecu d'argent	494
Demi-écu	83
One-fifth écu	8
One-sixth écu	1
One-twentieth écu	1
Sol of 15 deniers	2
Douzaine	6
12/24 denier	81
6 denier	2
Liard	16
Billon (unidentified)	33
Unidentified	3
	754

Spanish Coins

Mexican Dollar	400
Mexican Quarter	1
Peru Dollar	44
Guatemala Dollar	3
Chile Dollar	1
Cut Dollar	1
	450

British Coins

Guinea	5
Half-Guinea	1
Halfpenny	16
	22

Danish Coins

2 Skilling	1

Portuguese Colonial Coins

4 Escudo	4

Unidentified 2

Total	1,233

Chapter Two

**The Province of Quebec
Lower Canada
Upper Canada
The Province of Canada
and
The Dominion of Canada
1760 – 1900**

Sample of currency in Lower Canada, 1780–1800

guinea, 1787

moidore, 1723

Johannes, 1759

Spanish (Peruvian) dollar, 1790

louis d'argent, 1753

pistareen, 1722

bon, 1788

Bills of exchange

Bill of exchange drawn on Harley and Drummond   actual size: 191 mm x 98 mm

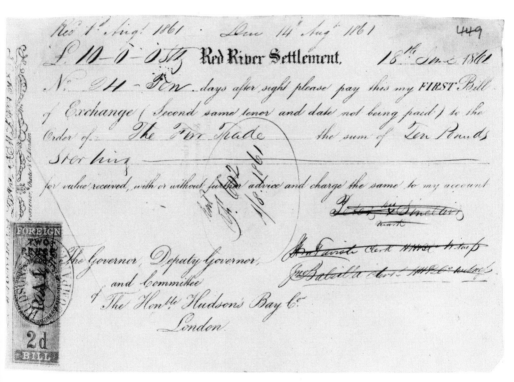

Bill of exchange drawn on the Hudson's Bay Company   actual size: 220 mm x 150 mm

Sample of coins and tokens in Upper Canada, 1830–1840

U.S. eagle, 1803

Mexican dollar, 1834

U.S. half-dollar, 1806

shilling, 1834

Bank of Montreal one-penny token, 1842

Brock token, 1816

Wellington token

Sample of paper money in Upper and Lower Canada, 1810–1830

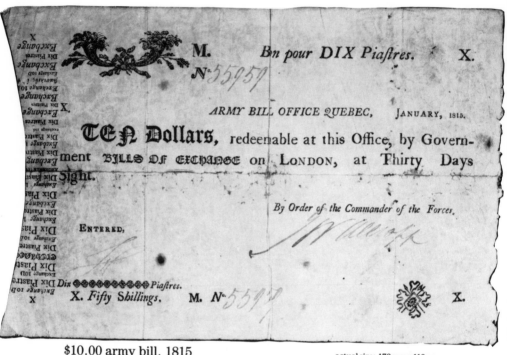

$10.00 army bill, 1815

actual size: 178 mm x 118 mm

$1.00 Bank of Montreal note, 1819

actual size: 171 mm x 69 mm

25s./$5.00 Bank of Upper Canada note, 1826   actual size: 171 mm x 66 mm

10s./$2.00 City of Toronto note, 1838   actual size: 176 mm x 70 mm

Sample of Central Canadian circulation, 1867

U.S. eagle, 1847

sovereign, 1829

U.S. half-dollar, 1861

Canadian 20-cent piece, 1858

U.S. dime, 1857

Canadian 10-cent piece, 1858

U.S. half-dime, 1853

Canadian 5-cent piece, 1858

$1.00 note, Province of Canada   actual size: 190 mm x 74 mm

$2.00 note, Gore Bank, 1852   actual size: 178 mm x 74 mm

At the same time that General Murray forbade the circulation of the old paper money he provided for a new rating of the principal coins in Quebec. A year later the military governors of Montreal and Three Rivers also established rating systems for the coins in their districts (see Table 4). The systems established at Three Rivers and Montreal were not on the same basis as that established in Quebec. Murray had arrived with the army from Halifax and Louisbourg and he based the Quebec City rating on the Halifax system in which the Spanish dollar was rated at 5 shillings currency, 11.11% above its accepted sterling value of 4s, 6d. (For the development of Halifax currency, see Chapter 3.) All other coins were rated roughly in proportion. Amherst, the commander at Montreal and his governor at Three Rivers, Burton, had come overland from New York, and they based their systems on New York currency, which rated the Spanish dollar at 8 shillings, or 77.7% above its accepted sterling value. The New York merchants who followed Amherst and set up business in Montreal also favoured the New York rating and ensured its acceptance in the Montreal area.

The difference in the rating of coins in Montreal and Quebec City led to inconvenience in trade and to speculation in money. Coins were shipped to the city where they were most highly valued. In 1762, Gage, the Governor at Montreal, raised the value of the French crown or silver écu and the sols marqués, noting that in consequence of their being undervalued they had been shipped out of the area.[1] The French crown was also undervalued in Quebec City. It was rated equal to the dollar at 5 shillings although it contained 9% more silver than the dollar. Similarly the louis d'or was undervalued when compared to the English guinea by about 2s. 7.5d. The ratings for other French coins were presumably also too low. Although their later prominence indicates that there were substantial supplies in hoards, they did not circulate freely.

Table 4 Ratings of Coins Under Military Rule[2]

	Ratings in Quebec City		Ratings in Three Rivers		Ratings in Montreal
	Currency (£/s./d.)	Livres/ Sols/ Denier	Currency (£/s./d.)	Livres/ Sols/ Denier	Currency (£/s./d.)
Dollar	5/0	6/0/0	8/0	6/0/0	8/0 or
Guinea	1/3/4	27/0/0	–	–	6 livres
Half-Johannes	2/0/0	48/0/0	3/4/0	48/0/0	–
Moidore	1/13/0	36/0/0	–	–	–
Sp. Pistole	18/0	21/10/0	–	–	–
Louis d'or	1/0/0	24/0/0	–	–	35/0
French Crown	5/0	6/0/0	5/6	6/12/0*	8/10.5*
Sol marqué of 6 liards	0/.69	1/4	Halifax*	–	0/1.5*
Sol marqué of 9 liards	0/.86	1/8	–	–	0/2*
Half-Dollar	–	–	4/0	3/0/0	–
Fifth-Dollar	–	–	1/7	1/4/0	–
Eighth-Dollar	–	–	1/0	15/0	–
Sixteenth-Dollar	–	–	0/6	7/6	–
Copper Pieces	–	–	–	1/0	

*These were adjustments upwards, made in 1762, in the value of French coins
  which had been undervalued. In Three Rivers the French crown had
  previously been equal to $1.00.

Sources of coin

In the years of military government army pay and army
purchases were the principal source of coin in the country. The
army was normally paid in silver, usually in silver dollars valued
at 4s. 8d. (see Appendix C for an explanation of "army
sterling"). Dollars and Portugese Johannes were imported by
the army paymasters from New York and London. They were
the most common coins in circulation during the period of
military rule and for some years afterwards until the increase
in the rating of French silver brought it back into circulation.
In an effort to prevent the re-export of the specie the army
began to sell bills of exchange on the paymaster-general in
England to local merchants.

When these sales failed to raise sufficient cash for the
army's needs, specie continued to be imported from England,
Nova Scotia and the West Indies and in peacetime from New

York and Boston. Often the importation of specie from the Thirteen Colonies and from the United States was handled by merchants who purchased bills in Canada, sent them to the United States for sale at a profit and shipped specie from the United States to Canada to purchase more bills. Although the sale of bills could not always provide all the specie required by the army, it continued to be the major factor in British army finances for nearly a century as well as being a major element in the financing of Canadian trade with Britain.

In establishing a rating for coins in 1759 – 60 Murray and Burton gave ratings both in Halifax or Quebec currency and in livres and sols. The rating in livres and sols gave official recognition, if not legal force, to the keeping of accounts by the French system. Although subsequent laws on coinage did not set ratings in livres and sols, many accounts in Quebec, particularly in smaller centres, continued to be kept in the old way. As late as 1834 the official Blue Books, in giving the ratings of coins in circulation, gave rates both in Halifax currency and in livres and sols and the accounts of the Contrecoeur Isles et Communes seigneury were kept in livres until at least the 1850s.[3] Six livres, Canadian money of account, were equal to 1 dollar; 24 livres were equal to £1 Halifax currency. It should be noted that French coins which continued to circulate in Canada were usually referred to by their value in terms of money of France, not in Canadian money of account. Thus the écu was often called a piece of 6 livres although in terms of Canadian money of account it was, after 1777, worth 6 livres 12 sols.

Quebec currency

In spite of minor adjustments such as those made by Burton and Gage in 1762, the three separate rating systems remained in force until Murray was appointed civil governor of the whole colony in 1764. Shortly after his appointment he issued an "Ordinance for establishing and regulating the currency of this province". The ordinance, which came into effect 1 January 1765, abandoned both the Halifax and New York standards and set the Spanish dollar at 6 shillings, one-third above its sterling value, with other coins in proportion. The exact reason for choosing this level is not known. It was, however, the traditional rate in New England and the maximum rate authorized by

Queen Anne's proclamation of 1704. A convenient feature of the rating was that one shilling currency was very nearly equal to one livre Canadian money of account. The difference was so small that they were defined as being equal, at least in contracts made before 1765 (see Table 5).[4]

Table 5   Ratings of Coins Established by the Ordinance of 14 September 1764

Coin	Weight* (troy grains)	Rating (£/s./d.)	Purity	Precious Metal Content (grains)	Grains per Shilling
Gold					
Johannes of Portugal	438	4/16/0	.9166	401.47	4.18
Moidore	162	1/16/0	.9166	148.49	4.12
Carolin of Germany	137	1/10/0	–	–	–
Guinea	124	1/8/0	.9166	113.66	4.06
Louis d'or	123	1/8/0	.9166	112.74	4.03
Pistole, Spanish and French	100	1/1/0	.9166	91.66	4.36
Silver					
Dollar, Seville, Mexico and Pillar	420	6/0	.9166	384.97	64.16
French crown or 6-livre piece	460	6/8	.9166	421.64	63.25
French coin, currently passing at 4s. 6d. Halifax currency (écu of of 1718 and 1723)	376	5/6	.910	342.16	62.21
British Shilling	(92.9)	1/4	.925	85.9	64.43
Pistareen	(88.5)	1/2	.8125	71.91	61.63
French 9d. piece	–	1/0	–	–	–
20 British Coppers	–	1/0	–	–	–
48 Sols Marqués	–	1/0	–	–	–

Silver/Gold Ratio = 15.31:1

*Through the remainder of this book, weights are given in troy measure. Weights which are not enclosed in brackets in these tables are supplied by the statute and are usually the minimum weight at which a coin was legal tender. Weights in brackets and purities have been obtained from other sources, generally from Appendix A in Robert Chalmers' *History of Currency in the British Colonies* (London: Printed for H.M. Stationery Office by Eyre and Spottiswoode, 1893). A. Bonneville, *Encyclopédie Monétaire: ou Nouveau Traite des Monnaies d'or et d'Argent en circulation Chez les Divers Peuples du Monde* (Paris: A. Bonneville, 1849) has been used as a second source.

Use of the new rating system was not made compulsory. If parties to an agreement wished, they could specify the use of another currency system in their dealings, but failing such an agreement the rating system of 1765 was to apply. Nor did the ordinance apply to private accounts; these could continue to be kept in Halifax or in New York currency.

In order to prevent the importation of excessive quantities of copper coin, British coppers and sols marqués of all types were undervalued, and a limit of one shilling was placed on payments in sols marqués. The ordinance also forbade the cutting of coins, particularly dollars, into pieces to obtain subsidiary coinage. This was a common practice in the English colonies and had been sanctioned in the government of Montreal where an ordinance of 1761 had forbidden the cutting of dollars into smaller parts than one-eighth.[5]

Prior to 1765 French coins were undervalued and so did not circulate. Under the new rating they were deliberately overvalued so as to bring them out of their hoards and keep them in circulation.[6] Based on the rating given the dollar the French crown was rated about 1.25 pence too high and the light écu of the issues of 1718 and 1723 was rated about 2.25 pence too high. Similarly, the louis d'or was rated about 2.5 pence too high when compared to the guinea; on the other hand the Portuguese Johannes and gold *moidore* were undervalued. Because of this overrating, the French coins, especially the silver écus and their fractions, quickly became the preferred coins in which to make payments and hence the most common. The ordinance also underrated gold against silver; gold disappeared and silver became the dominant coinage.[7] In Lower Canada the dominance of French silver was to last into the 1830s although pistareens also played an important role as small change. In Upper Canada, and to a lesser extent in the Montreal area, dollars played an important role.

In addition to underrating gold the rating of 1765 had underrated copper coins so as to prevent an influx of unwanted copper. Although this underrating was partially corrected by an ordinance of 15 May 1765 which made 18 copper half-pennies equal to 1 shilling currency, copper coins remained underrated and disappeared from circulation.[8] In response to the dearth of small coin the merchants began to issue their own notes for use as change. Because most of these notes began with the phrase "Bon pour..." so many sols or pence, they were known as "bons". By 1767 the practice had become so common that one enterprising merchant applied to the council for the exclusive right to issue bons. Although the government refused him the monopoly it felt it had no alternative but to tolerate the issue of bons by private merchants.[9]

The new rating, being a compromise between the systems in use in Quebec and Montreal, failed to satisfy merchants of either city and within a month of its coming into force petitions were submitted requesting a return to Halifax currency. Murray's response was to strengthen the original ordinance. By the ordinance of 15 May 1765 he provided that from 1 July the new currency was to be the sole one used in all formal financial transactions. Any agreements made in other currencies would not be admitted as evidence in court.

In spite of this setback the merchants continued to press for a return to the Halifax standard. After Murray left the colony a draft of a revised ordinance was submitted to London for approval but was disallowed. In 1768 Guy Carleton, the new governor, took much of the impetus out of the drive for a change in the currency law by revoking the ordinance of 15 May 1765. As a result, merchants could keep their accounts and make agreements in any currency they wished; only if no currency was specified in an agreement did the rating of 1 January 1765 come into effect.[10]

From the later history of Upper Canada where many merchants kept accounts in New York or York currency up to the 1820s it seems probable that some merchants in Montreal returned to the use of York currency in their accounts, if indeed they had ever abandoned it. Government officials at the upper posts kept their accounts in York currency until at least 1784. Many Quebec merchants used Halifax currency throughout the period; a petition dated 1767 when the 6 - shilling dollar was the only legally enforceable rating, declared that two-thirds of the merchants continued to keep their books in Halifax currency.[11] Throughout the period the army pay contractors did all of their calculations in Halifax currency.

The public accounts of Quebec present a bewildering array of ratings. In 1765 many of the accounts did not specify the currency in which they were submitted. Almost as many accounts were in Halifax currency and smaller proportions were in Quebec currency or in "lawful money of the province". Some accounts were given in sterling, two were in livres and sols with "lawful currency" equivalents, and one in York currency. In the accounts for 1766, when only the new currency could be legally enforced, most accounts were "lawful money" or did not specify a currency; some were still submitted in Halifax currency, livres, or sterling and then converted to lawful currency. After 1768 the proportion of accounts submitted in currencies other than the new currency increased. By 1773 most of the private accounts were in Halifax currency or, in one or two cases, dollars, although many government officials continued to submit their accounts in Quebec currency. The public accounts committee converted all accounts to sterling and prepared its report in sterling.

Another problem which faced Canadians in this and later periods was light coinage, the result either of normal wear or of deliberate debasement. Several of the coins mentioned in Murray's ordinance had not been minted for many years, the moidore not since 1732, and the light écu not since 1723. Those which remained in circulation in the 1760s must have been quite worn. In the British colonies to the south, where most of Canada's Spanish and Portuguese coins came from, clipping and sweating coins was widely practiced and many of the underweight coins found their way to Canada. So many light half-Johannes were imported that merchants refused to accept them at $8.00 Halifax currency. To solve the problem the government encouraged the merchants to set an acceptable rate and after some discussion they agreed to take half-Johannes weighing 9 pennyweight (which was almost the full weight) at $8.00 but to deduct 5 coppers for every grain deficiency in the coin. The problem of the half-Johannes pointed up a serious weakness in the rating of 1765. It did not provide any remedy for lightweight coins; consequently light coins passed at the same rate as heavy coins and the heavier coins were driven out of circulation.

Not all clipped or sweated coins were a result of importation; there were domestic clippers as well. In 1780, 41 Quebec merchants offered a reward of £100, in addition to the reward offered by law, for information leading to the conviction of clippers or sweaters. The advertisement announcing the award noted that new money imported by the government only a year previously was already debased below the limits set by the currency ordinance of 1777.[12]

Supply of coinage

Although there were shortages of specific types of coins in Quebec during the time from the end of the Seven Years' War to the American Revolution, there is not much evidence of an overall shortage of coin. The needs of the colony were small: one estimate places the total circulation of the colony in 1771 at about £8,000.[13] The British government brought a certain amount of coin into the country and raised the rest in Canada by the sale of bills of exchange. The situation changed with the outbreak of the American Revolution. Government expenditures increased beyond the capability of the colony to supply coin at the same time as a former source of coin, trade with the American colonies, was cut off. To meet its expenses in Canada the British government forwarded at least £255,000 in coin to the colony in 1776. Shipments of coin continued until the autumn of 1779 but from then until 1782 no specie was received in the colony.[14]

From 1779 to 1782 the government financed its operations through the sale of bills of exchange in Canada. Many of the bills had to be sold on credit, which suggests that the supply of coin was not completely adequate to meet the needs of the army. In 1782 the army forwarded £128,549 in coin to Quebec. When the Quebec merchant community discovered that Governor Haldimand had applied for further supplies of coin in 1783 it requested that bills of exchange be sent instead as there was no shortage of coin in Quebec and bills of exchange were in great demand.[15]

The increase in government expenditures in Canada during the American Revolution increased commercial activity in the colony several times over. Prices almost doubled and merchants expanded their operations, largely on the basis of bills of exchange. When the war ended and prices fell there was a series of major bankruptcies in Quebec City.

Halifax currency

During the Revolutionary War, Canada dropped the unpopular New England or Quebec rating, adopted in 1765, and introduced the Halifax rating throughout the colony (see Table 6). The Halifax rating valued the Spanish dollar at 5 shillings, one-ninth above the accepted rating of 4s. 6d. sterling. The rating of the gold coins, assuming full weight, was reasonably accurate (except for the doubloon) but gold was undervalued against silver and consequently did not circulate. The act allowed 2.25 pence to be deducted for every grain lacking in the weight of gold coins but no allowance was made for light silver. Among the silver coins the British shillings and crowns were heavily undervalued against the dollar. The dollar and the French crown were rated equitably based on their full weights, but on the basis of the weight of circulating coins the dollar was undervalued. The rate for the écu of the issue of 1718 and 1723, seems too low based on its mint weight but these coins had been in circulation for 50 years and must have been very worn. All silver was undervalued against the pistareen, a debased Spanish coin. In theory the pistareens should have driven the French crowns and other silver out of circulation; in fact, the crowns and half-crowns remained a major part of the circulating medium in Lower Canada. (Why this was so is not clear. It is possible that the French coins were more debased than we know or that there simply were not enough pistareens to supply the need.)

French silver and pistareens became the dominant coins in Canada. Dollars, which were the usual form of army pay, were another important component of the circulation. An analysis of the coins listed in the estate inventory of a major Three Rivers merchant in 1801 showed that dollars were almost 50 times more common than French crowns. Pistareens formed an insignificant part of his estate. Although the contents of an estate cannot be taken as typical of the circulating medium, the inventory indicates that dollars were available in Quebec even if they did not circulate.[16]

Table 6 Ratings Established by 17 George III, an Ordinance for Regulating the Currency of the Province of Quebec, 1777.

Coin Gold	Weight (grains)	Rating (£/s./d.)	Purity	Precious Metal Content (grains)	Grains per Shilling	In Effect Until
Johannes of						
Portugal	438	4/0/0	.9166	401.47	5.02	1836–42
Moidore	164	1/10/0	.9166	150.32	5.01	1836–42
Doubloon or						
4-Pistole piece	408	3/12/0	.9166	373.97	5.19	1796
Guinea	128	1/3/4	.9166	117.32	5.02	1836–42
Louis d'or	123	1/2/6	.9166	112.74	5.01	1808–9
Silver						
Spanish Dollar	(417.6)	5/0	.903	377	75.4	1842
British Crown	(464.5)	5/6	.925	429.6	78.11	1826–42
French Crown, or						
piece of 6 livres	(455)	5/6	.9166	417	75.82	1830–42
French piece of						
4 livres, 10 sols						
(écu of 1718)	(374.9)	4/2	.910	341.16	81.88	1830–42
Shilling	(92.9)	1/1	.925	85.9	79.29	1826–42
Pistareen	(92)	1/0	.8125	74.75	74.75	1830
French piece of						
36 sols	–	1/8	–	–	–	1830–42
French piece of						
24 sols	–	1/1	–	–	–	1830–42

( ) = weight taken from Chalmers or other sources (see Table 5)

Copper coins legal tender to 1s.
Others to pass in proportion
Silver/Gold Ratio = 15.38:1

The 36- and 24-sol pieces were probably thirds and fifths of écus.

Bons

The rating of 1777 remained in force until 1796. During this period there was a gradual depletion of coin in circulation, as the withdrawal of a large part of the British army after the Revolutionary War curtailed the major source of imported coin. Payments for imports also took coin out of the country. The shortage was most acute in the area above Montreal. The upper country was tributary to Montreal, and to a lesser extent to New York; consequently very little coin entered it, and what there was went out to pay debts. A great part of the business was done by barter and with book credits; what could not be handled by credits was usually settled by notes or bons issued by the merchants. In 1792 a merchant noted that, in settlement of a debt of £25, he had received the bills of 12 different people scattered throughout Upper Canada.[17] The Duke de la Rochefouchault wrote that even the troops in Upper Canada were

> paid in paper money, that everyone makes to any amount he chooses, and which nevertheless is universally received with a degree of confidence, equal to that which obtained in France in the second year of the revolution. There are notes of this kind of only two pence in value. They are small slips of paper, either written or printed.[18]

John McGill, a commissariat officer in Upper Canada, was less sanguine about the credit of the bons. Writing from Queenston in 1793 he noted that

> The normal money in circulation here, for the payment of all kinds of produce, is nothing more than notes of hand (or what is termed Bon) on small scripts of paper from 3.25 Sterling to thirty six shillings Sterling issued by people in trade payable on the 10th, 15th, & 25th October annually subject to no interest, and generally pass in the neighbourhood where the issuer resides. It however frequently happens, that the holder of some of this paper currency finds it necessary to realize it into specie, and for that purpose has recourse to the issuer, who will not give specie for his own notes unless he receives Nine Dollars for Eight or at a rate of 12.5 per cwt discount...[19]

According to McGill the notes were also discounted in trade. "At Niagara wheat cannot be purchased for less than 3/9 in specie and not under 4/4.5 and 4/8.25 per bushel in paper [money or] 5/ payable in goods." Governor Simcoe saw the bons as a means by which the merchants monopolized government contracts for flour. He proposed to break the monopoly by purchasing flour directly from the producers and paying for it either in coin or in transferable government notes.[20] There is no evidence that these notes were ever issued.

Another source of paper currency in the last decade of the eighteenth century was American bank notes. By 1800 a total of 29 banks had 15.5 million dollars worth of notes in circulation. After the War of 1812, American bank notes became quite common in Canada but they may have been less common before the war. Adam Shortt states that prior to 1810 their circulation in Canada was impeded by the fact that there was no Canadian law prohibiting their forgery.[21]

Although the coin famine was most severe in Upper Canada it also existed in the lower province. In 1788 the collector of customs at Quebec testified that "It is very rare I receive at my office either Gold or Silver... I generally accept notes."[22] In 1792 the shortage of coin or reliable notes prompted three of the leading fur-trading partnerships, Phyn, Ellice and Inglis, Todd, McGill and Company, and Forsyth, Richardson and Company to give notice that they intended to establish a banking company in Quebec City which would take deposits, issue notes, and discount (make loans). Although the bank may have come into operation briefly it does not seem to have issued any notes. It was nevertheless the first attempt to organize a note-issuing bank in Canada.

The Currency Act of 1796

In 1796 the problem of the export of gold as a result of its underrating had become so serious that a new rating was established in both Upper and Lower Canada in an attempt to bring the silver/gold ratio into balance (see Table 7). The new statutes made no change in the rating of silver coins, although the United States dollar was added to the list of legal tender coins. The rating of the Spanish doubloon was raised and the minimum acceptable weights of the Johannes, moidore, and guinea were lowered slightly thus raising their relative value. The silver/gold ratio was increased slightly from 15.38 under the 1777 ordinance to 15.47:1 under the 1796 act. In order to prevent the importation and circulation of lightweight gold coins the acts provided that 2.25 pence should be allowed for every grain over or under the specified weight. To simplify larger transactions the acts provided that in payments of over £50 gold could be weighed in bulk at the option of either party. After 1 June 1797, British, Portuguese and United States gold was to be allowed 89s. currency per ounce and French and Spanish gold was to be allowed 87s. per ounce when weighed in bulk.

78

Surprisingly the acts did not provide for any remedies for lightweight silver coins, and as a result silver remained the dominant coinage. Among the silver coins the shilling and British crown were clearly underrated and can hardly have circulated. The light écu was also very underrated. However, it is quite possible that its worn state made up for the rating. The Spanish dollar, the United States dollar, the French crown and the pistareen were all rated equitably, assuming they were of full weight, but the worn state of French crowns may have given them an edge in circulation.

Copper coins were limited as legal tender to payments of 1 shilling or less. This restriction may have been in response to the importation of large quantities of old worn copper coin of the period 1770-75. Although export of "base Copper Coin and base Foreign Coin" to the colonies was prohibited by an imperial act in 1798 it continued to be a profitable enterprise through the first half of the nineteenth century.[23]

The act of 1796 undervalued the doubloon, the louis d'or and French pistole. In order to correct this undervaluation the Lower Canadian legislature revised the currency law in 1808; the Upper Canadian legislature made similar revisions in 1809 (see Table 8). The revisions brought the coins closer to their proper evaluation; they did not, however, correct the underlying overvaluation of silver against gold, so silver remained the dominant metal.

The currency acts of 1808-09 also included some minor revisions to the 1796 acts. The allowance for heavy or light French or Spanish coins was reduced to 2.2d per grain over or under the official weight. When coins were weighed in bulk the French and Spanish coins were to be allowed 87s. 8.5d. per ounce. In order to protect those who acquired coins in bulk by weight but dispensed them individually, a deduction of 0.5 grain per coin was allowed when weighing coins in bulk.

Table 7   Ratings Established by 36 George III, C.5, 1796, Lower Canada and 36 George III, C.1, 1796, Upper Canada

Coin	Weight (grains)	Rating (£/s./d.)	Purity	Precious Metal Content (grains)	Grains Per Shilling	In Effect Until
Gold						
Guinea	126	1/3/4	.9166	115.49	4.95	1836–42
Moidore	162	1/10/0	.9166	148.49	4.95	1836–42
Spanish milled Doubloon or 4-Pistole piece	408	3/14/0	.9166	373.97	5.05	1808–9
Louis d'or, pre-1793	124	1/2/6	.9166	113.66	5.05	1808–9
French Pistole, pre-1793	100	18/0	.9166	91.66	5.09	1808–9
U.S. Eagle	270	2/10/0	.9166	247.48	4.95	1858
Johannes	432	4/0/0	.9166	395.97	4.95	1836–42
Silver						
British Crown	(464.5)	5/6	.925	429.6	78.11	1826–42
Shilling	(92.9)	1/1	.925	85.9	79.29	1826–42
Spanish milled Dollar	(417.6)	5/0	.903	377.0	75.4	1842
French Crown (pre-1793)	(455)	5/6	.9166	417.0	75.82	1830–42
French piece of 4 livres, 10 sols (écu of 1718)	374.9	4/2	.910	341.16	81.88	1830–42
French piece of 36 sols	–	1/8	–	–	–	1830–42
French piece of 24 sols	–	1/1	–	–	–	1830–42
U.S. Dollar	(416)	5/0	.8924	371.25	74.25	1842
Pistareen	(92)	1/0	.8125	74.75	74.75	1830s

( ) = weight taken from Chalmers or other sources (see Table 5)

Other coins in proportion
Copper coins were legal tender to 1 shilling
Silver/gold ratio = 15.47:1

Table 8   Revised Rating for Doubloons, Louis d'or and French Pistoles. Established by 48 George III, C.8, 1808, Lower Canada, and 49 George III, C.8, 1809, Upper Canada

Coin	Weight (grains)	Rating (£/s./d.)	Purity*	Gold Content (grains)	Grains per Shiling	In Effect Until
Doubloon	408	3/14/6	.9166	373.97	5.02	1836–42
Louis d'or	124	1/2/8	.9166	113.66	5.01	1836–42
French Pistole	100	18/3	.9166	91.66	5.02	1836–42

*The purity of these coins gives some difficulty. Assays indicate that the louis d'or was commonly closer to .9 in purity than .9166. The French pistole was presumably the louis d'or introduced in the reign of Louis XIII and last minted in 1709. The coins in circulation in 1808–9 must have been very worn and hence overrated. They must also have been quite rare. Assays showed that the pistoles were usually closer to .904 in purity rather than .9166. The mint purity of doubloons was reduced to .901 in 1772 and to .875 in 1786 although its gross weight remained unchanged. All three types of doubloon might have circulated in Canada in 1808–9. Depending on which level of purity was present, one shilling's worth of gold in a doubloon might weigh 5.02 grains, 4.93 grains or 4.79 grains. It seems probable that by 1808–9 most doubloons in Canada were either the newer issues and hence well overrated or the old issue and hence worn and only slightly overrated.

Trade in bills of exchange

In 1783 the merchants of Quebec had complained that there was too much coin in the colony and too few bills of exchange. By the 1790s the situation was well on its way to being reversed. The British government attempted to supply most of its financial needs in Canada by forwarding bills of exchange on London to Quebec and selling them for coin with which it paid its bills. By the end of the century bills of exchange on London tended to be in oversupply at Quebec and often traded at a discount, in some cases as much as 10% below par. Although bill prices revived between 1803 and 1805, bills were generally at a discount until after the War of 1812. During the war itself they were discounted as much as 20-25% in spite of large imports of specie by the government. Partly the discount was a result of European conditions. The Bank of England suspended specie payments in 1797 and did not resume them until 1821. Suspension, combined with wartime inflation, weakened sterling against other currencies and the exchange rate tended to fluctuate according to the fortunes of war as well as to the supply of bills of exchange. Successful Canadian trading ventures, particularly the export of wheat to Britain, also reduced the demand for bills of exchange by creating sterling credits in Britain.[24] Although Canada enjoyed a favourable balance of trade with Britain in the decade before the War of 1812, its balance of trade with the United States was not as good. Canadians imported timber, beef, wheat and horses from the states which bordered the Great Lakes or were served by the Richelieu River. These imports were largely the result of numerous small purchases and were generally paid for in silver, particularly in silver dollars. The visible imbalance in the commodity trade with the United States was at least partially balanced by a trade in bills of exchange. During the years 1799–1810 sterling prices were lower in Quebec City than they were in Boston or New York. If the difference was great enough (about 3–3.5% in 1807) it became profitable to ship bills from Quebec to New York or Boston, sell them, and ship the coin back to Quebec.[25] In Quebec the coin reentered circulation through the medium of army pay and purchases; in all likelihood much of it was eventually exported to the United States, thus completing the cycle.

Government agents sometimes travelled to the sterling markets in New York and Boston to acquire coin but it was more common for them to limit their risk and involvement by selling their bills to private firms in Quebec. These firms shipped the bills to New York or Boston to purchase coin which was then used to purchase more bills in Quebec. By the 1790s this trade had been in effect for many years. Phyn, Ellice and Company of Schenectady were purchasing bills in Quebec for the New York market during 1774–76 and Lawrence Ermatinger may have been involved in a similar trade as early as 1770. The army paymasters imported coin from New York as early as October 1760 but commercial exchange business may not have been established for some time after.[26] The trade was interrupted by the American Revolution but was probably revived after the war as soon as the surplus of coin in Canada reported in 1783 was depleted. By the turn of the century the trade was well developed. The correspondence of John Hale, the Deputy Paymaster-General at Quebec, indicates that by 1800 at least three firms, James and Andrew McGill and Company, Forsyth, Richardson and Company, and Lester and Company were regularly involved in purchasing bills in Quebec and selling them in the United States. As well some Boston and New York merchants took the initiative and shipped coin to Quebec to purchase bills on London which they required.

The War of 1812 completely disrupted this system. The United States was cut off as a source of coin supply at the same time that rising military expenditures increased the demand for coin. The exchange rate which had fallen below par in 1810 plummeted to as much as a 20–25% discount in 1812 and 1813. Very early in the war the colonial government sought an alternative to importing money from the United States or raising it at ruinous rates in Canada. Coin was imported from Halifax which in turn raised money for the government in Quebec by the sale of bills of exchange in the Caribbean. However, the sums raised in this way were far from sufficient to carry on the war and in the summer of 1812 the government decided to issue a form of paper money for circulation in Canada.

Army bills

In July the Executive Council of Lower Canada approved the issue of up to £250,000 currency in paper money to be known as "army bills". The bills were to be of two types. Small bills of $4.00 were to be payable in cash at Quebec. Larger bills, from $25 upwards, were redeemable in cash or in bills of exchange on London at the option of the government. The rate of exchange paid was established fortnightly by a special commission. Although the small bills did not bear interest the larger bills did at a rate of 4%. In order to preserve the credit of the bills they were to be received as specie in payments at all public offices. An act of the legislature further strengthened their credit by rendering void all contracts which made a distinction between army bills and coin and by forbidding the export of gold or silver in any form from the colony. In addition the colonial government guaranteed the bills and agreed to pay the interest to a maximum £15,000 annually.[27]

The original issue soon proved insufficient, and one year later a second act of the legislature doubled the limit. It also provided for the issue of up to £50,000 of 1, 2, 8, 10, 12 and 16-dollar bills which were similar to the $4.00 bills of the first issue. In 1814 the upper limit on bills issued was raised to £1.5 million currency, with up to one-third of this being authorized for issue in small bills of 1, 2, 3, 5 and 10 dollars. Early in 1815 a bill was introduced in the assembly which would have raised the limit to £2 million but the legislative council refused to agree to the increase. The small bills issued in 1814 did not bear interest nor were they payable in cash but they could be used to buy bills of exchange on London or exchanged for larger, interest-bearing bills. The provincial government had guaranteed the principal on the earlier bills but it refused to guarantee the principal on later issues.[28]

In 1813 the bills were made legal tender in Upper Canada as well as in Lower Canada and throughout the war they circulated freely in both provinces. Upper Canada also authorized the issue of £100,000 of its own bills but they were never issued.

The army bills were well accepted in the early years of the war. In September 1812 a Quebec merchant advertised that he preferred them to cash in payment of debts. In October, Assistant Commissary-General Robinson reported that they had succeeded beyond expectations; of nearly £200,000 in large-denomination bills which he had put into circulation, only £16,000 had been exchanged for bills on London.[29] There were, however, problems. The fortunes of war could affect the bills' credit. In June 1813 with American forces advancing on all fronts Governor-in-Chief Sir George Prevost wrote gloomily that in the uncertain state of affairs paper money had lost its effect and only specie could command the country's hidden resources. A year later Major-General Riall wrote that people on the Niagara frontier had no faith in the commissary and would not sell goods without "money down".[30] There is also some evidence that the bills depreciated: in January 1814 three government officials petitioned for an increase in their salaries partly on the grounds that army bills, with which they were paid, were depreciated by 20%.[31] Forgeries were also a problem; some forged notes were evidently put into circulation by the American army in an attempt to discredit the bills.[32] However, the problems seem to have been minor in comparison to the benefits resulting from the bills. Some Canadians would have liked to see the army bills continue to circulate after the war. However, the bills were largely an imperial military responsibility and there was little incentive for the military to keep them in circulation beyond the time they served a purely military need. The colonial government's contribution only paid about one-third of the interest on the total value of the bills outstanding in 1814; the remainder, about £33,000, was paid from the military chest. Moreover the colonial guarantees on the bills were scheduled to expire in August 1817. It was anticipated that once the war ended, military expenditures would be drastically reduced, sterling exchange rates would return to a normal range, and there would be no further need for the finance provided by the bills. As the end of the war drew near there was an influx of coin from the United States. Exchange rose steadily from a 20% discount in January 1814 to a 2.5% discount in December. During the winter of 1814-15 the government began to retire the bills and by November 1815 it began to redeem bills in coin instead of in bills of exchange. The redemption of the bills went on steadily from 1815 to 1817. In 1817 the ban on the export of specie was lifted and although the Army Bill Office continued in existence for another three years, almost all of the bills had been withdrawn by the end of the year (see Table 16).

The army bills had been identified with the prosperity of the war years and their success may have encouraged individuals who had been interested in the possibility of establishing a bank before the war to continue their efforts after the war. The idea of establishing a note-issuing bank was not a new one. In England banks had been issuing paper money for over a century. In the United States banking had expanded rapidly from only three banks in 1784 to 89 in 1811. In the same period bank-notes increased from 17% to 48% of the total circulation of the United States and by the end of the war, bank-notes and treasury notes formed 77% of the total American circulation.[33]

The rise of Canadian banks

Although the attempt to establish a Canadian Bank in 1792 failed, the idea did not die. In Upper Canada, Robert Hamilton investigated the possibility of establishing a bank in 1800, and in 1810, Kingston residents petitioned the legislature to charter a bank. In Lower Canada, bills to charter banks were introduced in the legislature in 1808, 1816, and 1817. All failed; the third failure prompted a group of Montreal merchants to establish a private bank without the benefit of a charter.

Articles of association were signed, shares subscribed, a bank staff and premises hired, and in November 1817 the Montreal Bank, later the Bank of Montreal, opened for business. This was followed in 1818 and 1819 by the Quebec Bank at Quebec City, a second bank at Montreal named the Bank of Canada, and a bank at Kingston. In addition, the Bank of Montreal opened an office of discount and deposit in Quebec City and appointed an agent in Kingston. All began business as private partnerships but all applied to their respective legislatures for charters. All except the Kingston bank (which later failed from lack of capital) received charters in 1821. As well, a chartered bank, the Bank of Upper Canada, was established at York.[34]

Of the four chartered banks the Bank of Montreal and the Bank of Upper Canada at York quickly emerged as the dominant institutions in their provinces. The Bank of Montreal usually had double or treble the value of notes in circulation of its three rivals combined. In addition the Bank of Montreal was the major dealer in foreign exchange in Lower Canada, and the government banker. The Bank of Canada never had a very large circulation and seems to have concentrated its efforts on dealing in foreign exchange. In Upper Canada the Bank of Upper Canada was the only bank until 1833. For some years the government was a shareholder and the bank served as the government bank. After 1833 it was the British commissariat banker as well.[35]

Although the banks were incorporated by separate acts of the legislature, the acts of incorporation were quite similar. The banks were limited in their business to dealing in bills of exchange and to discounting. They were not to deal in real estate, nor were a bank's debts, not including deposits, to exceed three times its paid-up capital. The first bank charters placed no limitation on the value of bank-notes which a bank could place in circulation, other than the limitation that total debts were not to exceed three times the paid-up capital; renewals of the bank charters in 1841 limited the issue of notes to the total of the bank's paid-up capital. In order to maintain the notes' credit the acts of incorporation provided that all bank-notes should be redeemable on demand in gold or silver legal tender coin. Although the banks received deposits they did not initially pay interest on ordinary deposits.

The main sources of bank profits were dealings in bills of exchange, commercial loans and the issuing of bank-notes. The issuing of bank-notes and the making of loans were intimately connected. Typically bank-notes were put in circulation by means of loans or discounts. For example, a merchant requiring a loan of £1000 for three months, a typical period for commercial loans, would offer the bank his promissory note for £1000, payable in 90 days, and countersigned by two other merchants. If the bank accepted his note (commonly referred to as commercial paper) it would credit his account with a sum, say £985 4s. 1.5d. When the credit was withdrawn it would be paid in the bank's notes which would be put into circulation. The difference, £14 15s. 10.5d., between the value of the note and the value of the credit, represented three months' interest at 6% annually, paid in advance. Because the bank had, in effect, purchased the merchant's note at a discount, the entire process was referred to as discounting.

The effective interest which banks collected on loans made in their own notes was potentially much greater than it would have been had they loaned actual coin. Intrinsically the notes were worthless; they cost the bank no more than the cost of paper, ink and labour. Their value lay in the fact that they were evidence of a debt owed by the bank and when they were returned to the bank their face value had to be paid in gold or silver coin. If it should happen that the £985 4s 1.5d. worth of notes loaned to the merchant remained in circulation for 90 days, or until after the merchant had paid off his note, the bank did not have to put up any coin to finance the loan. In effect it had bought the merchant's note with interest-free credit and the £14 15s. 10.5d. interest which the bank collected, less operating costs, was profit. Operating costs included the cost of producing the bank-notes, wages, and rent, but they did not include a lost opportunity cost as they would have if the bank had loaned coins instead of bank-notes.

In the example given it was suggested that the £985 4s. 1.5d. in bank-notes issued in satisfaction of the loan might all stay in circulation until after the merchant had repaid his loan, in which case the bank would not have to put up any of its own coin to execute the loan. In fact this was unlikely, and banks had to keep reserves of coin on hand to redeem their notes as they were returned. However, the specie reserve, as it was known, was only equal to a fraction of the amount of the notes outstanding. The actual ratio of notes in circulation to specie on hand varied from time to time and from bank to bank; in the early 1840s the ratio in central Canada ranged from 2:1 to about 6:1. The higher the ratio of circulating notes to specie the greater the bank's opportunity for profit, but higher ratios also increased the risk. So long as all of the outstanding notes were not brought in for redemption at one time the bank would be solvent, and so long as people were confident that the notes could be exchanged for coin there was little reason to exchange them for the more cumbersome coin. If, however, confidence in the ability of the bank to redeem its notes failed, and there was a run on the bank (that is, all of its outstanding notes were brought in for redemption at once) the bank would have to refuse to redeem them. Quite frequently this would only confirm the panic, with the end result that the bank would fail. To enable banks to deal with minor runs, charters were amended to allow banks to suspend payments for up to 60 days, but any further suspension led to a loss of the bank charter.

Bank-note circulation

The first issue of Bank of Montreal notes were in 1, 5, 10, 20- and 100-dollar denominations; 2-dollar notes were issued later. The Bank of Canada issued notes in 1, 2, 5, 20, 50- and 100-dollar denominations and the Bank of Quebec in 1, 3, 5, 10- and 100-dollar denominations with a 2-dollar bill in a subsequent issue. By the time it went bankrupt the Bank of Upper Canada (Kingston) had roughly £20,000 currency in circulation in 1, 5, 20, 50- and 100-dollar denominations. The Bank of Upper Canada (York) was the only bank to issue its early notes in pounds and shillings: in the 1820s it had 5s., 10s., £1 5s. and £2 10s. notes in circulation. From the 1830s to the 1850s it used both dollar and pound/shilling designations on its notes. The Quebec Bank also issued 5-shilling or 6-sous notes but in general, central Canadian banks used dollar denominations.

Bank-notes very rapidly became the dominant form of money in both the Canadas. In 1823 J.B. Robinson noted that "for several years past all payments in Upper Canada, not only by Individuals but by civil and even Military departments of the public service have been generally made in the paper of the different banks".[36] In the same year the compiler of the official Blue Books estimated that the total circulation of Upper Canada was about £100,000 currency of which about £75,000 was bank paper from Upper and Lower Canadian banks. Lower Canadian banks were active in Upper Canada. By 1818 both the Bank of Canada and the Bank of Montreal had agencies at Kingston and the Bank of Montreal had an agency at York. Bank of Montreal notes circulated widely in Upper Canada. A letter in the Kingston *Chronicle* in 1824 noted that the troops at Kingston were paid in Bank of Montreal notes.[37] These incursions were viewed with displeasure by the proprietors of the Bank of Upper Canada, and in 1824 they succeeded in having "An act to prohibit banks from carrying on business in this province that do not return their notes in specie within the same" passed. As neither the Bank of Montreal nor the Bank of Canada were prepared to conform to the act they closed their offices in Upper Canada until the act expired in 1830. The act did not prevent Lower Canadian bank-notes from circulating and they continued to form an important part of the circulation in Upper Canada throughout the 1820s. Probably because of the nature of commerce between Upper and Lower Canada relatively few Upper Canadian bank-notes circulated in Lower Canada.

In addition to local bank-notes, American bank-notes also circulated in Canada, particularly in Upper Canada. In 1819 Lieutenant-Governor Maitland described the province as "over-run with American paper"[38] and suggested that the formation of a provincial bank would drive the American paper out of circulation. In 1815 the Kingston *Gazette* carried an advertisement for a lost pocketbook containing 28 ten-dollar bills, 1 twenty-dollar bill, 1 five-dollar bill, 1 three-dollar bill, 1 seventy-five-dollar bill and one half-Eagle, "all American".[39]

The copper money which circulated was even more varied than the paper. Much of it was not legal coin but copper trade tokens manufactured commercially in England and imported as a profit-making venture. Some tokens were also manufactured in Canada. Quantities of these tokens, many bearing a likeness of the Duke of Wellington, were imported during the war and quickly fell into such disrepute that they interfered with trade. In 1817 the Quebec and Montreal merchants petitioned the legislature to regulate the use of copper coin. Nothing was done and the variety of copper in circulation continued to grow as its quality declined. John McTaggart, a clerk on the Rideau Canal in the 1820s, estimated that there were 120 varieties of copper coin and tokens which passed as half-pennies in Canada.[40] In 1830 a committee of the Upper Canadian assembly stated that the current copper currency consisted of Wellington and Brock halfpence weighing about 3 pennyweight each (compared to a full weight halfpence which weighed about 6 pennyweight), old worn British halfpence which "were cried down at home many years ago", old buttons and farthings beaten smooth, Nova Scotia halfpence weighing 5 pennyweight, 22 grains, English and Irish halfpence of about the same weight and a few Congress cents weighing 7 pennyweight each.[41]

French coinage in Lower Canada

After the division of Quebec into the provinces of Lower and Upper Canada in 1791 the two provinces passed parallel currency legislation in 1796 and in 1808–09 with the result that coins circulated in the two provinces at the same rate. In 1819 Lower Canada made a number of postrevolutionary French coins legal tender (see Table 9). In this case Upper Canada did not follow the lower province's lead and as a result a rift opened between the currencies in the two provinces. The rift was to grow wider with subsequent legislation in the 1820s and 1830s.

Table 9   Ratings of Post-Revolutionary French Coins Made Legal Tender in Lower Canada by 59 George III, C.1, 1819, Lower Canada

Coin	Weight (grains)	Rating (£/s./d.)	Purity	Precious Metal Content (grains)	Grains per Shilling	In Effect Until
Gold						
40-franc piece	198	£1/15/2	.9	178.2	5.07	1842
20-franc piece	99	18/1	.9	89.1	4.93	1842
Silver						
6-livres coin	(455)	5/6	.9166	417.0	75.82	1842
5-franc piece	(385.8)	4/8	.9	347.2	74.41	1842
Fractions in proportion						

( ) = weight taken from Chalmers or other sources (see Table 5)

The Lower Canadian legislation of 1819 made the gold 40-
and 20-franc and silver 5-franc and 6-livre pieces legal tender.
The 40-franc piece was undervalued and can hardly have
circulated but the 20-franc piece was equitably valued in
relation to other gold coins. The 5-franc piece was overrated
at 4s. 8d. but it remained uncommon. The common coin in
Lower Canada was the 6-livre piece or French crown and its
half. The crown had first been rated at 5s. 6d. currency in 1777.
At that time it was overvalued and as it became more worn
the rating became increasingly unrealistic. A legislative
committee estimated that the crowns in circulation in Lower
Canada in the late 1830s were 2.1% below their mint weight and
the half-crowns were 8.9% below mint weight. By 1828 it was
estimated that there was £50,000 in French silver in circulation
in Lower Canada, mostly half-crowns and crowns.[42] One reason
for the prominence of the half-crown and crown may have been
importation by the banks. The banks were accused of evading
the obligation to redeem their notes in coin by redeeming them
in debased coins, particularly pistareens, old French crowns
and half-crowns, and old English crowns and shillings.[43] As early
as 1820 the Bank of Montreal refused to accept the notes of
the Bank of Canada because they could only be redeemed in
overvalued half-crowns.[44] In 1829 the Bank of Montreal had to
defend itself against the charge that it imported worn half-
crowns and issued them at the official rate of 2s. 9d.[45] The
practice of redeeming notes in overvalued coins seems to have
been general among the banks and was probably the cause of
bank-notes being received at a discount in Canada. In 1827 the
Blue Books for Upper Canada reported that British gold brought
a premium of 8-9.5% Portuguese and American gold 4-6% and
silver 7% over paper money, principally paper money of the
Bank of Upper Canada.

Although Upper Canada did not follow Lower Canada's
lead in making postrevolutionary French coins legal tender, it
did act to eliminate one source of confusion between the
currency systems of the two provinces. Since the 1760s, when
Upper Canada had been tributary to Montreal, some merchants
had continued to keep accounts in New York currency, rating
the dollar at 8s. currency instead of in the official Halifax
currency which rated it at 5s. currency. In 1821 the legislature
passed an act reaffirming the use of Halifax currency and
providing sanctions against the use of York Currency. After

1 July 1822 only accounts kept on the basis of five shillings currency per dollar would be accepted by the provincial government and contracts using the old York currency would not be binding. In spite of the act the use of York currency continued to be common for some years. Thomas Fowler, a visitor to Upper Canada in 1830, seems to have used York currency as often as he used Halifax, and J. Macaulay, the Inspector-General, reported in 1840 that York currency was still used in the rural parts of Upper Canada.[46] Terms such as a "York shilling", equal to 12.5 cents or a "bit", continued in popular use even longer.

British currency reform

In the 1820s the British government, in one of its periodic attempts to impose some uniformity on the empire, attempted to establish a common monetary system throughout the empire by encouraging the use of British coinage. Because the imperial government had delegated authority to establish local currency rates to the colonial legislatures, this had to be brought about through example rather than direct legislation. As a first step, in 1825, the government ordered that in future all troops serving in the colonies should be paid in British silver or copper coin. Realizing that this change could not be brought about immediately the government allowed that, where the Spanish dollar was by law or practice legal tender, it could be used to pay the troops at a rate of 4s. 4d. per dollar if British silver was not available. The directive also allowed the use of the five-franc piece at 4s. sterling. To encourage the use of British silver the government directed that bills of exchange on the treasury, which were sold to raise coin in the colonies, should be sold for British coin at a fixed rate of £103 of coin for a £100 bill of exchange. If British coin was not available other coin could be accepted but the market rate for exchange would prevail.

From the Canadian point of view the change had several undesirable effects. British silver coinage did not circulate freely in Canada and could only be obtained at a premium. By reducing the sterling value of the dollar the regulations undermined the theoretical foundation of the Halifax currency system, both in the Canadas and in the maritime colonies, and upset long-established practices. Halifax currency was based on a dollar valued at 4s. 6d. sterling; by reducing the dollar's sterling value by 2 pence the British government inflated Halifax currency by about 4%. One important effect of this inflation was an upward pressure on the currency price of sterling bills. A more immediate effect of the reduction in the sterling value of the dollar was that it abolished army sterling in which the dollar was valued at 4s. 8d. The result was an increase in costs to Canadians doing business with the army. A further blow came in 1828 when the treasury directed that imperial customs duties should also be collected in British coin or in dollars valued at 4s. 4d. sterling. After 31 January 1831 only British coin was to be accepted in payment of customs. For nearly 50 years Canadians had been accustomed to paying customs in dollars rated at 4s. 6d. sterling or in some cases at 4s. 8.75d. (see Appendix C). Finally the premium on exchange at 3% exceeded the cost of shipping coin to England. Consequently government bills were unsaleable until 1827 when the premium was reduced to 1.5%.[47]

Although the home government could not unilaterally change Canadian laws regarding currency it did put pressure on the local governments to encourage the circulation of British coins in Canada. The Upper Canadian legislature responded half-heartedly in 1826 by increasing the rating of British silver about 15% above its sterling value. The rating of the crown was increased to 5s. 9d. currency and the shilling to 1s. 2d. currency with higher and lower denominations of British silver in proportion (see Table 10). The act also provided that 17s. 4d. of British silver and copper coins should be valued at 20s. currency, a ratio of £115.38 currency to £100 sterling. This provision seems to have been ignored in practice and most accounts continued to be kept on the assumption that £111.11 currency was equal to £100 sterling.

Table 10   Ratings Established For British Silver by 7 George IV, C.4, 1826, Upper Canada

	Weight (grains)	Rating (s./d.)	Purity	Silver Content (grains)	Grains Per Shilling	In Effect Until
Shilling (old)	(92.9)	1/2	.925	85.9	73.63	1836–42
(new)	(87.3)	1/2	.925	80.7	69.17	1836–42
Crown (old)	(464.5)	5/9	.925	429.6	77.71	1836–42
(new)	(436.36)	5/9	.925	403.63	70.2	1836–42

( ) = weight taken from Chalmers or other sources (see Table 5)

On the surface the rating was roughly equitable since at 5s. the dollar was 15% above its new sterling value of 4s. 4d. However, the change did not bring British silver into general circulation. According to R. Chalmers there were three reasons for this. First, the dollar was still overvalued and British silver undervalued. Second, because British silver was in demand for the purchase of bills of exchange on England, it was bought up and returned to the government coffers before it could circulate widely. Third, the extensive issue of paper money drove coin out of circulation. As a result the dollar remained the common coin in Upper Canada and paper money the common medium of exchange.[48]

In Lower Canada the legislature refused to make any changes in its currency laws to encourage the circulation of British silver. The Legislative Council argued that British silver was already overrated under the act of 1796 because when it was used in making remittances to Britain it was treated as bullion and fetched the market price, about 5s. per ounce of standard silver in the 1820s. Thus a new crown, nominally worth 5s. sterling, was worth only about 4s. 6.5d. sterling when remitted in bulk to Britain. On the basis of this market valuation the currency rating of the crown, 5s. 6d., represented an advance of 21% on its true value compared to an advance of 15% or 19% on the dollar, depending on whether the dollar was valued at 4s. 2.3d. or 4s. 4d. sterling. The council also pointed out that the Spanish dollar was convenient for paying seigneurial dues, which were calculated in livres and sols, because it was valued at 6 livres.[49] No change was made in the rating of British silver in Lower Canada although imperial officials, chiefly the army and customs officers, adopted the new rating for dollars. As a result of the changes in Upper Canada the divergence between the currency systems of Upper and Lower Canada, which had begun in 1819, widened. It was to grow wider still in the next few years.

Monetary reform in Upper Canada

In 1796 the pistareen had been overrated at 1 shilling in both Upper and Lower Canada. Over the years with continued wear this overrating increased with the result that it became, along with the half-écu, the dominant coin in circulation in Lower Canada and an important coin in Upper Canada. The pistareen also circulated in the United States, New Brunswick and Nova Scotia. Following a report by the United States mint in 1827 the rating at which pistareens were accepted was reduced from 20 cents to 18 cents or 17 cents. At about the same time their rating in Nova Scotia and New Brunswick fell to 10d.[50] In order to avoid being flooded with pistareens both Upper Canada and Lower Canada moved to adjust the values of the pistareen. In Lower Canada pistareens were reduced in value to 10d. and half-pistareens to 5d. in 1830. At the same time Upper Canada undertook a general housecleaning and demonetized the pistareen and all French silver and it provided that any British silver under 96% of its legal weight should not circulate as legal tender. The practical effect of the changes in the rating of the pistareen is not completely clear. Adam Shortt contends that the need for small coins was so great that the circulation of pistareens was not greatly reduced. Writing in 1837, J. Buchanan stated that the pistareens were bought up, shipped to Spain and replaced by United States half- and quarter-dollars.[51] Overall, the changes in legislation between 1826 and 1830 meant that French coins, among the most common coins circulating in Lower Canada, were not current in Upper Canada, and British silver circulated at different rates in each province. Only the dollar and its parts continued to circulate at the same rate in both provinces.

The close relationship which had developed between the American and Canadian monetary systems was illustrated a second time when the United States revalued its coins in 1834.

When the United States established its coinage in 1792 it took the Spanish dollar as its model and established the pure silver content of its new dollar at 371.25 grains, the average content of a sample of circulated Spanish dollars. At the time the silver/gold price ratio was 15:1 so the pure gold content of the basic gold coin, the eagle worth $10.00, was set at 247.5 grains. Shortly after the United States set this ratio and began minting coins, the price of silver began to fall and for the next 30 to 40 years the silver/gold ratio was closer to 15.5:1 or 16:1. As a result, gold almost never circulated in the United States. At the same time silver, although overvalued in the United States, was even more overvalued in the West Indies and seldom remained in circulation long. Spanish dollars and foreign gold coins were legal tender in the United States and formed a part of the general circulation. In 1834 an attempt was made to correct the silver/gold imbalance by reducing the gold content of the eagle from 247.5 to 232 grains. The new price for gold was above the world market price and gold flowed into the United States mint. To correct for this the precious metal content of both the silver dollar and gold eagle were adjusted slightly in 1837. The change was not great enough to alter the balance and American silver generally stayed out of circulation until 1853.

These changes had an immediate effect on Canadian circulation, particularly on the circulation of Upper Canada which had close trade ties with the United States. The increased value of gold in the United States quickly drained off what little gold circulated in Canada. This was particularly true because neither the sovereign, which had replaced the guinea as the principal British gold coin after 1817, nor the new eagles, were legal tender in Canada and both circulated according to market rates. Silver tended to be drawn to the United States by trade.

In response to this flight of coin Upper Canada completely revised its coinage rating system in 1836 (see Table 11). All gold coins except British and American ones were demonetized. The ratings for the guinea and the old eagle were increased, the new eagle was made legal tender at 50s. and the British sovereign at £1 4s. 4d. Spanish, Mexican and United States dollars were left at their traditional rating, but British silver was rated substantially above its proportionate value. In particular the shilling and the sixpence were rated very much above their worth in relation to other silver and to gold. The law also provided that when gold coins lost 4% of their legal weight they ceased to be legal tender.

Table 11   Ratings Established by 6 William IV, C.27, 1836, Upper Canada

	Weight (grains)	Rating (£/s./d.)	Purity	Precious Metal Content (grains)	Grains Per Shilling	In Effect Until
Gold						
Guinea	129.5	1/5/6	.9166	118.70	4.65	1842
Sovereign	123.5	1/4/4	.9166	113.20	4.65	1858
Eagle, pre-1834	270.0	2/13/4	.9166	247.48	4.64	1858
Eagle, post-1834	258.0	2/10/0	.900	232.20	4.64	1858
Silver						
Crown (old)	(464.5)	6/0	.925	429.60	71.61	1842
Crown (new)	(436.36)	6/0	.925	403.63	67.27	1842
Half-Crown (old)	(232.25)	3/0	.925	214.83	71.61	1842
Half-Crown (new)	(218.18)	3/0	.925	201.82	67.27	1842
Shilling (old)	(92.9)	1/3	.925	85.90	68.70	1842
Shilling (new)	(87.3)	1/3	.925	80.70	64.60	1842
Sixpence (old)	(46.45)	0/7.5	.925	42.97	68.75	1842
Sixpence (new)	(43.64)	0/7.5	.925	40.38	64.59	1842
Dollar, Spanish	(417.6)	5/0	.903	377.00	75.40	1842
Dollar, U.S.	(416)	5/0	.8924	371.25	74.25	1842
Dollar, Mexican of 1831-33	(416.73)	5/0	.8963	373.52	74.70	1842

Silver/gold ratio, 15.05:1
( )=weight taken from Chalmers or other sources (see Table 5)

The changes in Upper Canada improved its currency in relationship to the American market but put it even more out of joint with Lower Canada. In Lower Canada the need for currency reform was becoming increasingly obvious but the political pressures which were soon to lead to rebellion and the financial turmoil created by the panic of 1837 delayed reform. In 1839 both Upper and Lower Canada passed currency acts which would have given the same ratings to most of their major coins, but the bills were reserved and were not confirmed by the British government. It was not until 1841 that the Legislature of the Province of Canada adopted a uniform coinage for the whole province.

The growth of banks

During the 1830s the role of banks in the monetary system continued to increase. In 1833 the Bank of Montreal was made the banker for the British military in Lower Canada and at Kingston and the Bank of Upper Canada became the army bank in the rest of Upper Canada.[52] The appointments greatly increased the banks' opportunities to put their notes into circulation. For all banks the value of bank-notes in circulation in Lower Canada increased from £214,000 currency in 1829 to £512,000 in 1841; in Upper Canada the increase was from £140,000 to £403,000 (see Table 16). Two new chartered banks began business in Upper Canada: the Commercial Bank of the Midland District and the Gore Bank; and three new ones in Lower Canada: the City Bank of Montreal, the Banque du Peuple, and the Bank of British North America. The last had a royal charter and branches in Quebec City, Montreal, Toronto, Saint John, N.B., St. John's, Newfoundland, and Halifax. In addition to the new chartered banks several joint stock banks began operations without charter: the Farmer's Bank, the Bank of the People, the Niagara Suspension Bridge Bank and the Agricultural Bank. Although the private banks issued notes they did not report consistently to the legislature and it is impossible to estimate their circulation.

The decade saw the introduction of several measures to control the issue of bank-notes. In general these measures were directed towards controlling the issue of small notes which, it was believed, drove coins out of circulation. In Lower Canada the issue of notes for less than $5.00 by people or organizations other than chartered banks was forbidden in 1830. Although the prohibition was evaded by the Banque du Peuple which issued its notes as drafts on the firm of Viger, Dewitt and Company, the law marked the beginning of regulation of the issue of bank-notes.[53] In the same year, when the charter of the Bank of Montreal was renewed, it included a provision prohibiting the issue of notes for less than 5s. currency and limiting the issue of notes for less than £1 5s. ($5.00) currency to less than one-fifth of the bank's paid-up capital. As other bank charters were renewed similar provisions were included in them. In 1839 the lower limit for notes issued by unchartered banks was raised to £5 currency and all banks or individuals were forbidden to issue notes of less than 5s. In Upper Canada, regulations did not limit minimum note size to 5s. until 1840. In 1837 Upper Canada restricted the right to issue notes to chartered banks and to private banks which were already issuing notes: the Farmer's Joint Stock Bank, the Agricultural Bank, the Bank of People, the Niagara Suspension Bridge Bank, and the Bank of British North America (which was chartered in Britain). In 1838 the Agricultural Bank failed and lost the privilege of note issue.

The panic of 1837

The great banking event of the 1830s was the panic of 1837 and the subsequent suspension of specie payments by the banks. This dramatic event, which involved overextended creditors calling in their debts and refusing to give new credits, began in England and quickly spread to North America. In New York the banks suspended specie payments on 10 May 1837. This immediately put pressure on Canadian banks which, so long as they continued to redeem their notes in coin, would be called upon to supply at least part of the hard money which was no longer available from New York banks. Such a drain would have quickly depleted their supply of coin and left their bank-notes unsecured. To avoid this the Lower Canadian banks stopped payment in coin the next week and did not resume payment until the following May.

In Upper Canada the bankers were also in favour of suspension, but Lieutenant-Governor Head would not permit it except under very disadvantageous terms. Only the Commercial Bank of the Midland District accepted them and stopped specie payments in September 1837. The other banks were able to weather a run by their noteholders but were forced to reduce their circulation by about 25%.[54] In March 1838, when American and Lower Canadian banks were preparing to resume specie payment, the Upper Canadian bankers obtained permission to suspend theirs. The move had little to do with the panic and was largely designed to free the Bank of Upper Canada's coin reserves for speculation in foreign exchange. In the end the chartered banks in Upper Canada did not resume specie payments until November 1839.[55]

The early stages of the panic sharply reduced the amount of paper money in circulation (see Table 16). Coin was still required for many payments such as customs duties, but it could only be obtained by purchase in the market, usually at a premium. Within a week of suspension in Lower Canada, silver dollars were at a premium of 6% and French crowns at a premium of 3%.[56]

Because bank-notes had customarily been redeemed in small coins (so as to discourage redemption) a shortage of small coins developed. This encouraged many merchants to revive the practice of issuing bons or, as they were called by the English Canadians, "shinplasters". The most common denominations were 10¢ (6d.), 12.5¢ (7.5d.), 25¢ (1s. 3d.),and 50¢ (2s. 6d.).

In addition to the bons, the cities of Montreal and Toronto put municipal notes in denominations of 6d. or 12 sous, $1.00, $2.00 and $4.00 into circulation. The issue of these notes was probably illegal, but they circulated with little hindrance until specie payments were resumed.[57] Toronto municipal notes continued to circulate (or perhaps were reissued) until 1851 or later. In 1838–39 Upper Canada planned an issue of £250,000 in inconvertible treasury notes which would have circulated in much the same manner as treasury notes in the maritime colonies. However, the imperial government refused assent to the bill and with the passing of the financial crisis the idea was dropped.

Copper coinage

Throughout the 1830s the condition of the copper coinage in both provinces continued to deteriorate. Virtually anything with a resemblance to copper coin was put in circulation. Lord Aylmer, in a letter recommending the issue of a special copper coinage for Lower Canada, sent the Colonial Office a sample of the copper circulating in Lower Canada which included a regimental button of the Royal Fusiliers.[58] Sir Duncan Gibb, a prominent early Canadian coin collector, remembered that when he had begun collecting he had

> succeeded in obtaining a Greek copper coin of Alexander the Great, in ordinary change from Mr. Peter Dunn, a grocer; a large brass of Domitian, much worn, and another coin of Constantius Chlorus, also in ordinary change, but such occurrences were very rare.... Half crowns of Charles II were not rare and frequently sixpences and shillings were met in ordinary change. Spanish, Portuguese and French silver were the common medium of exchange, associated with that of the U.S.A. and Mexico. Copper of all countries found Canada the real land of circulating freedom.[59]

To correct the situation in Upper Canada, Lieutenant-Governor Colborne requested that about £50,000 of copper coinage be shipped to Upper Canada. It seems probable that Colborne expected a distinctive issue of coinage in both copper and small silver change. The treasury reduced the issue to only £5000 in copper, and instead of issuing distinctive Canadian coins merely forwarded a special minting of standard British copper. Some or all of the coins were shipped to Quebec in 1832, and a quantity was offered to the Bank of Upper Canada for distribution. The bank refused to take the coins except at the rate of 60d. per Spanish dollar while the British officials insisted they were worth 52d. per dollar. Other possible distributors evidently reacted the same way and it seems that few of the coins ever entered into circulation.[60]

About 1836 the banks began to refuse the lightweight copper coinage. The Bank of Montreal and Banque du Peuple imported small quantities of 1-sou tokens and put them into circulation. These proved so popular that the Bank of Montreal introduced £20,000 worth of penny and halfpenny tokens in 1837. These were widely imitated (or forged); as many as 40 different varieties have been identified.[61] The tokens were not legal tender, but an ordinance of the special council in 1839 gave them a privileged status in Lower Canada. The ordinance forbade the importation of any copper or brass token or coin except for the lawful copper coin of the United Kingdom. Copper coin could be manufactured in Lower Canada if permission was granted by the council and if the coins had the same relative value as those issued by the Bank of Montreal. Fifteen days after the ordinance came into effect no coin was to be passed by anyone except for lawful coin of the United Kingdom, tokens of the chartered banks and of the Banque du People, American cents and other lawfully produced coin.

In essence the ordinance was reaffirmed by an act of the provincial parliament in 1841. Although these acts were not enforced as stringently as they might have been, they seem to have reduced the problem of spurious copper. Subsequent importations of copper tokens by the Bank of Montreal in the 1840s and by the Bank of Upper Canada and the Quebec Bank in the 1850s also improved the condition of the copper coinage but it remained diverse almost to Confederation. R.W. McLachlan described the state of the coinage when he began collecting about 1858:

> Besides the bank tokens, the only authorized copper money, we had any number of sous, Tiffins, Harps, Wellingtons, Ships, and Blacksmiths along with a goodly sprinkling of less common Canadians. Of British coins there were plenty of worn halfpennies of George II and George III and many varieties of 18th and 19th Century trade tokens. Of United States coins one found always present some of the large cents, although worth more than a halfpenny each. A few Colonials, an occasional Fugio and Nova Constellatio, and considerable numbers of the State issues of Connecticut, Vermont, and New Jersey; rarely, a specimen from Massachusetts, New York or Virginia turned up. We always found, too, quite a few Jacksonian and "Hard Times" tokens.
>
> In addition, foreign coins seemed to be present in considerable numbers. Three, especially, hailed from as many different countries: the one skilling of Denmark, dated 1771; the one kreuzer of Austria for 1816 and the Norwegian one skilling, 1820. I have often wondered how so

many of these particular items came to be circulating in Canada, but have never yet got the true reason. French, Spanish and Portuguese abounded, as well as some of the other European countries. German coins were rarer because of their smaller size, which precluded them from circulating.[62]

Restoration of a common standard

The union of the provinces in 1840 provided an opportunity to restore a common standard of coinage. The first session of the legislature considered the matter at length, and obtained the views of some of the leading bankers and businessmen of the province. Although very few of those questioned favoured retaining the system of Halifax currency, there was no agreement on a substitute. Almost equal numbers favoured the adoption of the American decimal system for reasons of commercial convenience or the adoption of the sterling system for political and sentimental reasons. As a result the Halifax system was retained, with an adjustment in the ratings assigned coins (see Table 12).

The new ratings came into effect 27 April 1842. The worst of the old coins, the French crowns and half-crowns, were dropped from currency. Gold coin of France, Spain, Portugal and the South American states was only legal tender if taken by weight in payments of £50 or more. The sovereign, American eagle, all dollars and half-dollars were legal tender to any amount but the smaller fractions of dollars and British silver were only legal tender to £2 10s.

The currency act of 1841 made dollars, British silver, and U.S. fractional silver the dominant coins in Canada during the 1840s. Although gold coins were equitably rated against each other, gold was slightly undervalued against silver. The silver/gold price ratio established by the act was about 15.45:1 compared to a ratio of 15.7:1 or more on world markets. The act set a minimum weight for all dollars of 412 grains; most dollars in circulation exceeded the minimum and were equitably rated against each other. British silver was overvalued to degree actually greater than that shown in Table 12 because no minimum weight was established for it and British silver in Canada, particularly the shilling, was badly worn (see Table 13).

103

Table 12   Ratings Established by 4–5 Victoria, C.93, 1841, Province of Canada

	Weight (grains)	Rating (£/s./d.)	Purity	Precious Metal Content (grains)	Grains Per Shilling	In Effect Until
Gold						
Sovereign	(123.27)	1/4/4	.9166	113.	4.64	1858
U.S. Eagle, pre-1834	270	2/13/4	.9166	247.5	4.64	1858
U.S. Eagle, post-1834	258	2/10/0	.900	232.2	4.64	1858
Multiples and divisions in proportion.						
Silver						
Spanish Dollar	412	5/1	.903	372.04	73.19	1853
U.S. Dollar	412	5/1	.900	370.8	72.94	1851
Mexican Dollar	412	5/1	.896	369.15	72.62	1853
Central Amer. Dollar	412	5/1	–	–	–	1853
South Amer. Dollar	412	5/1		–	–	1853
Half-Dollar	–	2/6.5	–	–	–	1857
Quarter-Dollar	–	1/3	–	–	–	1851
Eighth-Dollar	–	7.5	–	–	–	1851
Sixteenth-Dollar	–	3.5	–	–	–	1851
5-franc piece	384	4/8	.900	345.6	74.06	1851
British Crown	(436.36)	6/1	.925	403.63	66.35	1858
Shilling	(87.3)	1/2.5	.925	80.7	66.77	1858

Silver/gold ratio = 15.45:1.

( ) = weight taken from Chalmers or other sources (see Table 5)

In payments of £50 or more, gold of the following types is legal tender by weight:

British and pre-1834 American at 94s. 10d. currency per oz. troy
Post-1834 American, at 93s. currency per oz. troy
French at 93s. 1d. currency per oz. troy
Doubloons
  Spanish, Mexican and Chilian at 89s. 7d. currency per oz. troy
  La Plata, Columbia at 89s. 5d. currency per oz. troy
  Portugal, Brazil at 94s. 6d. currency per oz. troy

Table 13   Average Weight of Principal Coins in Circulation in Lower Canada c.1830 and 1840 Compared to Their Mint Weight*

1830	1830 Average Weight (grains)	Lacking	1840 Average Weight (grains)	Lacking	Mint Weight
French Crown	445.4	2.1%	443.9	2.4%	455.0
French Half Crown	207.17	8.9	206.2	9.4	227.5
Spanish Dollar	415.0	0.6	412.4	1.1	417.6
Spanish Quarter	99.5	4.7	97.5	6.4	104.4
U.S. Dollar			414.0	0.5	416.10
U.S. Half-dollar	207.8	0.1	206.2	0.9	208.001
U.S. Quarter			103.1	0.9	104.10
Mexican Dollar			415.6	1.4	421.292
British Crown			431.5	1.1	436.36
British Half-crown			213.3	2.2	218.18
British Shilling			83.0	4.9	87.3
Pistareen	77.18	14.2			90.0 (Avg.)

The weights for the American coins are for pre–1837 coins; the post–1837 dollar weighed only 412.5 grains.

The Mexican weight is that given by Bonneville, *Encyclopédie Monétaire,* for the issue of 1824.

* from Chapman, *Thoughts on the Money...* p.7; Province of Canada, Journals of the Legislative Assembly, 1841, Appendix 0.

These inequities were partially mitigated by the limitation of British silver's legal tender status to small payments. United States dollars enjoyed an advantage in Canada unrelated to their silver content. Ten U.S. dollars, which were equal to one eagle in the United States, were worth 50s. 10d., whereas the eagle was worth only 50s. The difference made it profitable to export eagles and import dollars.

The act of 1841 put a further strain on the traditional par between Halifax currency and sterling. Par was based on the relative values of the silver dollar at 5s. currency and 4s. 6d. sterling; the new act rated the dollar at 5s. 1d. The relationship between currency and sterling had been undermined when the British government reduced the sterling rate at which it would receive the dollar to 4s. 4d. in 1825 and to 4s. 2d. in 1838. To the extent that the dollar formed the basis of Halifax currency, the changes altered the par value of Halifax currency from the traditional £111.11 to £115.38 currency per £100 sterling in 1825 and to £120 currency in 1838. The increase in the currency rating of the dollar to 5s. 1d. when it was valued at 4s. 2d. sterling implied a Halifax currency par value of £122. However, the act had valued the pound sterling, as represented by the sovereign, at £1 4s. 4d. currency; on this basis £121.67 currency was equal to £100 sterling. Which conversion rate was to be used in practice was not specified.

Although the British military establishment had adjusted its accounts to the changes in the true par in 1825 and 1838, the colonial government and colonial merchants ignored the changes and continued to keep their accounts on the basis of the old par.[63] After 1842 the army, as well as some of the Canadian merchants, adopted £121.67 as the new par. The banks and exchange brokers announced that they would adopt the new par as well and for several years some sources gave exchange quotations based on the new par.[64] However, newspaper exchange rate quotations continued to be based on a par of £111.11 to £100 and the provincial accounts continued to be kept in the old currency except in cases where actual foreign exchange dealings were involved such as payments of the provincial debt in Britain. In such cases the new par of £121.67 per £100 was usually used. As a result of the failure of the government to adopt the new par, exchange dealers and perhaps the merchant community returned to the old system, which was generally accepted in Canada until decimal currency was adopted in 1858.[65]

Growth of the decimal system

Perhaps the most important development of the 1840s was the growing popularity of the decimal system. In an 1840 report, the Inspector-General of Public Accounts, J. MacCaulay, noted that in many of the rural parts of Upper Canada, decimal currency and York currency were regularly used for keeping accounts.[66] The committee which drafted the new currency law called 23 witnesses from banking, commercial and government establishments. Of these, only two favoured retaining

106

Halifax currency. Ten were in favour of adopting the American decimal system and eleven favoured the adoption of sterling. The new rating system encouraged the use of decimal notation because the currency rating of all major coins involved fractions of shillings or pence if sterling notation was used. Some of the more awkward fractions were probably ignored; for example, the correct rating of the shilling in proportion to the crown was 1s. 2.6d. Even 1s. 2.5d. was considered too inconvenient and a meeting of the Kingston Board of Trade recommended it be accepted at 1s. 3d. and the sixpence at 7.5d.[67] In Lower Canada a rate of 1s. 3d. for the shilling and 7.5d. for the sixpence was adopted unofficially by merchants and bankers as early as 1838–39, anticipating confirmation of the currency ordinance of 1839. In June 1840 a Montreal merchant advertised that he was continuing to take sixpence at 7.5d., shillings at 1s. 3d., half-crowns at 3s. and crowns at 6s. currency. Correspondence between the military secretary and the deputy commissary-general indicates that 1s. 3d. was the commonly accepted rate for the shilling and 7.5d. the rate for the shilling until at least 1852.[68]

The 1841 session of the legislature also considered the introduction of a provincial paper currency. Lord Sydenham proposed a government bank which would have had the exclusive right of issuing bank notes. Since this would have deprived the banks of their major source of profit, the proposal was strenuously opposed and eventually defeated. As an alternative the banks were forced to accept an annual tax equal to 1% of the banknotes in circulation.[69] The question of issuing government notes arose again in 1847–48. During the depression of those years the government found itself virtually unable to raise loans at home or abroad and began to issue interest-bearing debentures for sums as low as £2 10s. or $10.00. By May 1850 over £630,000 in $10.00 and $20.00 debentures were in circulation; however, they were all withdrawn from circulation during the year.

In 1850 the United States government reduced the rate at which Spanish and Mexican quarter, eighth- and sixteenth-dollars were accepted by about 20% and demonetized other foreign coin. Two years later it reduced the silver content of its subsidiary silver coins, which had not been in general circulation, so that they came into circulation. (A fall in the price of gold also contributed to this.) As had been the case in 1834,

Canada was forced to respond to these changes. To prevent an influx of small Spanish and Spanish-American coin from the United States, Canada lowered the rate at which they were received. The quarter dollar was lowered from 1s. 3d. to 1s., the eighth-dollar from 7.5d. to 6d., and the sixteenth-dollar from 3.5d. to 3d.

In the same session the legislature began to work towards a more general reform of the currency. The rate at which dollars and half-dollars were to pass was reduced from 5s. 1d. and 2s. 6.5d. to 5s. and 2s. 6d. respectively, thereby eliminating the inequity in the rating of the American dollar and the eagle. The act also provided for the issue of distinctive Canadian silver and gold coins in denominations which would have been compatible with a decimal currency system. The act was disallowed, largely on the grounds that coinage was a royal prerogative; in spite of the disallowance the Blue Books of 1851 and 1852 treat the act as though it had come into effect and it is possible that the new rating for dollars was adopted early in 1851.

Certainly some change in the relative value of the dollar occurred in 1851. During the 1840s, dollars, half-dollars and bank-notes formed the principal contents of the various military chests scattered throughout Canada. However, during 1851 the dollars and half-dollars were almost completely replaced by American eagles and their parts, and British silver. Silver dollars also disappeared from general circulation at about the same time. The disappearance of the dollars from circulation would have been compatible with a reduction in the value of the dollar from 5s. 1d. to 5s. currency since at the lower rate there was no incentive to export eagles and import dollars.

In June of 1851, representatives of the provinces of Canada, Nova Scotia and New Brunswick met in Toronto and agreed to work towards a common currency based on the decimal system. In response to the resolution, the Canadian legislature passed an act directing that provincial accounts should be kept in dollars and cents with the dollar equal to 5s. and the pound sterling equal to £1 4s. 4d. or $4.866 currency. The act also provided that Her Majesty, rather than the Governor-General, might have coins representing dollars or multiples or fractions of dollars struck for use in Canada. The British government delayed confirmation of the act while it attempted to persuade

Canada and the other North American colonies to adopt a system based on the pound, shilling and pence which would at the same time be compatible with the dollar.

Finally in 1853 the legislature passed a compromise act incorporating the pound, dollar, shilling, pence and cent as units of Canadian currency. The pound currency was defined as being equal to 101.321 grains of standard British gold compared to the 123.27 grains in £1 sterling. The sovereign was made legal tender at £1 4s. 4d. currency, the old eagle at £2 13s. 4d. or $10.666 and the new eagle at £2 currency or $10.00. Other foreign gold coins could be proclaimed legal tender at the rate of 92.877 grains of pure gold per pound currency. British silver was to remain legal tender until a proclamation established which silver coins were allowed. Silver was not to be legal tender for more than £2 10d. British copper coins were legal tender to 1s.; the penny was to be equal to two cents and the halfpenny to one cent. The act provided for the striking of provincial silver and copper coinage. Public accounts were to be kept either in dollars and cents or in pounds, shillings, and pence as directed by Her Majesty (see Table 14).

Table 14   Ratings Established by 16 Victoria C.158, 1853, Province of Canada

	Weight (grains)	Currency Rating (£/s/d.)	Decimal Rating ($)	Purity	Metal Content (grains)	Grains per Shilling
Sovereign	(123.27)	1/4/4	4.8666	.9166	113.0	4.64
Eagle, pre-1834	270.0	2/13/4	10.6666	.9166	247.5	4.64
Eagle, post-1834	258.0	2/10/0	10.00	.9000	232.2	4.64
Crown	(436.36)	6/1*	1.2167	.925	403.63	66.35
Shilling	(87.3)	1/2.5*	.2433	.925	80.7	66.79
Sixpence	(43.64)	0/7.25*	.1217	.925	40.37	66.37

( )=weight taken from Chalmers or other sources (see Table 5)
*In proportion to the sovereign.
From 1 January 1858 only the decimal rating was legally authorized.

The currency act of 1853 was proclaimed 1 August 1854. The act did not have any immediate practical effect but it provided legal authority for later changes. British gold and silver coins and American gold coins continued to be acceptable at the same rates they had had since 1841. All other foreign silver was demonetized but it continued to circulate. Although only British copper was named legal tender, bank tokens remained the major copper currency until at least 1870. Much completely spurious copper continued to circulate as well.

Shortly after the currency act came into force in 1854 Francis Hincks' ministry fell and a new government took its place. The new government was evidently less interested in currency reform than was the old one for it was several years before any action was taken on the enabling clauses in the act. In 1855 the public accounts committee recommended that public accounts be kept in a decimal currency based on the U.S. dollar rather than on the sovereign, and in 1857 an act was passed which provided that all accounts submitted to the government as well as accounts kept by the government should be in dollars and cents. Although it provided for the use of sterling notation in a second column it effectively ended the widespread use of both sterling notation and Halifax currency in the Province of Canada. When the currency act was revised in 1871 and extended to Nova Scotia, sterling notation was eliminated as an alternative to decimal notation.

At about the same time as decimal currency was adopted the government received permission from the home government to issue a special colonial coinage. The new coins, silver 5, 10- and 20-cent pieces and bronze cents, were made legal tender on 10 December 1858. The new coinage was not an immediate success as many people preferred the British shillings and sixpence which at their popular, although not their legal, ratings were overrated (see Table 15).[70]

110

Table 15 Customary and Legal Ratings in Canada, 1860

	Weight (Grains)	Rating ($)	Purity	Precious Metal Content (Grains)	Grains per Dollar
Sovereign	123.27	4.866	.9166	113.0	23.22
Eagle	258.0	10.00	.900	232.2	23.22
Shilling	(87.3)	.25	.925	80.7	322.8
Sixpence	(43.64)	.125	.925	40.37	323.0
Canadian 5¢	(17.93)	.05	.925	16.59	331.8
Canadian 10¢	(35.86)	.10	.925	33.17	331.71
Canadian 20¢	(71.73)	.20	.925	66.35	331.75
American 5¢	(19.2)	.05	.900	17.28	345.75
American 10¢	(38.4)	.10	.900	34.58	345.58
American 25¢	(96.0)	.25	.900	86.4	345.6
American 50¢	(192.0)	.50	.900	172.8	345.6

( )=weight taken from Chalmers or other source (see Table 5)

In the 1860s British silver was rapidly overshadowed by American fractional silver. The American revaluations of 1853 had reduced American silver, except for the full dollar, to a token currency intrinsically worth about 2.5% less than its face value in gold. American fractional silver became increasingly common although the dollar was rare. Shortly after the outbreak of the Civil War the American government suspended specie payments and began to issue treasury notes known as "greenbacks". These quickly fell to a discount: in July of 1864 they were worth only 40 cents on the dollar. American silver, particularly the token silver, was used to make payments in Canada. Although the coins were not legal tender in Canada and were not intrinsically worth their face value, they were by custom accepted at face value in Canada. As the amount of American silver in circulation increased, the Canadian banks began to refuse to accept it or accepted it only at a discount. To protect themselves, Canadian merchants had to follow a similar course. In January 1863 the Post Office refused to accept American quarters at more than 23¢, dimes at 9¢, and 3¢ pieces at 2¢. At the same time the Post Office lowered the rate on British shillings to 24¢. Most merchants, at least in western Canada, followed or had anticipated this move, although many of them accepted quarters at 24¢ and 50-cent pieces at 48¢. The

Montreal business community was not able to come to a consensus on the question and so was inundated with both American and British silver. Although the discounting of American and British silver eased the problem, foreign silver remained overabundant until 1870 when the Dominion government in concert with the banks bought up $5 million worth at a discount of 5% to 6% and shipped it out of the country. It was replaced by a second issue of Canadian silver in 5, 10, 25- and 50-cent denominations as well as some 25-cent paper notes.[71]

Dominion notes

The financial crisis of 1857-59 resulted in the failure of two small Toronto banks, the International Bank and the Colonial Bank. These failures led to a demand for improved government supervision of banks at the same time as difficulties in government finances made the prospect of a government note issue attractive. In 1860 the government introduced a bill designed to end, over a period of years, the banks' right to issue notes, in favour of government notes issued through the banks. The banks objected to this proposal, which would have denied them their most profitable activity. It was defeated but resurfaced in 1866 as 29-30 Victoria, C.10, "An act to Provide the for Issue of Provincial Notes".[72] The act called for the issue of $5 million in provincial notes, backed 20% by coin and 80% by provincial debentures. A further discretionary issue of up to $3 million was provided for, to be backed 25% by coin and 75% by debentures. The notes were redeemable in coin at Toronto and Montreal; elsewhere they were legal tender. In order to encourage the circulation of these provincial notes, banks which withdrew their own notes from circulation and substituted provincial notes were exempt from the need to hold government securities as part of their reserve fund and were also compensated by a payment equal to 5% of their average circulation. In spite of these inducements, only the Bank of Montreal, the largest bank in the country, agreed and as its notes were withdrawn in 1866 and 1867 over $4 million in provincial notes were put in circulation.

The issue did not have as great an impact on the general circulation as might have been expected. Because the provincial notes were legal tender they could be used in place of the traditional specie reserve, and by the end of 1867 almost half of the $4 million issued remained in bank vaults as part of their reserve fund. The new bank act of 1870 ensured that a large part of all dominion notes would remain out of general circulation because it required that, in general, 50% of all bank reserves should be held in dominion notes.

Following Confederation, the provincial notes were renamed "dominion notes" and in 1868 they were made redeemable in Halifax and Saint John as well as in Montreal and Toronto. In 1876 the dominion note acts were extended to Prince Edward Island, Manitoba and British Columbia. It was evidently not until 1886 that the acts were extended to the Northwest Territories although the notes were certainly in circulation from the mid-1870s.

The authorized issue of dominion notes was gradually increased. In 1870 the normal limit on notes issued was increased to $9 million, 20% backed by specie and 80% backed by government debentures. Issues beyond $9 million had to be 100% backed by specie. In 1875 the normal maximum issue was increased to $12 million, and in 1880 the limit was raised to $20 million. As noted above, all of these notes did not enter circulation: in 1891, of approximately $16 million in dominion notes actually issued, $10 million were held as bank reserves.[73]

Following Confederation there were relatively few important changes in Canadian banking related to note issue. The provisions of the provincial note act which had been intended to encourage banks to give up their note issue were extended to banks in Nova Scotia and New Brunswick in 1868. However, no bank took advantage of the inducements offered, and in fact the Bank of Montreal resumed the issue of its own notes following the passage of new bank acts in 1870-71. The acts brought banks in all four provinces under common regulations. Minimum note denomination was set at $4.00, all notes were to be payable in specie or in dominion notes at the head office, and suspension of payment involved the loss of the bank charter. Bank-notes in circulation were not to exceed the paid-up capital of the bank. Banks were to hold, as nearly as possible, one-half of their reserve in dominion notes and never less than one-third.

In 1880 the minimum note denomination was raised to $5.00, and the minimum proportion of dominion notes to be held as part of the bank reserve was raised to 40% of the whole reserve fund. With the exception of these two changes the provisions of the bank act of 1871 relating to notes remained unchanged until the end of the century. A number of new banks were incorporated and others ceased operations so that the total number of banks in operation in 1900 was only slightly higher than in 1867. The value of bank-notes in circulation increased from approximately $15 million in 1870 to over $45 million in 1900. In the same priod the dominion notes issued rose from about $7 million to over $25 million; however, many of these were held in bank reserves and bank-notes formed the most common circulating medium.[74] Coins were used largely as change and as bank reserves; gold was practically noncirculating.

In 1871 an act was passed to provide a uniform currency for Canada. Essentially it reenacted the Canadian currency act of 1857 and extended it to Nova Scotia. The act also established a legal currency in Manitoba. Denominations were to be the dollar, cent and mill; pounds, shillings and pence were no longer accepted as an alternate method of accounting. The sovereign, at $4.866 and its parts continued to be legal tender but British silver was demonetized by a provision which gave legal tender status only to silver, copper and bronze coins struck for Ontario, Quebec or New Brunswick or to new coins which Her Majesty might have struck. Silver coins were only legal tender to $10.00; copper to 25¢. Until provided for by proclamation, the post-1834 eagle, rated at $10.00 and its parts were to be legal tender. The act provided for the minting of Canadian gold coins in multiples of $5.00, but none was struck until after the establishment of a mint at Ottawa in 1908. In 1875 the Uniform Currency Act was extended to the Northwest Territories and in 1881 to Prince Edward Island and British Columbia.[75]

Although no gold coins were minted under the provisions of the act before 1908, large quantities of copper cents and silver 5, 10, 25- and 50-cent pieces were put in circulation after the passage of the act. Following the withdrawal of American fractional silver in 1870–71, these and 25-cent paper notes formed the dominant and legal fractional currency of the dominion. Bank-notes and dominion notes formed the principal currency.

Table 16   Paper Currency in Circulation in Upper and Lower Canada and the Province of Canada, 1812–1855 (Expressed in local currency)[76]

	1812	1813	1814	1815
Army Bills	£250,000*	£500,000*	£1,500,000*	£396,778 D

	1816	1817	1818	1819
Army Bills	£72,527 D	23,607 D	–	–
Bank of Montreal	–	–	–	–
Quebec Bank	–	–	–	–
Bank of Canada	–	–	–	–
Bank of Upper Canada (Kingston)	–	–	–	–
Bank of Upper Canada (York)	–	–	–	–

	1820	1821	1822	1823
Army Bills	Ceased operation December 1820			
Bank of Montreal	–	–	£92,727 B	£82,638 Ja
Quebec Bank	–	–	25,565 B	46,493 Ja
Bank of Canada	–	–	39,206 B	31,971 Ja
Bank of Upper Canada (Kingston)	–	–	–	18,176 F
Bank of Upper Canada (York)	–	–	–	–

	1824	1825	1826	1827
Bank of Montreal	£92,727 Ja	137,580 F	133,005 F	88,543 F
Quebec Bank	25,565 Ja	28,427 F	36,416 F	28,393 F
Bank of Canada	39,206 Ja	11,447 F	24,127 F	8,432 F
Bank of Upper Canada	–	–	87,339 D	–

	1828	1829	1830	1831
Bank of Montreal	£148,639 D	171,405 B	178,552 F	223,558 F
Quebec Bank	44,328 D	39,071 B	38,713 F	47,980 F
Bank of Canada	3,505 D	3,487 B	3,487 F	1,911 B
Bank of Upper Canada	122,858 F	140,483 M	156,296 F	187,039 Ja

Table 16 (Continued)   Paper Currency in Circulation in Upper and Lower Canada and the Province of Canada, 1812–1855 (Expressed in local currency)[76]

	1832	1833	1834	1835
Bank of Montreal	£260,970 D	£194,684 B	£190,297 Ja	£155,898 M
Quebec Bank	65,721 D	47,787 B	46,752 Ja	39,360 M
Bank of Canada		Absorbed by Bank of Montreal		
City Bank of Montreal	–	–	34,235 Ja	75,541 M
Bank of Upper Canada	–	189,708 Ja	197,209 Ja	220,265 Ja
Commercial Bank of the				
Midland District	Inc.	81,400 D	70,000 Ja	113,450 Ja
Gore Bank	–	–	–	Inc.

	1836	1837	1838	1839
Bank of Montreal	212,298 B	275,200 B	212,717 B	176,265 B
Quebec Bank	64,611 B	74,891 B	47,292 B	32,014 B
City Bank	105,278 B	119,369 B	77,827 B	83,461 B
Bank of British	–	Offices		
North America	–	Opened	19,350 B	35,360 B
Banque du Peuple	–	–	–	56,018 B
Bank of Upper Canada	208,753 Ja	202,710 Ja	80,079 Ja	286,040 Ja
Commercial Bank	123,425 Ja	166,265 Ja	169,392 Ja	209,422 Ja
Gore Bank	27,913 N	35,848 Ja	18,135 Ja	57,313, Ja
Farmer's Bank	17,000 Ja	31,000 Ja	–	–
People's Bank	4,219 Ja	22,141 Ja	–	–
Agricultural Bank	23,875 Ja	26,193 Ja	Failed	–
Suspension Bridge				
Bank	–	6,117 Ja	–	–

	1840	1841	1842	1843
Bank of Montreal	222,842 B	218,072 D	250,950 D	307,562 D
Quebec Bank	39,205 B	43,697 D	31,920 D	38,876 D
City Bank	64,818 B	109,682 D	85,994 D	106,227 D
Bank of B.N.A.	22,974 B	77,049 D	74,974 D	80,910 D
Banque du Peuple	68,502 B	64,117 D	43,970 D	61,354 D
Bank of Upper Canada	156,749 Ja	149,831 D	97,031 D	124,049 D
Commercial Bank	202,570 Ja	152,077 D	67,791 D	137,076 D
Gore Bank	41,760 Ja	86,664 D	56,287 D	69,123 D
Farmer's Bank	–	14,350 Ja	–	–

Table 16 (Continued) Paper Currency in Circulation in Upper and Lower Canada and the Province of Canada, 1812–1855 (Expressed in local currency)[76]

	1844	1845	1846	1847
Bank of Montreal	398,059 D	563,034 D	455,637 D	396,683 D
Quebec Bank	40,787 D	70,774 D	70,964 D	63,184 D
City Bank	168,488 D	216,089 D	215,819 D	175,255 D
Bank of B.N.A.	91,111 D	216,239 D	232,546 D	222,017 D
Banque du Peuple	84,352 D	83,704 D	86,808 D	80,711 D
Bank of Upper Canada	172,404 D	186,558 D	180,618 D	175,071 D
Commercial Bank	156,436 D	199,016 D	197,320 D	184,107 D
Gore Bank	78,393 D	97,406 D	72,996 D	68,739 D
Farmer's Bank	–	–	–	–

	1848	1849	1850	1851
Bank of Montreal	£420,149 O	£349,286 Ja	£441,943 J	£581,697 Ma
Quebec Bank	52,584 O	44,911 Ja	56,922 J	65,690 Ma
City Bank	111,393 O	116,001 F	100,476 Au	96,435 Ma
Bank of B.N.A.	213,153 O	185,834 Ja	170,810 Ju	200,584 Ma
Banque du Peuple	44,168 O	32,144 Ju	49,898 J	70,508 Ma
Bank of Upper Canada	163,541 O	149,610 Ju	194,216 Ju	251,035 J
Commercial Bank	190,416 O	157,049 Ja	187,988 Ju	224,029 Ma
Gore Bank	67,634 O	–	107,678 Ju	133,184 Ma
Farmer's Bank	–	–	–	–

	1852	1853	1854	1855
Bank of Montreal	607,195 Au	–	1,191,007 Au	–
Quebec Bank	94,508 Au	–	210,639 S	–
City Bank	109,080 Au	–	259,007 Au	–
Bank of B.N.A.	265,572 Au	–	–	–
Banque du Peuple	60,757 Au	–	126,706 S	–
Bank of Upper Canada	363,422 Au	547,618 S	665,367 Au	–
Commercial Bank	242,123 Au	–	443,813 Au	–
Gore Bank	120,795 Au	–	266,491 S	–
Farmer's Bank	–	–	–	–
Molson's Bank	–	–	–	–

*Limit authorized by law. Because of a miscalculation in the Army Bill Office, the figures for 1815 and 1816 are about £20,000 too low. I am indebted to Professor Douglas McCalla for bringing this information to my attention.

The circulation figures are followed by letters indicatng the month to which they apply. Ja = January, F = February, M = March, A = April, Ma = May, J = June, Ju = July, Au = August, S = September, O = October, N = November, D = December. "B" indicates that figures are from the Blue Books and the date to which they apply is unknown.

From 1856 on, figures on bank-note circulation are available in C.A. Curtis "Statistics of Banking", *Statistical Contributions to Canadian Economic History*, Vol. 1 (Toronto: Macmillan, 1931), p. 80.

Chapter Three

Acadia
Ile Royale
and
Nova Scotia

Sample of coins in Nova Scotia, 1830

Chilean doubloon, 1819

Spanish (Mexican) doubloon, 1804

U.S. dollar, 1799

British half-crown, 1820

Province of Nova Scotia halfpenny token, 1823

Commercial Change halfpenny token, 1815

Paper money in Nova Scotia

£1 treasury note, Province of Nova Scotia, 1854   actual size: 184 mm x 106 mm

The basis of the French claim to Acadia was laid with Champlain's settlements in Passamaquoddy Bay in 1604 and at Port Royal in 1605. Over the next sixty years the province, twice taken by English forces and twice returned to France, grew to a total population of less than 500 settlers clustered in the Annapolis Valley, on the isthmus of Chignecto and along the Saint John River valley. With a small population engaged principally in farming, fishing and fur trading it is doubtful there was much money of any sort in the area. If there was, it would probably have been French silver and perhaps some Spanish coin brought by fishermen or adventurers from New England.

In theory the government of Acadia was subordinate to the government of Canada but in practice it was so isolated that Canada only occasionally interfered in its affairs, and the Acadian government usually reported directly to France. Although the currency edicts of the council at Quebec might in law have applied to the settlements in Acadia, there is no evidence that they were applied in practice: specifically there is no evidence that the edicts of 1654, 1661 and 1662 which created a special money of account or monnoye du pays in Canada were applied in Acadia.

There was some use of locally issued card money in Acadia. The first known issue was made in 1703 in connection with fortifications at Port Royal. The justification for the issue was the same as that used in Canada: the appropriation supplied by the home government had been inadequate to the task. The reaction of the home government was also typical. It ordered the withdrawal of the card money and forwarded 10,000 livres in addition to the regular appropriation to retire it. 10,295 livres 10 sols was withdrawn from circulation.[1] In the winter of 1706 - 07 a second small issue of 6,000 livres in cards was made but the home government ordered it withdrawn and absolutely forbade further issues. Since these directions were repeated several times up to 1710, it seems probable that the issue of 1706 - 07 remained in circulation for several years.

An incident in 1705 suggests that there may have been proportionately more coin in Acadia than in Canada although it did not circulate freely. De Brouillan, commanding the troops at Port Royal, was reprimanded for having a quantity of shillings and dollars melted down and made into plate. As a result of de Brouillan's actions, according to the treasurer, dollars and most other silver in Acadia had disappeared from circulation. Several years later the local governor, de Subercase, noted that there was "beaucoup d'argent a l'Acadie mais que les habitans ne le mettent pas dans le commerce".[2]

With the loss of Port Royal in 1710 and the cession of Nova Scotia to Britain by the Treaty of Utrecht in 1713, the sphere of French influence was narrowed to the small settlements on the isthmus of Chignecto, fur traders and missionaries in what is now New Brunswick and, by far the most important, the new settlements around Louisbourg on Ile Royale. Little is known of the financial and monetary affairs of the French inhabitants of the mainland after 1710. Trade with Louisbourg probably brought some coin into the area. In 1745 Sieur Marin de la Malgue led an expedition from Quebec against the English settlements around the Minas Basin. He purchased his supplies from the Acadians with coin and with notes on Quebec and Louisbourg. With the fall of Louisbourg the French were unable, at least temporarily, to redeem all of the notes. When a subsequent expedition was sent against the English in Acadia in 1746 the Acadians, although sympathetic, were reluctant to accept notes and demanded payment in coin. Some notes left by these expeditions in Acadia remained unpaid until at least 1752.[3]

Following the establishment of Fort Beauséjour in 1751 with its small garrison it is probable that a regular but small supply of specie was sent to the area as pay for the troops. In addition the government supplied 50,000 livres to aid in the construction of dikes in the area; whether this amount was paid in coin, notes or supplies is not known. With the capture of Fort Beauséjour in 1755 and the loss of Louisbourg three years later this source of specie disappeared.

Louisbourg

The island fortress of Louisbourg was in a very different position from the tiny settlements in Acadia or the much larger colony at Quebec. First, Louisbourg was a garrison town. The garrison of regular troops was larger in proportion to the total population than was the garrison at Quebec and the influence of its pay was proportionately greater. In addition, expenditures on public buildings and fortifications were proportionately greater; C. Moore has calculated that in the 1730s the French government spent about 77 livres per head in Ile Royale compared to 9 livres per head in Canada.[4] Doubtless some of these expenditures would have been settled by means of bills on France or by cash raised from sales from the king's stores but, to a much greater extent than was true in Canada, government expenses in Louisbourg were met by importing coin. In 1749, when the governor returned to take possession of the colony for France, he brought with him nearly one-half million livres in specie to meet the needs of the government.[5]

The second factor which distinguished Louisbourg's economy from that of Canada was that it was a trading economy. Ile Royale was much less self-sufficient than Canada: it imported all of its manufactured goods and most of its provisions, from Canada, from Acadia, from France and from the British colonies to the south. On the other hand, Louisbourg controlled a lucrative cod fishery which made it almost as valuable economically as all of Canada. Ile Royale's export earnings in 1737 have been estimated at 370 livres per colonist, compared to 40 livres per colonist for Canada.[6] Although much of this trade would have been settled by means of bills of exchange and barter, some would have been on a cash basis, and since Ile Royale, unlike Canada, frequently had a favourable balance of trade, some of this coin would have come to the colony.

Prizes were a third source of income and hard money for the colony. Although a complete record of prizes does not exist, in the short period from August to October 1757, Louisbourg privateers brought in 39 vessels valued at over 800,000 livres.[7] Prizes were a source of income only available in wartime but they periodically gave a boost to the local economy and supplied an infusion of cash when their cargoes included specie.

As a result of these three factors, monetary conditions in Louisbourg were very different from those in Canada. Coins were in much more general use and although coin shortages were reported in the 1740s and 1750s, the government was never forced to resort to the issue of card money,[8] and never found it necessary to establish a special monnoye du pays in Ile Royale. With a few exceptions coin circulated at the same rate as it did in France.[9]

The actual selection of coins which circulated at Louisbourg seems to have been similar to those which circulated in Canada. Excavations at Louisbourg have unearthed approximately 695 identifiable coins, most of which are copper. On the basis of this sample, P. Moogk hypothesized a typical "pocketful of change at Louisbourg". It included two liards, probably minted in the 1650s, a sol minted in the 1690s, a double sol from about 1740, a bronze "dardenne" worth 6 deniers and perhaps a two reales Spanish coin, or quarter-dollar, struck in the 1720s. The pocketful of change is that of an ordinary colonist and does not include more valuable silver or gold coins. Silver and gold coins have not been found in large numbers in excavations at Louisbourg although from documentary evidence there is no doubt that they were present. Estate descriptions mention silver écus of various types and, less frequently, louis d'or. A substantial amount of Spanish silver including quarter-dollars also found its way to Louisbourg as a result of trade with the English colonies, the French West Indies or southern France.[10]

New England currency

After New England troops captured Port Royal in 1710 it became the principal British settlement in the new colony of Nova Scotia. In Brebner's opinion Nova Scotia was New England's outpost. Until the establishment of Halifax the area was generally provisioned by New England and was largely settled by New Englanders. To a degree it also became part of the sphere of New England currency although so long as the Acadian influence lasted the actual coin in use was often French.

By 1710 New England currency, which for practical purposes may be identified with Massachusetts currency, was greatly depreciated in terms of sterling. Until the 1630s New England money had been the same as sterling but in 1642 Massachusetts had created a monnoye du pays by raising the value of coined money in the colony by one-ninth so that £111.11 of Massachusetts currency was equal to £100 sterling; this process of devaluation continued until 1705 when £154.85 Massachusetts currency was declared equal to £100 sterling. During the same period Massachusetts and the other colonies gradually adopted the Spanish dollar as their basic coin in place of English coins. By a royal proclamation of 1704, the Spanish dollar was made equal to 4s. 6d. sterling; its local value under the Massachusetts legislation of 1705 was 6s. 11.5d. However, the legal changes in the value of Massachusetts currency had been overtaken by other events.

In 1690 when the Phips expedition returned after its unsuccessful attempt to take Quebec, the Massachusetts government, faced with paying off the troops, had issued paper bills of credit. These were made legal tender and as subsequent issues were made they drove all coins out of normal circulation and paper money became the basic circulating medium. Until about 1715 the bills of credit maintained their legal value, about £150 currency per £100 sterling, but then they began a rapid process of devaluation which, by 1720, had raised the real exchange rate to about £220 currency per £100 sterling. By 1730 the rate was about £340, by 1740 about £525 and by 1750 over £1,000 currency per £100 sterling. In 1750 Massachusetts returned to the silver dollar at 6 shillings as the base of its currency and recalled all of its paper currency at the rate of £7 10s. paper currency (Old Tenor) for £1 currency (New Tenor).[11]

Circulation in Nova Scotia

Money of account (and to a lesser extent real money) in the portion of Acadia controlled by the British, consisted of a confusing mixture of Massachusetts currency, French currency and sterling. The garrison at Port Royal drew most of its supplies from Boston and in dealing with Boston used Massachusetts currency. Massachusetts bills circulated locally around Port Royal where they were reluctantly accepted by the Acadians in return for supplies. The Acadians also carried on a clandestine trade with Louisbourg from which they received small supplies of silver, most of which was hoarded but some of which entered circulation. The garrison at Annapolis (formerly Port Royal) was paid by Britain, and in dealing with Britain accounts were kept in sterling. However there were no (or few) actual shipments of money from Britain to the post; money was raised in Boston by the sale of bills of exchange on London. The money raised was usually in the form of Boston bills which were issued as pay to the garrison and to the Acadians for the purchase of supplies.

The negotiation of the bills of exchange proved a constant problem. Besides dealing with the fluctuation of Massachusetts currency the officers had to cope with the dilatory habits of the British treasury. In 1711 Samuel Vetch reported that public bills sold for 20% less than private bills because of the difficulties experienced in having them paid at the treasury.[12] In order to obtain supplies at all, successive commanders were forced to pledge their private credit.

Reports from Annapolis in the first decade of British occupation indicate that hard money was in very short supply. Boston bills were reportedly the only money in circulation.[13] Conditions in the 1720s evidently improved slightly, for the council felt it necessary to introduce regulations governing the rates at which coin should circulate. In 1727 the council at Annapolis, having found that the local merchants were endeavouring to lower the value of French coin, "the only currency we have amongst us", resolved that all coins be continued at their former value, particularly the new French crowns stamped with four double Ls which were to circulate at 12s. 6d.[14] The "écu aux deux L" was the issue of 1724 - 26 which contained 334 grains of pure silver. Its sterling value compared to the shilling was only about 3s. 11d., hence the currency value was about 320% of the sterling value. This was a greater advance than the Massachusetts-London exchange rate which averaged about 290% of sterling in 1727. The overrating, even in terms of Massachusetts currency, may have been an attempt to keep or bring coins into circulation at Annapolis.

If it was it could have only been successful temporarily for New England currency was steadily declining in value. By 1730 - 31 the average New England/sterling exchange rate was about £335.50 to £100 and Nova Scotia was forced to devalue its currency again. A proclamation of 11 March 1730 directed that all French and foreign silver was to pass for no more than 18s. per ounce and that New England bills were to be legal tender in all contracts.[15] At this rate the "écu aux deux L" should have passed for 13s. 6.5d. and the dollar for about 16s. These rates may have been sufficient to bring coin into circulation at the time but as New England currency became more and more inflated coin could only have been kept in circulation by further adjustments in the ratings of coins, and there is no evidence that those adjustments were made.

Following this proclamation little is known of currency in Nova Scotia. The identification of Nova Scotia currency with that of Massachusetts was reaffirmed in 1742 and Boston bills continued to be the dominant currency. Surreptitious trade with Louisbourg continued to introduce French silver into the area throughout the period; there was a particularly large influx in 1746, when some of the bills which French expeditions against Annapolis in 1745 and 1746 had introduced were paid off. The use of French money of account continued to be common among Acadians.[16]

British influences

During the British occupation of Louisbourg (from 1744 to 1749), coined money was more common in British Nova Scotia than it had been before. In addition to the French money which had circulated freely at Louisbourg, Admiral Peter Warren brought at least 100,000 silver dollars to the town in 1744.[17] The British garrison at Louisbourg was generally paid in coin and Boston bills did not obtain currency there. This was not the case at Annapolis where payment of wages in depreciated Boston bills provoked a mutiny or strike in 1747.[18]

The establishment of a large settlement at Halifax combined with the deportation of the Acadians and their replacement by New Englanders changed the character of the province. Prior to 1749 the British presence in Nova Scotia had been largely military and mercantile. There were few settlers other than the Acadians. After 1749 there was a substantial English-speaking civilian population. Moreover, the military and naval presence at Halifax changed the orientation of the colony. Although it maintained very close contact with New England its ties with England became much stronger: strong enough, in fact, to keep it loyal (or at least neutral) during the American Revolution.

This change in orientation had an effect on the currency. The increased British involvement and expenditure in Nova Scotia made hard money more common than it had been previously. Nova Scotia began to break away from the New England currency bloc. The bloc was greatly weakened in 1750 when Massachusetts retired its paper bills and returned to a silver coinage but New Hampshire, Rhode Island and Connecticut did not. In reestablishing silver as its basic currency, Massachusetts rated the dollar at 6s., an advance of one-third on its sterling value. For some reason Halifax did not follow this rating, and as early as 1750 dollars were generally accepted at a rate of 5s. currency in Halifax.[19] In 1758 this rating was given legal sanction by an act of the first legislature which established that all Spanish dollars, the Seville, Mexico and Pillar dollars weighing 420 grains, were to be accepted at 5s. currency in payment of all debts and contracts. The home government objected to the act on the grounds that giving the dollar what amounted to legal tender status at 5s. contravened the colonial currency act of 1707. When the assembly refused to amend the act the home government disallowed it in 1762.[20] The disallowance had little practical effect for the dollar continued to be received at 5s. although it did not regain the status of a legal tender until 1842. Although the act of 1758 dealt only with the dollar, the 9:10 ratio between the dollar's accepted sterling value, 4s. 6d., and its value under the act, 5s., became the basis for the entire currency system. The accepted way of converting sterling money of account to Halifax currency was to add one-ninth to the sterling value; to convert from Halifax currency to sterling money of account one subtracted one-tenth of the currency value. The system was also applied to individual coins: the British crown, worth 5 shillings sterling, was frequently valued at 5s. 6d., an increase of slightly less than one-ninth on its sterling value. Halifax currency was adopted in Quebec, Prince Edward Island, and New Brunswick, and persisted with some modifications into the 1850s, long after the original basis of the calculation, the dollar worth 4s. 6d. sterling, had vanished. As the silver content of the dollar decreased and as other coins replaced the Spanish dollar as the principal coin in circulation, the use of the 9:10 ratio became increasingly unrealistic and in commercial

130

exchange was compensated for by large premiums on sterling exchange.

The use of the dollar as the basic coin in Halifax currency suggests that it was the most common coin in the colony. What references there are to tend to confirm this; there is a report of 6,000 silver dollars being shipped from Boston to Halifax in 1750 and another report of £4562 10s. in dollars and halfpence being shipped from England in 1752.[21] In addition to dollars and halfpence there were some cut pistareens in the colony: in 1750 the master of the *Huzza* was charged with selling over 3,000 of them to Halifax merchants at rates ranging from 1s. 2d. to 1s. 4d. In response to this the council decreed that no part of a pistareen should pass in payment except the half- at 6d. and the quarter- at 3d.[22]

The sale of cut pistareens suggests that there was a shortage of small coin in the colony and indeed only two months before the incident involving the master of the *Huzza* the governor had proposed that he issue small notes for the payment of workmen. These would be redeemed in coin, if it was available, or in bills of exchange when presented in amounts of £50 or more. The bills of exchange would only be issued in redemption if 25% of the value of the bills were paid in dollars. The merchants baulked at this last requirement and no notes were issued.

In order to encourage settlement in the 1750s, the Nova Scotia government granted bounties, or subsidies, to certain activities such as fishing, haying and building fences. It was expected that the bounties could be paid by excise taxes and import duties on beer, wine and alcohol. However, revenues fell short of expenses and the province was forced to take out loans to meet its obligations. In 1763 it was £10,000 in debt with an annual income of £5,000; by 1766 it was £20,000 in debt and its income had fallen to £4,000 per annum. Virtually bankrupt, the province considered every feasible method of financing itself, including lotteries.[23]

Provincial treasury notes

In 1763 the provincial surveyor, Charles Morris, suggested that rather than take out loans to pay off the bounties and other expenses the debts should be paid directly by issuing transferrable, interest-bearing certificates, or notes. He compared them to bank-notes and suggested that they might help solve the colony's coin shortage as well as pay off debts.[24] The scheme proposed by Morris may already have been in effect, for in 1762 the province had authorized a loan of £4,500 to pay off various bounties and had provided that if the cash could not be raised the bounties might be cancelled by issuing interest-bearing receipts. Morris' idea was definitely incorporated in an act authorizing a loan for £4,000 in 1763 which provided that interest-bearing certificates for as little as £5 each might be issued in return for cancelling bounty warrants. For a loan of £2,900 in 1764 the minimum amount of the receipt was lowered to 20s.; a further loan in 1764 lowered the limit to 10s. Finally in 1765 the legislature provided that notes of as little as 5s. might be issued to replace notes of £10 or more or warrants on the provincial treasury.

By 1768 over £20,000 currency of these notes had been issued under various acts. Although the interest-bearing notes were not technically money, nor did they have the status of legal tender, there is no doubt that the province intended that they should pass in lieu of money. Several measures were taken to encourage their circulation. In 1765 the Executive Council resolved that the import and excise tax collectors should take three-quarters of their collections in provincial notes; a year later customs collectors were directed to take half their duties in cash and half in provincial notes. This regulation was dropped in 1767 and all duties thereafter were collected in gold or silver.[25]

The most probable reason why the province refused to accept its own notes in payment of duties after 1767 is that the notes had fallen below their face value. In an address to the lieutenant-governor in 1765 the assembly requested that steps be taken to retire some of the outstanding notes, upwards of £16,000, so that the rest would circulate as currency. Presumably they were not circulating because they had depreciated. More evidence of this is found in a letter from Lieutenant-Governor William Campbell to the Lords of Trade, probably dated 1767, in which he stated that provincial funds were trading at 25% discount.[26] In spite of the weakness of the notes the government in 1768 directed that the interest on the warrants granted for bounty certificates would be paid in provincial notes.[27] This would have further depreciated both the notes and the warrants, but the province's finances were so tenuous that no alternative was available.

By 1774 the notes had depreciated to about half of their face value.[28] In spite of this they evidently continued to circulate, for acts of 1773 and 1776 empowered the treasurer to issue new notes to replace worn or defaced ones. By 1777 the old treasury notes had almost all been exchanged for new ones.[29]

In spite of their weaknesses the treasury notes may have formed the principal circulating medium of the province. In an address to the governor in 1775 the assembly estimated the total circulating medium of the province, by which they probably meant coin, at only £1,200;[30] at the same time about £20,000 in treasury notes were outstanding.

Sterling exchange remained at a discount in Halifax during the first decade of the colony's existence. In 1750 the governor had been forced to give a London bill of exchange of £635 sterling for 2,540 Spanish dollars, a rate of 5s. sterling per dollar or an 11% advance on the accepted rate of 4s. 6d. per dollar. According to Joshua Mauger this rate, £100 sterling for £100 Halifax currency, was typical of the 1750s. Other sources indicate that in the late 1750s and early 1760s a more typical rate was £100 sterling for £102 to £105 currency.[31] In 1763 the British government contracted with Mauger to deliver up to £10,000 in dollars to Nova Scotia annually at a rate of £105 currency for £100 sterling bills at 30 days – a discount of 5.5% for sterling bills. How long this arrangement continued is not known, but later in the year Mauger petitioned the Board of Trade for relief, as the province's bills were being refused in London.[32]

In order to relieve the shortage of hard money, the government considered the issue of a paper currency in addition to or as substitute for the treasury notes. In 1766 the assembly and council made a joint address to the king requesting permission to issue £40,000 in paper currency although a study by their joint committee had reported that the province could make no provision for retiring it.[33] Nothing seems to have come of this proposal, but the idea of paper currency was not forgotten. In 1775 the assembly proposed the establishment of a provincial loan office which would make loans of up to £20,000 secured by mortgages on land. The notes issued would have the status of legal tender. The scheme did not win the support of the council or governor and was shelved for the time.

Impact of the American Revolution

In some respects the American Revolution proved the temporary salvation of the colony. Imperial expenditures increased with the outbreak of war and climbed further after the evacuation of Boston in 1776, when a large part of naval operations were transferred to Halifax. Increased military presence and expenditures augmented the provincial revenues and enabled the government to reduce the provincial debt which had peaked at £23,000 about 1775.[34] Wartime expenditures also partially relieved the shortage of specie. In 1775 sterling bills on London traded at about 10 - 11% below par. Even at these rates it was difficult to raise cash and the governor requested that coin be sent out to pay the troops and officials. By mid-1776 the situation had changed dramatically, and the governor reported that it would not be necessary to send cash as bills of exchange would now bring a premium.[35]

In 1777 the governor in his speech from the throne congratulated the legislature on having paid off the old debt, discharged arrears in interest, reduced the public debt and left money in the treasury. Progress was not uninterrupted, however, for in the years 1779 - 80 the specie shortage reappeared and the price of sterling bills fell to a discount again. At the same time prices rose to double prewar levels. The specie shortage was relieved in November 1780 when a supply ship which had been unable to reach Quebec put into Halifax. The £63,000 in coin which it carried was appropriated for the service of Nova Scotia, temporarily relieving the specie shortage and driving bills of exchange to a premium.[36] However, the supply of coin was soon exhausted and by the end of the war sterling exchange had once again fallen to a 10 - 11% discount (see Table 41).

In addition to increased revenues the war also brought increased expenditures, not all of which were borne by the home government. In 1779 the colonial government authorized the expenditure of £5,000 for outfitting a small armed vessel to protect the province. The money was raised by an issue of treasury notes bearing interest similar to the earlier issues. In

134

spite of this issue the province was able to decrease the total outstanding provincial debt to about £15,000 by the end of the war.[37] A resolution by the House of Assembly in 1784 that 10% of all import and excise duties be put into a sinking fund to retire treasury notes demonstrated the province's determination to retire all of its debt and in fact the debt was reduced to about £9,000 in the mid 1780s.[38]

In the late 1780s the colony once again began to pay bounties and the debt grew again to a peak of £22,500 before the government took steps to reduce it. As a result of the increased debt treasury notes fell to a 25 - 40% discount by May of 1792. Provincial officials who were paid in treasury notes or warrants lost heavily. The province also lost since the depreciated securities had to be accepted at face value in payment of provincial duties.[39] In order to restore its credit the province provided for the funding of the provincial debt in 1792 and for the withdrawal of treasury notes and warrants from circulation. New taxes provided for the regular payment of interest on the funded debt and for its gradual retirement. As a result the credit of the treasury notes was fully restored by 1793; they were gradually withdrawn from circulation and by 1800 the entire public debt was paid off.

Currency act of 1787

After the disallowance of the currency act of 1758 in 1762, Nova Scotia had no legal tender. In 1787 a legal rating system was established for British silver coins based on the Halifax currency system of an advance of one-ninth on the sterling value of coins (see Table 17). The crown was rated at 5s. 6d. currency, the half-crown at 2s. 9d. and the shilling at 13d. with smaller coins in proportion. The act declared that the coins should "pass current" at the rates prescribed but did not state that they should be legal tender; however, it was later interpreted as having made them legal tender.[40] The act also forbade the circulation of copper coins which were not legal tender in Great Britain.

Table 17 Ratings Established by 28 George III, C.9, 1787
Nova Scotia

	Weight (grains)	Rate (s./d.)	Purity	Precious Metal Content (grains)	Grains Per Shilling	In Effect Until
Crown	(464.5)	5/6	.925	429.6	78.11	1826
Half-Crown	(232.25)	2/9	.925	214.8	78.12	1826
Shilling	(92.9)	1/1	.925	85.9	79.29	1826

( ) - weight taken from Chalmers or other sources (see Table 5)

The act did not provide a rating for British gold coins; the earliest rating for them is given in a report on prices in Nova Scotia in 1805 at which time guineas were rated at £1 3s. 4d. and dollars at 5s. As these ratings were described as "invariable" it may be assumed that they had been in effect for some time. On this basis an exchange table, circa 1805, has been prepared (see Table 18). The dollar was clearly the best silver in which payments could be made. At a ratio of 14.85:1 the silver dollar ws substantially overvalued compared to gold; the average ratio in Europe for the years 1790 – 1810 was very close to 15.5:1. Consequently it is not surprising that in 1799 Governor Wentworth reported that dollars were the common coin:

> Dollars and the parts of dollars and pistareens are the principal money in use – none base or counterfeit appear – very little gold is in currency – light gold coins, by custom are refused, whatever of these are imported are generally purchased by the Merchants and immediately exported.[41]

Table 18 Customary and Legal Ratings of Coins in Nova Scotia, c. 1805*

	Weight (grains)	Rate (£/s./d.)	Purity	Precious Metal Content (grains)	Grains Per Shilling	In Effect Until
Gold						
Guinea	(129.4)	1/3/4	.9166	118.6	5.08	–
Half-Johannes	(221.3)	2/0/0	.9166	202.9	5.07	–
Doubloon	(417.6)	3/12/0	.875	365.4	5.08	c.1812
Silver						
Dollar	(417.6)	5/0	.903	377	75.4	c.1842
Crown	(464.5)	5/6	.925	429.6	78.11	1826
Shilling	(92.9)	1/1	.925	85.9	79.29	1826

( ) - weight taken from Chalmers or other sources (see Table 5)

Average Silver/gold ratio = 15.29:1

* Based on 28 George III, C.9, 1787, N.S. and PAC, MG II, C0217, Volume 80, p.47

As the treasury notes were withdrawn from circulation in the 1790s the shortage of coin in the province became more acute. Available coin was hoarded or applied to speculation in prize goods and vessels. Excess money was also shipped to the United States, where there were greater opportunities for investment. To combat the loss of coin, as well as to provide a circulating medium, a proposal to establish a local bank was put forward in the assembly in 1801 but was rejected. The following year the governor, in speaking of the extreme scarcity of money in the country, recommended the establishment of a bank but nothing was done. The idea of a bank seems to have been dropped for the time but in 1806 the assembly resolved that a provincial currency receivable at the treasury should be established. Once again nothing resulted from the resolution although the shortage of coin had grown serious enough that money for payment of the troops could no longer be raised in North America and had to be shipped out from Britain and the West Indies. A further proposal to establish a bank in 1811 came to nothing. In the same year the local merchants agreed to raise the rate at which the doubloon was accepted from £3 12s. to £3 17s. 6d. currency. The changes may have been made in an attempt to attract doubloons from the West Indies, which had become Nova Scotia's principal North American trading partner. It may also have been intended to prevent merchants who accepted doubloons at the higher rate in the West Indies from taking a loss on them. Since both the provincial government and the army agreed to accept doubloons at the new rate, it gained nearly universal acceptance.[42]

Under the new rating the doubloon was overvalued by about 5s. 6d. when compared to the guinea. If one assumes that the prevailing silver/gold ratio remained about 15.5:1, the doubloon was also overvalued against the dollar, since the silver/gold ratio in Nova Scotia, based on the metal content of the dollar and doubloon was about 16:1. Whether this advantage was sufficient for the doubloon to drive the dollar out of circulation in Nova Scotia is not clear but the tendency was in that direction. During the War of 1812 the commissariat sent silver from Nova Scotia to central Canada and kept gold, which was undervalued in Canada, in Nova Scotia. After the war a decision to accept doubloons at £4 currency completed the rout of the dollar and made the doubloon the dominant coin in Nova Scotia.

During the early years of the nineteenth century the shortage of coin put pressure on exchange and kept sterling bills trading at or below par. In 1810 J.N. Inglefield, the naval commissioner at Halifax, wrote that in the eight years he had been at the station only two bills had been sold above par and that the exchange rate had fallen as low as a 10% discount.[43] Just before and during the War of 1812 sterling exchange fell to 15% and 20% discount for the best government bills and even more for private bills. Inglefield attributed the coin shortage and the consequent unfavourable rate of exchange to the export of coin to the United States to pay for flour imports.[44]

During the war another factor in the low rate of sterling exchange may have been the need to supply at least a part of the coin needed in Canada, which had lost its normal source of supply, the New York market, with the outbreak of war. Most of the several hundred thousand dollars of coin which were shipped from Halifax to Quebec during the war were actually raised in Bermuda and the Caribbean, not in Nova Scotia, but the levy still put pressure on Nova Scotia exchange rates because the Caribbean was a traditional source of Nova Scotian coin. Finally, the effect of the suspension of specie payment in Britain from 1797 to 1821 cannot be ignored. Exchange, both in Nova Scotia and in Canada fell below par shortly after the suspension, and, with insignificant exceptions, did not rise to par or above until after the Napoleonic Wars when it was clear that specie payment would be resumed in the near future.

Wartime paper money

Like Canada, Nova Scotia responded to the war-induced shortage of coin by issuing paper money (see Table 19). Unlike the army bills issued in Canada, the Nova Scotia treasury notes were entirely the responsibility of the province and were paid out of the treasury in satisfaction of warrants and were received in payment of duties. The notes bore interest at 6% and were redeemable in coin at the treasury. £12,000 in notes of various denominations were authorized in 1812. The 20s. notes were used to pay the troops and were by far the most common denomination. In 1813 the entire issue was withdrawn and replaced with a new issue of 14,000 20-shilling notes and 3,000 40-shilling notes. As before, the notes were issued through the treasury or through the army paymaster and were receivable in payment of taxes and duties. There were not, however, legal tender. Unlike the earlier issue the notes issued in 1813 did not bear interest. They were, in theory, redeemable in gold or silver; however, if the treasurer was unable to redeem them when they were presented they could be converted into certificates bearing interest. The notes were probably accepted for the purchase of bills of exchange on the British treasury, for the commissariat accepted the bills in the military chest and issued them in army pay during the war.[45]

Table 19 Treasury Notes Authorized in Nova Scotia, 1812–62

Denomination	Number Issued						
	1812	1813	1817	1818	1819	1820	1821
£50	50	0	0	0	0	0	0
£20	100	0	0	0	0	0	0
£12	200	0	0	0	0	0	0
£5	400	0	1,000	–	–	–	–
£2/10/0	400	0	0	0	0	0	0
£2/0/0	0	3,000	0	–	–	–	–
£1/0/0	2,000	14,000	0	–	–	–	–
10/0	0	0	0	0	0	8,000	–
5/0	0	0	0	0	0	16,000	–
Total Value	£12,000	£20,000	£5,000	£15,000	£10,000	£20,000	–
Total Authorized	£12,000	£20,000	?	£40,000	?	£70,000	£66,227

	1823	1826	1828	1829	1830	1832	1846
£50	0	0	0	0	0	0	0
£20	0	0	0	0	0	0	0
£12	0	0	0	0	0	0	0
£5	0	0	0	0	1,000	0	0
£2/10/0	0	0	0	0	0	0	0
£2/0/0	–	0	0	0	0	0	0
£1/0/0	–	35,000	40,000	14,000	0	23,000	60,000
10/0	–	10,000	0	2,000	0	4,000	0
5/0	0	0	0	0	0	0	0
Total Value	£5,000	£40,000	£40,000	£15,000	£ 5,000	£25,000	£60,000
Total Authorized	?	?	£40,000	£55,000	£55,000	£80,000	£60,000

	1854	1856
£50	0	0
£20	0	0
£12	0	0
£5	0	0
£2/10/0	0	0
£2/0/0	0	0
£1/0/0	50,000	50,000
10/0	0	0
5/0	0	0
Total Value	£ 50,000	£ 50,000
Total Authorized	£110,000	£160,000

*Limited to amount already in circulation, about £60,000
?-amount uncertain – Number not known

The notes gained general acceptance and passed at their face value throughout the war. When it was suggested in 1817 that they should be withdrawn a group of Halifax merchants petitioned the Legislative Council in favour of retaining them. Rather than withdrawing the notes the legislature authorized new issues over the next four years on much the same terms as the issue of 1813. This decision to expand the issue of treasury notes in Nova Scotia following the war was in sharp contrast to the plan to withdraw them from circulation in Lower Canada. In part the difference may be traceable to the fact that the Nova Scotia notes were a purely local innovation while the Lower Canadian bills were the responsibility of the imperial military authorities. It may also stem from the fact that Nova Scotians had a long and rather mixed experience of government paper money; Lower Canadians had no actual experience of paper money but did have the unhappy memory of card money. The different attitude to government paper money continued to characterize the two jurisdictions almost to Confederation. Nova Scotia kept about £60,000 of government paper in circulation until the 1850s, and when it needed to raise money to build a provincial railway in 1854 and 1856 it authorized an increase in treasury notes to £160,000. Nova Scotia did not become seriously involved in traditional borrowing until 1857. The Canadas, on the other hand, made no significant issue of government paper money between 1814 and 1866 when provincial notes were introduced. Canadian deficits were financed through the sale of bonds and debentures.

The rapid expansion of the authorized paper in circulation caused some concern. In opposing the issue of 1818 the Legislative Council admitted that the notes had circulated without depreciating during the war, but argued that unless a fund was set up to guarantee the interest on the new issues, the credit of the notes would suffer.[46] At about the same time the deputy commissary-general in Halifax refused to accept treasury notes into the military chest. The refusal evidently had nothing to do with the notes' credit but was based on the personal liability of the commissary officer if forged notes were accepted or notes in his possession were destroyed by fire. As his refusal to accept the notes reflected on their credit, steps were taken to reassure him and he resumed accepting treasury notes in 1819 and continued until at least 1822.[47]

A third indication that there was some concern about the strength of the treasury notes may be found in a statute of 1818 which prohibited corporate bodies from issuing bills intended to circulate as money. This act may have been intended to control a growing issue of private paper in small denominations (similar to the Canadian bons) which was coming into circulation in Nova Scotia. But more significantly, it may also have been passed to forestall the establishment of a private note-issuing bank. A bank would have provided competition for the treasury notes and plans were afoot for the formation of a bank. In March 1819 a public meeting was called in Halifax to discuss establishing a bank. An application was made to the legislature for a charter and a bill passed the assembly but was lost in the Legislative Council.

The proposal for a bank may have helped revive an old idea. In 1775, at a time when there was a scarcity of circulating money, the assembly had proposed the establishment of provincial loan offices authorized to issue up to £20,000 in paper currency as loans secured by mortgages on land. The assembly drew its inspiration from the land banks of Pennsylvania and New York, and the governor, who suspected the assembly of being soft on revolution, dismissed the idea.[48] The idea was revived in 1818 during the debate on the issue of additional treasury notes, but it was not until 1819 that it was incorporated into legislation.[49] The act provided for an additional issue of £15,000 in treasury notes and for the establishment of loan offices in King's and Annapolis Counties and in Halifax. The notes issued under the act were in every other respect like the earlier treasury notes issued except that they were to be put into circulation by means of loans secured by land. This provision may have been intended to satisfy the objection of the Legislative Council in 1818 that the treasury notes were not adequately secured.

Shortage of change

Although there was concern about the soundness of the treasury notes, the notes did go a long way toward relieving the shortage of circulating money. However, the smallest notes issued before 1820 were for £1 currency and consequently they did nothing to solve a growing shortage of small change. The shortage resulted, as it had in Canada, in the importation of large amounts of

142

spurious copper coins or tokens and the production of small private notes similar to Canadian bons. Many of both the coins and notes were issued by respectable private firms and could be redeemed, but others were simply "shapeless buttons and pieces of copper hammered out as wafers".[50] One correspondent of the *Acadian Recorder* noted that many of the tokens bearing the name of a respectable firm were accompanied by similar tokens except that the firm's name was absent. "Who", the correspondent asked, "will redeem these?"[51]

In 1817 the provincial government decided to have a supply of copper halfpence minted for the province. All other copper, save that legal in Great Britain, was to be taken out of circulation. Although the home government was sympathetic to the intent of the act it disallowed it on the grounds that coining was a royal prerogative. It did, however, suggest another method of proceeding which would avoid the problem. The provincial legislature failed to act on the suggestions until 1823, and the base copper remained in circulation.

As has already been noted, an act of 1818 forbade corporate bodies from issuing bills intended to circulate as money on pain of forfeiture of their charter. Because most of the firms or individuals who issued the notes were not chartered, the prohibition can have had little effect. Two years after the act was passed, "Senex", writing in the *Acadian Recorder*, complained of "this dreadful inundation of little bits of paper of all shapes, of all names, of all values from fifteen pence to a dollar". Senex went on to say that a recent decision of the merchant community to raise the rating of the doubloon to £4 had exacerbated the problem by driving other coin out of circulation.[52]

Importance of the doubloon

The same meeting on 8 March 1819 which had agreed to increase the rating of the doubloon to £4 currency also agreed to raise the rating of the sovereign to £1 2s. 6d. For some reason the rating of the sovereign was not increased but the rate of the doubloon was. Based on its gold content it was overrated by about 8s. 2d.; if the sovereign was worth £1 2s. 2.5d., the rating at which it passed in Halifax currency in 1822 (see Table 20), then the doubloon was worth about £3 11s. 10d. The effect of the overrating was to drive almost all other coins out of circulation. Even the dollar, which had dominated the Nova Scotia coinage before the War of 1812, was undervalued in relation to the doubloon which became the dominant coin in the province.

Table 20 Customary and legal Ratings of coins in Nova Scotia, 1822

	Weight (grains)	Rating (£/s/d.)	Purity	Precious Metal Content (grains)	Grains per Shilling	In Effect Until
Doubloon	(417.6)	4/0/0	.875	365.4	4.57	1860
Half-Doubloon		2/0/0	–	–	–	–
Eagle	(270.0)	2/10/0	.9166	247.5	4.95	1860
Half-Eagle	–	1/5/0	–	–	–	–
Guinea	(129.4)	1/3/4	.9166	118.6	5.08	–
Half Guinea	–	11/8	–	–	–	–
Half-Johannes*	(221.3)	2/0/0	.9166	202.9	5.07	–
Sovereign	(123.27)	1/2/2.5	.9166	113.0	5.09	–
Dollar	(417.6)	5/0	.903	377.0	75.40	–
Crown, old*	(464.5)	5/6	.925	429.60	78.11	1826
Crown, new*	(436.36)	5/6	.925	403.63	73.63	–
Shilling, old*	(92.9)	1/1	.925	85.9	79.29	–
Shilling, new*	(87.3)	1/1	.925	80.7	74.49	–

(From the 1822 Blue Books with the exception of those marked*, which are from 28 George III, C.9, 1787, N.S. and from reports of prices current in 1803.)
( )= weights taken from Chalmers or other sources (see Table 5)
Silver/gold ratio based on dollar/doubloon ratings of 16.5:1.

The overvaluation of the doubloon also upset the old Halifax currency par. At £4 the doubloon was almost 24% above its sterling value. Because it was the dominant coin, a more accurate par currency after 1819 would have been £124 currency to £100 sterling. However, the traditional £111.11 par was retained for another 18 years. Commercial exchange rates adjusted to the new real par and compensated by giving sterling exchange a permanent premium of 10-12% (see Table 41).

The doubloon was too large a coin for everyday use and even its parts were too large for small change. The gap left by the flight of small silver was quickly filled by issues of small private paper and copper tokens. To combat these issues, the government passed two acts in the session of 1820-21. One banned all promissory notes, bills of exchange and similar instruments under 26s. unless they provided evidence of a genuine debt. The other provided for the issue of 8,000 10- shilling and 16,000 5-shilling notes.[53] The province also ordered a supply of special copper and silver coins to be minted. The imperial government refused permission for the minting of the silver but allowed 400,000 halfpennies and 217,776 pennies to be minted. These were put in circulation in 1824 and the base copper ordered withdrawn. The pennies, with additional issues in later years, seem to have satisfied the province's need for copper coinage prior to Confederation.

The overrating of the doubloon did have one beneficial effect. The commissariat refused to accept doubloons at the inflated rate and since no other coins were available it was forced for a time to accept treasury notes. The increased demand gave the notes a slight premium of 1-2%. The premium was maintained until at least 1822 when the notes came under increasing pressure.

One potential source of pressure was competing bank-notes. A proposal for a chartered note-issuing bank was brought before the legislature in 1822 and debated in the assembly but was defeated. One of the arguments used against the bank was that it would undermine the credit of the treasury notes in order to encourage its own notes to circulate. The idea of a bank was revived in 1825 and defeated once again. Faced with the impossibility of gaining a charter the leading backers of the bank organized a private bank, the Halifax Banking Company, and opened for business in September 1825. Because it was, and remained, a private bank until it was absorbed by the Canadian Bank of Commerce in 1904, relatively little is known of its internal operations. It is known that by 1830 it had about £90,000 currency in circulation (see Table 23). Contrary to what had been feared this circulation did not lower the credit of the treasury notes; if anything, it enhanced them because the Halifax Banking Company's notes were payable either in coin or in treasury notes.

A serious blow to the notes' credit came in February 1825 when it was discovered that a large number of forged treasury notes had been put in circulation. To avoid any more damage to the notes' credit the government decided to call in all of the notes and either stamp them so as to guarantee their authenticity or replace them with a new issue. As a result the total value of notes in circulation was reduced from about £60,000 to £30,000, a level which was maintained until 1829. In spite of this measure the commissariat office,which since the war had been a major supporter of the notes, refused to accept them unless the province would guarantee its officers against loss in the event of their accepting forgeries. When a guarantee was not forthcoming the commissariat stopped accepting them.[54]

The commissariat may not have been the only public office which refused to accept the notes. According to one writer only the excise office, of all public offices, would accept the notes in 1825.[55] If this was in fact the case it was corrected in 1826 when a new treasury note act directed that the notes should be accepted at face value at the treasury, import and excise offices. Warrants on the treasury were to be paid in gold or silver, if available, or in treasury notes at the option of the payee. The option of receiving payment of warrants in coin was withdrawn in a revision to the act in 1828.

Attempts to introduce British silver

The commissariat's refusal to accept treasury notes would presumably have been reversed if the provincial government had agreed to guarantee commissariat officers against losses from fire or forgery. However, the imperial government's plan to introduce British coinage into the colonies put an end to that possibility. The imperial order-in-council of 23 March 1825 which was designed as a first step in this scheme provided that, in general, the army should be paid in British silver and copper. To encourage the circulation of British silver in colonies where the Spanish dollar was common, the government reduced by 2d. the dollar's sterling rating from the traditional 4s. 6d. sterling to 4s. 4d., which was still, according to the treasury's calculations, marginally above its true value. The imperial government recognized that British silver was practically nonexistent in many colonies and made arrangements to forward an initial supply of coin to the colonies. To keep the coin in the colony it also provided that bills of exchange on the treasury would be sold in future for British silver at a fixed rate of £103 of silver for each £100 sterling bill. The order-in-council was published in Nova Scotia in July 1825 and immediately created problems and confusion.[56]

Because only British silver would be accepted in payment of bills of exchange on the treasury the order eliminated one of the chief supports of the provincial treasury notes at a time when their credit was already shaken by the existence of forgeries. Also, because British silver did not circulate in Nova Scotia but was required for the purchase of bills of exchange, it began to bring a substantial premium on the market. Moreover in setting the fixed rate at which bills of exchange could be purchased at a premium of 3%, the British treasury had underestimated the market rate of exchange in Halifax. In the year prior to March 1826 commercial exchange ranged from a premium of 6–12%. The difference between the market premium on bills and the fixed premium on bills sold by the commissariat added to the value of British silver. As a result, although the British silver which was imported to pay the army did stay in Nova Scotia it did not circulate widely but was bought up and used exclusively to purchase bills of exchange.

The second stage of the attempt to introduce British money in the colonies was initiated in 1827 by a circular from the customs office in London directing that in future only British coins or dollars of full weight rated at 4s. 4d. each would be accepted in payment of imperial customs. After January 1830 only British coin would be accepted. This change involved an increase in customs duties since, although imperial customs had always been paid in sterling money of account, customs officers had, since 1817, accepted payment in foreign silver at the rate of 5s. 6d. per ounce of standard silver at which rate the dollar was worth about 4s. 8d. sterling. In some cases the dollar was only taken at 4s. 6d., its traditional sterling value, but this was still 4% more than the new customs value. In reaction to this new policy Halifax merchants pointed out that because of the demand for British silver for bills of exchange, it could only be obtained at a premium of 12% to 13% and that Spanish dollars were difficult to obtain at any price. They requested the option to pay duties in doubloons or in treasury notes. After some delay the British treasury agreed to accept doubloons in Nova Scotia and New Brunswick at their market value which was estimated at $15.50 per doubloon. It would not, however, agree to accept treasury notes, and the merchants had to accept this compromise until 1835.

One effect of this change was to put downward pressure on the rate at which the doubloon was received. The treasury had agreed to accept it as equivalent to $15.50, but this was below the customary rate of 16 dollars or £4 currency to which the provincial government and Nova Scotians adhered. Because the commissariat and imperial customs officials only received the doubloon at the lower rate, it became difficult to pass it at £4 currency, and according to a report of the Halifax Commercial Society the doubloon had fallen to £3 14s. 7.5d. by February 1829.[57] The change put treasury notes at a discount since a doubloon would buy four 1-pound treasury notes but neither the doubloon nor the notes would pass for four pounds at the commissary or customs office.[58]

The second stage of the customs regulation, having duties collected only in British coin, was never implemented, and indeed the entire idea of having British coin circulate throughout the colonies was quietly shelved. British coins continued to circulate within the vicinity of the commissariat and customs offices until other changes brought them into wider circulation. These other changes had to do with the revision of the Halifax rating system which the order of 1825 had touched off.

Following publication in Nova Scotia of the order-in-council which set the new sterling rate for the dollar, there was confusion as to the proper currency rating for British silver. If the silver dollar was worth 4s. 4d. sterling and 5s. currency, then the British crown, worth 5s. sterling, should pass for 5s. 9.25d. or 5s. 10d., with the shilling at 1s. 2d. This would have been in contravention of the colonial currency act of 1787 which rated British crowns at 5s. 6d. and shillings at 1s. 1d.[59] Some merchants evidently began to accept British silver at the new rate, and after a short trial reverted to the rating set by 28 George III C.9.[60] In February 1826 the question was debated in the legislature with some speakers favouring the old system, or a modified version of it, and some suggesting that the entire concept of Halifax currency be abandoned and sterling adopted. In the end, the legislature compromised by declaring itself in favour of adoption of the sterling system but declining to make any change until the other British North American colonies adopted sterling. In order to remove the contradiction between the rates established for British silver by the act of 1787 and the rates established by the imperial order-in-council, the legislature repealed the clause which set rates for British silver "so that in future such coin may pass current in this Province according to the actual value".[61] This simply led to more confusion as some merchants accepted shillings at 1s. 1d. currency, others at 1s. 1.5d. and others at 1s. 2d. The situation

148

evidently persisted intil 1830, when in an effort to solve the older problem of a shortage of silver change in the province, provincial officials began to accept shillings at 1s. 3d. currency and sixpence at 7.5d. The increased value quickly attracted small silver and solved the silver change problem. It also formed the basis for a gradual revaluation of British coinage in the province. The Blue Books for 1830 indicate that crowns were passing for 6s. currency, half-crowns for 3s., and shillings for 1s. 3d. currency. By 1833 the sovereign was passing for as much as 25s. currency although its value fluctuated with demand.

Establishing a new par

In 1834 the rating of the shilling and sixpence at 1s. 3d. and 7.5d. was given legal status. At the same time the doubloon was made legal tender at £4 currency and the sovereign was declared to be the standard of money in Nova Scotia, although no rating was given it. The act was only intended as a temporary measure until a common British North American currency could be established, and it expired in 1836. However, the rating had become firmly established in practice and the idea that the ratio of Halifax currency to sterling was 1.25:1 rather than 1.11:1 gained gradual acceptance. A customs act passed in 1834 directed that all provincial duties should be collected in sterling rather than in currency, that in future 20s. treasury notes should be considered equal to 16s. sterling instead of 18s. as formerly, and that doubloons, rated 80s. currency, were to be accepted in payment of duties at 64s. sterling. All of these ratings included a 25% increase on sterling.

The 25% advance on sterling values was not applied uniformly even to British coin, for the crown and half-crown were still, in 1835, accepted at only 20% above their sterling value. The sovereign, generally accepted at 25s., fluctuated with demand and sometimes fell as low as 23s. 10d. or rose as high as 25s. 8d.[62] An act of 1836 did much to relieve the inequities in the ratings of British coins. It provided that the sovereign should be paid out of the provincial treasury, and received for duties, at 25s. currency with other British coins in proportion, and that doubloons should be paid at the rate of £4 currency each (see Table 21). Assuming that the act established the current rate in the province, crowns would have passed at 6s. 3d., shillings at 1s. 3d. and sixpence at 7.5d.

The act did nothing to adjust the rate of the dollar and it remained out of circulation; the shilling replaced the quarter-dollar. The rating also left the doubloon slightly undervalued.[63]

Table 21 Customary and Legal Ratings of Coins in Nova Scotia, 1836 and 1842

	Weight (grains)	Rating (£/s./d.)	Purity	Precious Metal Content (grains)	Grains Per Shilling	In Effect Until
Doubloon	415	4/0/0	–	360.0	4.50	1860
U.S. Eagle, pre-1834	(270.0)	2/10/0	.9166	247.5	4.95	1860
U.S. Eagle, post-1834	(285.0)	2/10/0	.900	232.2	4.64	1860
Sovereign	123.27	1/5/0	.9166	113.0	4.52	1860
Mexican Dollar (1832)	401.23	5/0	.903	362.31	80.25	1860
U.S. Dollar	412.5	5/0	.900	371.25	74.25	1860
Crown	436.36	6/3	.925	403.63	64.58	1860
Shilling	87.3	1/3	.925	80.7	64.56	1860
Sixpence	43.64	7.5	.925	40.37	64.59	1860
Peruvian, Columbian, Mexican and Spanish Dollars after 1842	416	5/2.5	–	373	71.62	1860

( ) = weights taken from Chalmers or other sources (see Table 5)

Inaccurate ratings of the doubloon and dollar caused several problems. Banks refused to redeem their notes in doubloons, preferring to issue sovereigns or British silver instead. Until 1835 imperial customs had received the doubloon at a rate of £3 7s. 2d. sterling but in 1836 the rate was reduced to £3 6s. Spanish and Mexican dollars were accepted at 4s. 4d. Revenues from imperial customs were transferred to the provincial treasury as part of the provincial revenue at the same rates. From 1836, doubloons could only be paid out of the treasury at the rate of £4 currency, equivalent to £3 4s.sterling, a loss of 2s. sterling per doubloon to the treasury. Similarly dollars, by custom (if not by law) could only be paid out of the treasury at the rate of 5s. currency (4s. sterling per dollar), a loss of 4d. sterling per dollar. To correct this situation an act in 1839 provided that when treasury notes were redeemed in dollars, the dollars would be issued from the treasury at the market rate for dollars. Strangely a similar rule was not applied to doubloons.[64]

In an attempt to correct the undervaluing of the dollar, all full weight (416 grains gross weight, 373 grains pure silver) Peruvian, Columbian, Mexican and Spanish dollars were made legal tender at 5s. 2.5d. currency in 1842; United States dollars were believed to be inferior in weight and were not made legal tender. At the same time the sovereign and doubloon were made legal tender at 25s. and £4 currency respectively. Doubloons, sovereigns and dollars were made legal tender to any amount but British silver was limited as legal tender to payments of 40s. or less. British pence and halfpence and the copper tokens imported by the province were made legal tender to 12d. currency.[65] The new rating still left the dollar undervalued in relation to British silver and it does not appear to have come into circulation although Mexican dollars could be purchased on the market at 5s. 3d. currency. The change did, however, remove the last links with the old Halifax system.

In keeping with this change the practice of converting sterling money of account to currency money by adding one-ninth to the sterling value was gradually abandoned in the 1830s and the more realistic system of adding one-quarter to sterling values was adopted. In the Blue Books the change was made in 1836. Commercial exchange rates continued in most cases to be quoted on the basis of the old par until after Confederation with the result that sterling exchange was always at a nominal premium of from 12% to 15%.

Treasury notes and the banks

During the years 1826 – 1836, when Nova Scotia was coping with problems of fluctuating currency, it was also troubled by problems with its treasury notes and banks. Following the discovery of forged treasury notes in 1825 the number was sharply reduced and remained at about one-half of pre-1825 levels until 1829 when, in spite of the fact that they were still not accepted by the commissariat or the imperial customs, the value of notes in circulation was increased from about £30,000 to £54,000 and in 1832 to £80,000 (see Table 23).

In 1828 outstanding notes were called in and £40,000 in new 20s. notes issued in their place; unlike previous issues these notes were not redeemable in coin on demand nor could they be exchanged for interest-bearing certificates. They were, however, to be accepted in payment of taxes, and the governor could call them in and pay them off in coin if the state of the treasury permitted it. Subsequent issues in 1829 and 1832 were issued under the same conditions. Because of their inconvertibility, or for other reasons, the notes were discounted against coin in 1829.

A more serious challenge to the credit of the treasury notes came in 1832 - 33 when they became involved in the crossfire of a bank war. The Halifax Banking Company, established in 1825, had been successful, and its success, as well as the suspicion that it favoured its friends, inspired imitators. For several years the opposition of the legislative council, five of twelve members of which were also partners in the Halifax Banking Company, blocked attempts to gain a charter for a new bank. However in 1832 a new bank, the Bank of Nova Scotia, was chartered and opened for business. Even before the new bank opened a fierce rivalry broke out between the two banks. Under the terms of its charter the Bank of Nova Scotia had to have £50,000 of its £100,000 capital paid up in silver, gold, or treasury notes before beginning business. In the process of raising this it collected £23,000 in Halifax Banking Company notes and presented them for redemption in coin. Halifax Banking Company notes were redeemable either in coin or in treasury notes and had always been redeemed in one or the other; however, it had never been clear in law whether the choice was at the option of the bank or of the customer. In this case the bank redeemed one-half of its notes in coin and one-half in treasury notes and then announced that in future it would not make any payments in coin. The Bank of Nova Scotia could not, by law, suspend payment of its notes in coin, so in order to protect itself from demands for redemption of its notes, it put as few of its own notes in circulation as possible. What loans it made employed treasury notes, although it refused to accept treasury notes in payment of the loans. The refusal of the bank to accept treasury notes lowered their credit and they traded at a discount, variously estimated at from 2% to 8%.[66]

In an effort to restore the credit of the treasury notes as well as to break the deadlock between the banks, the legislature passed two measures in 1833. One provided that treasury notes would again be redeemable in gold or silver if either was available; if not the notes could be converted to interest-bearing certificates. A second act prohibited the circulation of any bank-notes under £5 except for treasury notes. The same act revoked the requirement that the Bank of Nova Scotia redeem its notes in gold or silver and allowed it to redeem them in treasury notes.

None of these measures was successful in restoring the credit of treasury notes or of bank-notes which had also fallen to a discount, and in 1834 the legislature required that both banks resume payment in coin on demand. Treasury notes continued to be payable in specie if possible, but in May 1834 when one of the banks requested a specie payment for treasury notes it held, the treasury found it "inexpedient" to pay in specie. As a result both banks refused to accept treasury notes.[67]

The circulating medium

As noted earlier the doubloon had become the dominant coin in circulation after 1819; an inventory of the Halifax Banking Company vaults in 1830 gives some idea of the extent of this dominance:[68]

Spanish doubloons	£1,300
Parts of doubloons	£210
Patriot (South American) doubloons	£19,036
Parts of doubloons	£514 10s.
Half-eagles	£31 5s.
Small gold	£658 19s. 8d.
Silver change	£486 15s. 4d.
Pistareens	£550
British money	£305 9d.
Province paper (Treasury notes)	£9,261
New Brunswick notes	£17 10s.
Bank-notes	£7,274
Sundry	£558 10s. 8d.

Writing at about the same time as the inventory was taken, Captain W. Moorsom noted that the doubloons and their parts were current in rural areas and that sovereigns, Spanish and American dollars and their parts, along with British silver, were occasionally found in Halifax. He noted that the recent decision to rate the shilling and sixpence above their true value was bringing them into circulation beyond Halifax. In the eastern parts of the province English and Irish tokens as well as French silver were common and were generally accepted at a somewhat higher value than they were elsewhere. Paper and old British coppers also circulated. Barter remained common in many areas and "cash" prices and "goods" prices were quoted in accordance with the mode of payment.[69]

Moorsom makes only a passing mention of paper money although there were never less than £27,000 worth of treasury notes outstanding plus at least an equal amount of Halifax Banking Company notes. Most of the treasury notes were in 1-pound denominations; there had been a large issue of 5- and 10-shilling notes in 1821 but most of the 5s. notes had gone out of circulation by 1830; the 10s. notes continued to circulate into the 1830s (some forged 10s. notes were reported in 1832,[70] but they were less common than £1 notes. The need for paper change was probably reduced when British silver became more common after 1830.

Little is known of the Halifax Banking Company's circulation; it reached £90,500 by 1830, £30,000 more than the value of the treasury notes in circulation. An act of 1820 limited all private notes to sums of 26s. and up; the initial issue of the Halifax Banking Company was probably in much the same denominations as the Bank of Nova Scotia which issued £1 10s., £2, £2 10s., £5 and £10 notes in 1832.[71] The smaller denominations could not have remained in circulation for long, as an act of 1833 prohibited banks from issuing notes of less than £5. (The prohibition remained in effect until 1870 when Nova Scotian banks were brought within the scope of the Canadian Bank Act and were permitted to issue notes as small as $4.00.) One result of this prohibition was that small notes from New Brunswick banks began to appear in Nova Scotia to fill the gap between the £1 treasury notes and the £5 bank notes. In addition, some private notes such as those issued by the Cunard Company in Mirimachi continued to circulate: at least £4,000 worth of Cunard notes were in circulation as late as 1839 but they were being gradually withdrawn.[72]

Another result of the prohibition of bank-notes in denominations of less than £5 was that the banks began to issue notes in unusual denominations in order to facilitate making change. The

Halifax Banking Company issued £5, £6, £6 10s. and £7 10s. notes after 1833; these continued to circulate for thirty years. The Bank of Nova Scotia issued £5 10s., £6, £7, £7 10s. and £10 notes in the 1830s and 1840s.

Through most of the 1820s the supply of provincial copper coins imported into the colony in 1823 - 24 had been sufficient but by 1830 complaints began to appear in the newspapers that there was a shortage of halfpence in Halifax; this was attributed to speculators who shipped them to the United States where they could be passed as cents.[73] In 1832, 200,000 pence and 800,000 half-pence similar in design to those minted in 1823 - 24 were imported and seem to have supplied the need for copper for several years. Subsequent importations were made in 1840 and later.

Like the other provinces, Nova Scotia was affected by the panic of 1837. The two banks, so recently bitter rivals, quickly came to an agreement to suspend payment, evidently with the support of the local merchants. Payments were resumed after two or three months. About the same time the Bank of British North America opened a branch in Halifax.[74]

By 1842 the Nova Scotia currency and banking system had reached a stable if not entirely satisfactory position and little was done to change it over the next ten years. The one major develop-ment of the period was the consolidation in 1846 of the various acts relating to treasury notes. All the old notes, about £60,000 worth, were called in and replaced with £1 notes. The new notes were to be issued in payment of warrants on the treasury and received in payment of taxes but were not made legal tender and were not accepted by the banks because they were not redeema-ble in coin. The act provided that duties had to be paid into the treasury in coin; however, in 1848 this rule was relaxed and duties were accepted in treasury notes, doubloons or sovereigns. In 1854 and 1856 the legislature authorized the issue of a further £100,000 in treasury notes to support the construction of a provincial rail-way. Only about £60,000 of the notes were issued at the time; the remainder were apparently issued in 1866 - 67. In 1861 the province began to issue notes denominated in dollars and most of the old notes were replaced by $4.00 and $5.00 notes in the early 1860s.

Interest in currency matters, particularly in the adoption of a uniform currency for British North America, revived about 1850. A currency committee of the Nova Scotia legislature recommended the introduction of a common currency in 1850, and in 1851 Joseph Howe met with representatives of Canada and New Brunswick to discuss the matter. The representatives of the three colonies agreed to urge the adoption of a common currency: Canada and New Brunswick adopted common ratings for their coins in 1854. No changes were forthcoming in Nova Scotia and in spite of attempts at currency reform in 1856, 1857 and 1858 the ratings of 1842 remained in effect until 1859 – 60.

Adoption of decimal currency

In 1858, in addition to a bill to regulate the currency, a bill to adopt decimal currency was introduced. Both bills were defeated but the decimal currency bill was reintroduced and passed in 1859. The bill, which came into effect 1 January 1860, provided that all accounts submitted to the government were to be stated in dollars and cents (although a second column showing pounds, shillings and pence was permitted). The act did not change the legal tender ratings established in 1842 but it did establish dollar and cent rates for British coins. It did not provide for a decimal rating of the doubloon or dollar.

Inconsistencies between the two rates, such as the fact that the sovereign was worth $5.00 or 25s. currency but that 5 silver dollars at £5 2.5s. currency were worth £1 6s. 0.5d. currency, were eliminated in 1860 by 23 Victoria C.3 which effectively abolished the use of sterling notation and made the new decimal currency system mandatory (see Table 22). The sovereign, doubloon, and Peruvian, Mexican, Columbian and old Spanish dollars were made unlimited legal tender; British silver was made legal tender in payments of $10.00 or less. The old provincial penny and half-penny were to be received at the treasury at the rate of 60 pence or 120 halfpence per dollar. They were not to be reissued but were to be replaced by bronze or copper cents and half-cents which were legal tender up to 25 cents. Provincial treasury notes were to be rated at $4.00 each; they were not made legal tender.[75]

The new rating did not significantly alter the relative value of any of the coins; British silver remained about 11% overvalued against dollars. The sovereign and doubloon were equitably valued; previously the doubloon had been slightly undervalued. In effect, the old Halifax currency had been converted to a new Halifax currency expressed in dollars.

Table 22   Ratings Established by 23 Victoria, C.3, 1860. Nova Scotia

	Weight (Grains)	Rating ($)	Purity	Precious Metal Content (Grains)	Grains per Dollar
Sovereign	123.27	5.00	.9166	113	22.6
Doubloon	–	16.00	–	360	22.5
Dollar (Peru, Mexican, Columbian and old Spanish)	416	1.04	.8966	373	358.65
Crown	(436.30)	1.25	.925	403.63	322.91
Half Crown	(218.18)	.615	.725	201.82	322.91
Florin	–	.50	–	–	–
Shilling	(87.3)	.25	.925	80.7	322.8
Sixpence	(43.64)	.125	.925	40.37	322.94
4 pence	–	.08	–	–	

( ) - weights taken from Chalmers or other sources (see Table 5)

In spite of having changed to a decimal system Nova Scotia had not moved any closer to a common currency with Canada and New Brunswick. Both provinces had based their decimal system on the United States dollar and had rated the sovereign at $4.86 ⅔ compared to the $5.00 rating adopted in Nova Scotia. The two currencies remained incompatible until the Canadian currency system was extended to Nova Scotia on 1 July 1871. The sovereign was revalued at $4.86 ⅔ and Nova Scotian accounts were made convertible into Canadian accounts at the rate of 75 Nova Scotia cents for 73 Canadian cents. Notes payable in other than Canadian currencies were withdrawn and the Nova Scotia treasury notes were revalued at $3.89. As a result, the distinction between Nova Scotian and Canadian currency disappeared.

Table 23　Paper Money in Circulation in Nova Scotia, 1812–67 (Expressed in local currency)[76]

Year	Treasury Notes	Halifax Banking Company	Bank of Nova Scotia	Bank of British North America	Union Bank	People's Bank
1812	£11,119 D	–	–	–	–	–
1813	23,129 D	–	–	–	–	–
1814	18,941 D	–	–	–	–	–
1815	16,769 D	–	–	–	–	–
1816	13,447 D	–	–	–	–	–
1817	24,719 D	–	–	–	–	–
1818	39,691 D	–	–	–	–	–
1819	49,577 D	–	–	–	–	–
1820	58,227 D	–	–	–	–	–
1821	63,877 D	–	–	–	–	–
1822	63,127 D	–	–	–	–	–
1823	63,127 D	–	–	–	–	–
1824	61,627 D	–	–	–	–	–
1825	31,877 D	Opened	–	–	–	–
1826	30,877 D	–	–	–	–	–
1827	27,877 D	"Considerable"	–	–	–	–
1828	39,027 D	–	–	–	–	–
1829	53,999 D	–	–	–	–	–
1830	53,999 D	£90,500 F	–	–	–	–
1831	54,999 D	–	–	–	–	–
1832	79,999 D	113,871 F	Opened	–	–	–
1833	70,299 D	–	£16,613 F	–	–	–
1834	68,499 D	"Cons."	68,201 Ja	–	–	–
1835	59,968 D	–	45,352 Ja	–	–	–
1836	59,968 D	–	30,944 Ja	–	–	–
1837	59,968 B	–	48,818 Ja	Branch	–	–
1838	59,968 D	–	50,289 Ja	opened	–	–
1839	59,968 B	54,991 ?	60,124 Ja	–	–	–
1840	59,968 D	–	84,148 Ja	–	–	–
1841	59,968 D	–	88,939 Ja	–	–	–
1842	59,968 D	–	72,892 Ja	–	–	–
1843	59,962 B	–	45,858 Ja	–	–	–
1844	59,962 B	–	38,430 Ja	–	–	–
1845	59,864 D	–	54,828 Ja	£(55,000)	–	–
1846	59,846 D	–	65,946 Ja	–	–	–
1847	59,846 D	(52,500)	71,939 Ja	(60,000)	–	–
1848	59,846 D	(52,500)	71,457 Ja	(60,000)	–	–
1849	59,846 D	(52,500)	51,832 Ja	(60,000)	–	–
1850	59,846 D	(50,000)	53,927 Ja	56,772	–	–
1851	59,846 D	(50,000)	57,164 Ja	56,772	–	–

Table 23 (continued)
Paper Money in Circulation in Nova Scotia, 1812–67
(Expressed in local currency)

Year	Treasury Notes	Halifax Banking Company	Bank of Nova Scotia	Bank of British North America	Union Bank	People's Bank
1852	59,846 D	(50,000)	66,541 Ja	56,772	–	–
1853	–	–	76,648 Ja	–	–	–
1854	–	–	106,812 Ja	–	–	–
1855	59,682 D	–	156,981 Ja	–	–	–
1856	119,682 D	–	139,306 Ja	–	–	–
1857	119,682 ?	–	147,255 Ja	–	$ 32,425	–
1858	119,682 ?	(68,750)	113,736 Ja	(75,000)	35,975	–
1859	119,682 ?	(68,750)	107,793 Ja	(75,000)	34,185	–
1860	$447,458 ?	(68,750)	100,572 Ja	(75,000)	36,340	–
1861	447,458 ?	$(275,000)	$445,873 Ja	$(300,000)	$187,300	–
1862	447,458 D	(275,000)	425,422 Ja	(137,500)	191,200	–
1863	447,458 D	(290,000)	480,771 Ja	(138,000)	267,820	–
1864	–	(275,000)	625,562 Ja	–	220,000	$ 128,660
1865	487,458 M	(250,000)	562,455 Ja	–	218,340	250,420
1866	522,458 M	–	512,638 Ja	–	–	–
1867	622,458 M	–	497,606 Ja	–	–	–

*Ja = January; F = February, D = December, B = from the Blue Books. Figures in brackets are estimates from the Blue Books

Figures taken from the Blue Books have been converted from sterling to local currency pounds at the ratio of 1:1.25 or to dollars at the rate of 1:5

Chapter Four

New Brunswick

Paper money in New Brunswick

5s. note, Bank of New Brunswick, 1820   actual size: 171 mm x 67 mm

£5 note, Bank of New Brunswick, 1838   actual size: 187 mm x 83 mm

Prior to 1713 what is now New Brunswick was under French rule, although whether it was part of the colony of Canada or of Acadia is not entirely clear. After the cession of Acadia to Great Britain in 1713 the confusion continued, Britain claiming that the area was part of Acadia and France claiming that it was part of Canada and had not been ceded. In practice, France remained the dominant power in the area until the loss of Fort Beauséjour in 1755 and the expulsion of the Acadians. In 1763 the area was formally annexed to the government of Nova Scotia and remained a part of it until 1784.

In fact, these legal changes had little influence on currency in the area, for it was so sparsely inhabited and its commerce so primitive that money played little part in daily life. Prior to 1755 the only substantial settlement was around Fort Beauséjour; after its loss the Acadians who were not deported were scattered, some to the middle St. John River Valley, some to Gulf of St. Lawrence coasts and some to Ile St. Jean. So long as France maintained a military presence in the region, either formally or through guerilla warfare, a certain amount of French silver and a larger amount of paper money entered the area. The silver tended to go to hoards; it resurfaced at the end of the Seven Years' War and remained a factor in New Brunswick currency until the middle of the nineteenth century.

Following the expulsion of the Acadians from Chignecto in the late 1750s several thousand New Englanders settled on Acadian lands, and smaller numbers settled in the St. John River Valley. Presumably these settlers introduced the paper currency and coin, chiefly Spanish dollars, of New England to New Brunswick.

For most of the 20 years during which it was part of Nova Scotia, New Brunswick stagnated. By 1775 there were still fewer than 3,000 inhabitants in the St. John Valley. It was not until the end of the American Revolution when Loyalist refugees settled in the area that the population grew significantly. It was this growth, as well as other considerations, that persuaded the British government to establish the separate colony of New Brunswick in 1784.

The currency act of 1786

According to the first governor, Thomas Carleton, there was very little money in circulation when he arrived in 1784. He did not specify what types of coin were in circulation, but based on the origin of the settlers and on the provisions of the currency act passed in 1786, it seems reasonable to assume that there was some French, Spanish and British silver, and British and Portuguese gold in the province. The army imported most of the coin it needed from Nova Scotia.[1]

An act passed in the first session of the provincial legislature established a basis for the provincial currency which was to endure until 1852. Essentially it adopted the Halifax currency system, with most coins increased about one-ninth above their sterling value (see Table 24). Because the Spanish dollar of the time was not generally worth 4s. 6d. sterling but only about 4s. 4.66d. it enjoyed an advantage in circulation. The same was true of the French crown, the rating of which was evidently based on an assumed parity with the English crown. In reality the French crown of 1726 – 93 was only worth about 4s. 10.25d. when it was of full weight, and it is unlikely that most of the crowns circulating in New Brunswick were of full weight. The overvaluing of the French crown probably made it one of the more common coins in the province: many years later, in the 1830s, it was reported that New Brunswick banks imported the coins from the United States and used them to redeem their bank-notes.[2] The half-Johannes and the guinea were correctly rated against each other and were reasonably rated against the French crown and the dollar but were overvalued against British silver. It is unlikely that British silver could remain in circulation in competition with gold or other silver.

Like the other British North American colonies New Brunswick generally suffered from an adverse balance of trade with Britain and found it difficult to keep coin in circulation. Shortly after his arrival in 1785 Lieutenant-Governor Carleton reported that what little specie there was in the colony was remitted to England by merchants to pay their bills because bills of exchange were not available in the province. Carleton believed that he could sell bills on London at a premium of 2.5% but he was prevented from doing so by the military commander in the region who insisted that all military expenses in New

164

Brunswick be met by selling bills of exchange on the paymaster at Halifax. Since New Brunswick merchants had no need for bills on Halifax, these could only be sold at a loss of about 7.5%.[3] Following the appointment of Edward Winslow as Deputy Paymaster of Contingencies in New Brunswick in 1785, the attempt to raise specie in the province appears to have been abandoned and for some years specie was imported from Halifax.

Table 24 Ratings Established by 26 George III, C.16, 1786, New Brunswick

	Weight (grains)	Rating (£/s./d.)	Purity	Precious Metal Content (grains)	Grains per Shilling	In Effect Until
Guinea	(129.4)	1/3/4	.9166	118.6	5.08	1844
Half-Johannes	(221.3)	2/0/0	.9166	202.9	5.07	1852
English Crown	(464.5)	5/6	.925	429.6	78.11	1844
French Crown	(455)	5/6	.9166	417	75.82	1844
Shilling	(92.9)	1/1	.925	85.9	79.3	1844
Sixpence	(46.3)	6.5	.427	42.92	79.23	1844
Spanish milled Dollar	(417.6)	5/0	.903	377.0	75.40	1821

Average silver/gold price ratio=15.27:1
French crown/gold price ratio=14.9:1
( ) - weights taken from Chalmers or other sources (see Table 5)

The currency act of 1786 did not provide legal tender status for a very broad range of coin, and it is possible that coins other than those named in the act circulated at rates established by custom. A currency act of 1805 provides some indication of what these coins may have been. Evidently modelled on the Lower Canadian act of 1796, the act rated the guinea at £1 3s. 4d., the same rating it had had since 1786; the Johannes at £4, the moidore at £1 10s.; the milled doubloon at £3 14s., the pre-1793 Louis d'or at £1 2s. 6d., the pre-1793 French pistolle at 18s. and the U.S. eagle at £2 10s.. Multiples and fractions of these coins were to be rated proportionately. The act was designed to keep coins in circulation in the colony, but whether or not it would have worked cannot be known for it was disallowed in 1806. The disallowance may have been ignored in practice;

two officials of the Colonial Office, J. Pennington and R.C. Chalmers, who wrote works on colonial monetary systems assumed that it was in force.[4]

Issue of provincial treasury notes

The 1805 session of the legislature which passed the currency law also passed an act which provided for the issue of provincial treasury notes. The preamble of the act justified the issue on the grounds that several New Brunswick vessels had been captured and as a result provincial duties, almost the sole revenue of the province, were interrupted. To bridge the gap in revenues the act authorized the issue of £5,000 in treasury notes in denominations ranging from $4.00 to $20.00. The notes, which bore interest at the rate of 5%, were to be issued and received at the provincial treasury on the same basis as gold or silver. The act also denied currency to any bank-note or paper currency of any foreign state. The notes were to be paid off when coin became available. Two years later, a subsequent act noted that £3,623 10s. of the notes had been returned to the provincial treasury. These were ordered cancelled and a new issue of £1,500 in interest-bearing notes prepared. On 1 May 1807 the outstanding notes of the 1805 issue were to be called in and paid off with the new notes. New notes which were not put in circulation by this exchange were to be issued in payment of warrants on the provincial treasury and were to be received at face value by the treasury. As soon as the state of the treasury permitted, the entire issue was to be called in and paid off in gold or silver.[5] How long the notes remained in circulation is not known (see Table 25).

The 1807 notes were issued in $4, $2 and $1 denominations. The use of decimal currency in both the issue of 1805 and that of 1807 may be taken as an indication that the dollar was the dominant coin in the province and that the decimal system was commonly used. The fact that the notes were issued in small denominations probably indicates a shortage of change in the province. Indeed there seems to have been a general shortage of hard money in the province, for in 1808 the commissary clerk was sent to Halifax to raise money for the pay of the New Brunswick militia. He was unable to raise it in New Brunswick except at a discount of 5%. The discount was blamed on

166

collusion by the merchants and may have been unusual; from 1803 to 1805 exchange had been at par. During the War of 1812 exchange was generally stronger in New Brunswick than in Nova Scotia and bills were sent to New Brunswick from Nova Scotia to raise money. However, wartime conditions were extraordinary since Halifax was expected to raise as much money as possible both in Nova Scotia and the Caribbean and ship it to Canada.[6]

Table 25 Treasury Notes Issued in New Brunswick, 1805 – 1818

Denomination	Number Issued	
	1805	**1807**
$20.00	200	–
$10.00	400	–
$ 8.00	600	–
$ 6.00	600	–
$ 4.00	900	800
$ 2.00	–	800
$ 1.00	–	1,200
Total	£5,000	£1,500

Denomination (£/s./d.)	1818
5/0/0	260
3/0/0	400
2/10/0	1,000
2/0/0	500
1/10/0	1,000
1/0/0	1,000
10/0	1,000
5/0	2,000
Total	£10,000

Unlike Canada and Nova Scotia, New Brunswick did not issue army bills or treasury notes during the War of 1812, but in the depression which followed the war £10,000 worth of treasury notes, ranging from 5s. notes to £5 notes, were issued. The notes of 1818 did not bear interest. They were issued from the treasury in payment of warrants, although the recipients had the option of taking coin, and were received at the treasury and the provincial customs office at face value. They were to be called in as soon as money was available. The notes were not a success, and by July of 1818 they were so depreciated that the government decided not to issue any more until they could be backed by gold or silver in the treasury. In 1819 the decision not to issue any more was made permanent, and a year later those which remained outstanding, about £1,850 worth, were called in and cancelled.[7] New Brunswick did not issue treasury notes again although the possibility was debated in 1832, 1834, and 1848.

Revision of the currency act

In 1818 New Brunswick also revised its currency laws (see Table 26). The sovereign was made legal tender at £1 2s. 3d. currency. Other British gold was rated proportionately. The ratings for British silver were not changed; however, since the new coinage of British silver in 1816 weighed about 6% less than the old silver, the rating of British silver was effectively increased in comparison with other silver. The act also established a rating of £2 10s. for the U.S. eagle and of 5s. for the U.S. dollar. The rating adopted for the eagle, £2 10s., was the same as that proposed in 1805. In terms of the sovereign, the eagle should have been rated at about £2 8s. 9d. currency. The advantage evidently made it the most common gold coin in the colony; Chalmers states that "New Brunswick had, in fact, practically adopted the currency of the United States with its over-valuation of gold".[8]

The act did not come into force immediately; it was reserved for royal pleasure which was not finally received until 1821 (see Table 26). While awaiting royal assent the legislature undertook a further revision of the currency system in 1820. Doubloons, although not mentioned in the statutes, circulated in the colony at £4 currency and in some cases at £4 7s. 6d. Even at the lower rate they were driving other coins, especially the dollar out of circulation, much as they were doing in Nova Scotia. To correct this the legislature made a second revision of the currency laws in 1820. The doubloon was made legal tender at £4 currency with its parts in proportion and the Spanish dollar was raised from 5s. to 5s. 4d. with its parts in proportion.

168

The French 5- franc piece was made legal tender at 5s. After some delay the act was given royal assent and came into effect at about the same time as the act of 1818.

Table 26   Ratings in New Brunswick in 1821 as a Result of 26 George III, C.16; 58 George III, C.22 and 60 George III, C.25

	Weight (grains)	Rating (£/s/d.)	Purity	Precious Metal Content (grains)	Grains per Shilling	In Effect Until
Sovereign	(123.27)	1/2/3	.9166	113.0	5.08	1844
Guinea	(129.4)	1/3/4	.9166	118.6	5.08	1844
Half Johannes	(221.3)	2/0/0	.9166	202.9	5.07	1852
U.S. Eagle	(270.0)	2/10/0	.9166	247.5	4.95	1867
Milled Doubloon	416.0	4/0/0	.875	364.0	4.55	1826
British crown (new)	(436.36)	5/6	.925	403.63	73.38	1844
British crown (old)	(464.5)	5/6	.925	429.6	78.11	1844
Shilling (new)	(87.27)	1/1	.925	80.7	74.49	1844
Shilling (old)	(92.9)	1/1	.925	85.9	79.30	1844
Sixpence (new)	(43.64)	0/6.5	.925	40.37	74.52	1844
French Crown	(455.0)	5/6	.9166	417.00	75.82	1852
U.S. Dollar	(416.0)	5/0	.8924	371.25	74.25	1852
Spanish Dollar	(417.6)	5/4	.903	377.0	70.71	1826
5-franc piece	(385.8)	5/0	.900	347.2	69.44	1826

( )=weight taken from Chalmers and other sources (see Table 5)
Silver to gold price ratio=14.9:1
Spanish dolar to doubloon price ratio, 15.46:1.

Under the new acts the doubloon was overrated by 8s. against the sovereign, by about 6s. 5d. against the U.S. eagle and by about 8s. 2.5d. against the half-Johannes. Similarly the Spanish dollar and the 5-franc piece were overrated against all other silver. The Spanish dollar was about 3d. too high compared to its nearest rival, the U.S. dollar. The overrating of the doubloons and the Spanish dollar must have driven all other coins out of circulation unless other coins were allowed to pass at more than their legal rate. In fact, Robert Chalmers contends that British silver circulated at a premium based on the exchange rate on London.[9] Although the doubloon and Spanish dollar were reasonably well rated against one another on the basis of a gold/silver price ratio, the doubloon could be sold in the United States for the equivalent of £4 2s. 6d. New Brunswick currency. As a result it was exported and only the Spanish dollar remained. Merchants complained that the rating of 5s. 4d. was inconvenient in dealing with Nova Scotia and with the United States where the dollar had different ratings.[10]

The 1820 currency revision proved completely unsatisfactory and was repealed in 1826.[11] Except in cases where contracts entered into between 1821 and 1826 provided for payment at the rate of 5s. 4d., the Spanish dollar reverted, by custom if not by law, to a rate of 5s. currency under the original currency act. The doubloon and 5-franc piece both lost their legal tender status but, according to the Blue Books of 1826, continued to circulate, the doubloon at £3 17s. 6d. and the 5-franc piece at 5s. The Blue Books also note that in addition to coins which had legal tender status, the pistareen, the gold louis d'or, and the Napoleon 20-franc piece circulated at 1s., £1 2s., and 18s. 9d. respectively. The pistareen was overvalued at 1s. and in 1828, following the lead of the United States, the merchants agreed to accept it only at 10d.. Following the devaluation many pistareens were exported to Lower Canada where they passed for 12d. until 1830.[12]

The attempt by the home government to introduce British coins into the colonies had no great effect on currency in New Brunswick. News of the policy was published by proclamation in October 1825, and the governor urged the legislature to make changes in the law which would help to bring British coin into circulation. The legislature argued that British silver should be brought into circulation gradually and that the best way to do this would be to put a small additional value on it. It then contended that British silver, according to the system proposed by the home government, was already overvalued by so much that it would drive other coins out of circulation. If, the legislature reasoned, the dollar was only worth 4s. 4d. sterling, then the crown, on the basis of its silver content, should only be worth 4s. 8.5d.; if the dollar was worth 5s. currency, then the crown should only be worth 5s. 5.25d. instead of the 5s. 9.25d. which would be required under the ratio proposed by the home government. The legislature believed a rating for the crown of 5s. 6d., which was already in force in New Brunswick, was sufficient to keep British silver in circulation if the dollar was rated at 5s.; consequently it refused to take any action on the home government's currency proposals except to repeal the 1820 currency act, thereby reducing the rating of the Spanish dollar from 5s. 4d. to 5s. currency.[13]

Copper coinage

None of the New Brunswick currency laws had provided for copper coinage, and little is known of the early copper circulation in the province. The governor's response to a colonial office circular in 1798 warning of the exportation of fraudulent copper coins was that there were no complaints about base copper at that time. The situation had changed by the early 1820s when complaints began to appear in the newspapers about the quality of copper coin in circulation. According to the Saint John *City Gazette* in 1821 the passing of "bad coppers" had become a serious evil; in 1820 "certain persons" had imported a cask of farthings from Ireland and were passing them as halfpence. The Blue Books of 1822 reported that a vast variety of base coin was in circulation. In 1824 a public meeting in Saint John decided that only penny tokens, English and Irish copper of the reign of George II or later, and the new Nova Scotia copper should pass as currency. Whether this decision was sufficient to drive the bad coin out of circulation is not known, but no further complaints were heard until the late 1830s.

In 1820, presumably in response to a shortage of change and possibly in an attempt to combat the bad coppers, the City of Saint John began to issue small notes. The first issue was probably a 6d. note but in later years notes for 1s. 3d., 2s., 2s. 6d. and 4s. 10d. were issued. The notes were redeemable in gold or silver when presented in amounts of £4 or over. They circulated until at least 1840 when some merchants attempted to drive them out of circulation. In the 1830s they were joined by bank-notes and private notes for as little as 2s. 6d.[14]

Banking and bank-notes

In 1820, at about the same time that banks were being established in Lower Canada, the Bank of New Brunswick was incorporated in New Brunswick. The bank's initial capital was set at £50,000 and its debts were limited to double its paid-up capital. The bank's notes were binding on it but the act of incorporation did not specify payment in specie on demand.

The success of the Bank of New Brunswick led to imitators, but like the Halifax Banking Company directors, the supporters of the Bank of New Brunswick were able to resist attempts to incorporate a major rival for many years. In 1825 the Charlotte County Bank was incorporated but its capital was only £15,000 and it never challenged the lead of the older bank. In 1834 a rival group circumvented the legislature by obtaining a royal charter for the Commercial Bank. At the same time the legislature incorporated a fourth bank, the Central Bank of New Brunswick, and in 1836 two more banks, the City Bank and the Saint Stephen's Bank, were incorporated and began business. The Bank of British North America opened a branch in Saint John in October 1837.

The rapid increase in the number of banks led to a proportionate increase in the value of bank-notes in circulation in the colony. Total circulation of bank-notes rose from about £76,500 sterling in 1832 to £315,000 sterling in 1837 (see Table 29). The banks, with the possible exception of the Commercial Bank and the Bank of British North America, were not limited in the size of notes they could issue; most limited themselves to issuing notes of 5s. or higher but in 1837 the City Bank issued some for 2s. 6d. In addition to the banks, at least three private firms issued notes. Benjamin Smith, a Saint John merchant, issued 5- and 10-shilling notes about 1835, G.F. Williams and J.M. and C. Connell of Woodstock issued some 2s. 6d. notes in 1837, and the Cunard Company issued notes at Miramichi in the early 1830s before there was a bank there. Because the Cunard notes were redeemable in Halifax, Saint John and Charlottetown they were popular and occasionally traded at a premium. After a bank was established at Mirimachi the notes were gradually withdrawn and by 1840 no more than £4,000 worth remained in circulation.[15] Nova Scotia treasury notes and Halifax Banking Company notes also circulated in New Brunswick.

There was some concern that the uncontrolled issue of paper money would drive all coin out of the province, but it was not until after the panic of 1837 when all New Brunswick banks suspended payment that the province took some steps to limit the circulation of paper. In 1837, 8 William IV, C.6 prohibited the issue of bank-notes or tokens except by incorporated banking companies. 1 Victoria, C.18 limited the banks to issuing notes of 5s., 10s., 15s. and £1 currency and up. These restrictions remained in effect until New Brunswick joined Confederation.[16]

From 1840 to Confederation there was no significant change in banking legislation. The Charlotte County Bank and the Central Bank failed and two new banks, the Westmorland Bank and the People's Bank, opened for business. Six banks were chartered in the 1860s but none of them actually opened before Confederation.

New Brunswick bank returns are incomplete and it is difficult to determine accurately the total note circulation. It is probable that the figures given in the Blue Books (see Table 29) are estimates which include the circulation of the Bank of British North America, Nova Scotian treasury notes and Nova Scotian banks in New Brunswick. It is clear that total circulation was subject to very wide fluctuations.

Copper tokens

During the latter half of the 1830s spurious copper currency began to appear in the colony in large enough quantities to cause problems. At a meeting in June 1840 the Saint John merchants decided that all copper coins which had been in circulation three years previously (American cents, British pence and halfpence, Demarrara and Nova Scotian tokens, the old Fish penny and heavy manufacturing tokens of Britain) would be received at face value. Spurious copper introduced since 1837, that is, imitations of American, Nova Scotian and Canadian coppers, "Trade and Navigation" tokens and "one-stiver" pieces, would be received at one-half their face value. Buttons, medals and bits of uncoined copper would be rejected. At the same time customs officers seized a large shipment of spurious copper which was being imported for use in New Brunswick.[17] The province also made arrangements to put its own copper coinage in circulation; £3,000 was allocated to purchase the supply. A quantity of British coppers was imported, but for some reason not put into circulation. The entire supply was exchanged for provincial penny and half-penny tokens modelled on those of Nova Scotia. Most of the tokens were put into circulation in 1843; however, the government had misjudged the need for copper coinage, the issue was too large and the tokens, which were not legal tender, fell to a discount. A second minting of the tokens amounting to 480,000 halfpennies and 480,000 pennies was made in 1854. Apparently the second issue also overestimated the need for copper coinage and a large part of it was melted down in 1862.[18]

Currency legislation

When 60 George III, C.25 was repealed in 1826 the Spanish dollar was left without a legal tender status, although in practice it probably reverted to the rating of 5s. per dollar which had been established in 1786. Such a revision would also have put it on a par with the American dollar which, under 58 George III, C.22, 1818, was legal tender at 5s. In 1835 any uncertainty with respect to Spanish dollars was removed by 5 William IV, 2nd Session, C.7, which made the Spanish, Peruvian, Mexican, Chilean and Central American dollars legal tender at 5s. currency with their parts legal tender in proportion.

The repeal of 60 George III, C.25, which had overrated the doubloon at £4 currency, left the United States eagle at £2 10s., the most highly rated gold coin which had legal tender status, and it became the dominant large coin in New Brunswick. Between 1834 and 1837 the gold content of the eagle was reduced from 247.5 grains to 232.2 grains, making it even more overvalued against the sovereign.

There is some evidence that overvaluation of the eagle was compensated for in practice by allowing British gold and silver to pass above their legal rate. The same 1840 meeting that established which copper coins and tokens should be allowed to circulate, also led to an increase in the rate at which British silver would be accepted. The shilling was valued at 1s. 3d. with its parts in proportion. The increase was evidently made to apply to the crown and the British gold as well for a notice appeared in the New Brunswick *Courier* in 1842 to the effect that the trading community had decided to reduce the rate at which British gold and silver would be accepted. The new rates were to be 24s. 6d. for sovereigns, 1s. 2.5d. for shillings and 24s. 2d. per pound sterling for British silver in general.[19] These ratings, although described as reductions on the current rates, were still about 10% above the legal rate.

In addition to these informal measures, the colonial legislature in 1837 attempted to correct the inequities in ratings of coins. At the same time it raised the value of most coins so as to prevent their export to the United States. The rating of the major gold coins was equitable and would presumably have brought the sovereign into circulation. British silver was overvalued and might have driven dollars out of circulation; however the act was not confirmed on the grounds that a more general reform of the currency in the British North American colonies was under consideration.[20]

In 1843 the legislature again tried to bring the ratings of coins into proportion. The Colonial Office stated that if the dollar was to be rated at 5s., then the proposed ratings for the sovereign, £1 4s. 2d., and for the post-1834 eagle, £2 10s., were too high and refused royal assent to the bill. Further legislation a year later rated the sovereign at £1 4s. and the crown at 6s. with its parts in proportion (see Table 27). The bill made no change in the rate at which American eagles were to be accepted, but in spite of this the Colonial Office allowed it to come into force and contented itself with a suggestion that the rating of the eagle should be adjusted. The legislature considered the suggestion in 1845 and rejected it; the eagle continued to pass at £2 10s. currency until 1867.

Variety of coinage

In 1845 the Blue Books gave the following account of coins which were accepted in the colony:

Gold
British guinea and its aliquot parts
British sovereign and its aliquot parts
Portuguese Johannes
Spanish milled Doubloon

French Louis d'or
French Napoleon or 20-franc piece
American Eagle and its parts

Silver
British coinage
Spanish milled Dollar and its parts
Old French Crown
French 5-franc piece
Spanish Pistareen
American Dollar and its parts
Copper
British mint pence and halfpence and a provincial
coin recently imported from England

**Table 27   Ratings in New Brunswick in 1844 under 26
George III, C.16; 58 George III, C.22, s.3; 5 William IV, C.7,
and 7 Victoria, C.29**

	Weight (grains)	Rating (£/s./d.)	Purity	Precious Metal Content (grains)	Grains per Shilling	In Effect Until
Sovereign	(123.27)	1/4/0	.9166	113.0	4.71	1852
Eagle, pre-1834	(270.0)	2/10/0	.9166	247.5	4.95	1852
Eagle, post-1834	(258.0)	2/10/0	.900	232.2	4.64	1867
Half-Johannes	(221.3)	2/0/0	.9166	202.9	5.07	1852
Crown	(436.36)	6/0	.925	403.63	67.27	1852
Shilling	(87.27)	1/2.5	.925	80.7	66.77	1867
Sixpence	(43.64)	0/7.5	.925	40.37	64.59	1867
Spanish Dollar	(417.6)	5/0	.903	377.0	75.40	1852
Mexican Dollar (1843)	(416.66)	5/0	.902	375.83	75.16	1852
Peruvian Dollar (1822)	(416.66)	5/0	.902	375.83	75.17	1852
Chilian Dollar (1839)	(415.90)	5/0	.904	375.97	75.20	1852
Central American Dollar	–	5/0	–	–	–	1852
U.S. Dollar	(412.5)	5/0	.900	371.25	74.25	1852
French Crown	(455.0)	5/6	.9166	417.0	75.82	1852

( ) - weight taken from Chalmers or other sources (see Table 5)
Silver to gold price ratio, 15.05:1
Crown to new eagle price ratio, 14.5:1

How representative this listing is of the coins which actually circulated is not known. However, it is significant that the listing was not changed until the 1860s.

The guinea had not been coined since before 1816 and must have been rare. Unless it was treated as an aliquot (evenly divisible) part of the sovereign it was no longer legal tender after 7 Victoria C.29 came into force. If it circulated at all, it must have been at a customary rate, probably about £1 5s. 2d. It is equally unlikely that the sovereign or Johannes circulated in any quantity; the sovereign was uncommon even in England. Both were undervalued against the new eagle; the rating of the Johannes had not been changed since 1786. The Spanish doubloon, French Louis d'or, Napoleon and 5-franc piece were not legal tender and it is not certain at what rate they were received although the doubloon probably was accepted at £3 17s. 6d. at which rate it would have been overvalued by about 2d. compared to the sovereign.[21] The Louis d'or (which had not been minted since before the revolution) should have been rated at £1 2s. 11.75d., the Napoleon at about 19s. 0.25d., and the 5-franc piece at about 5s. 2d.

The act of 1844 left British silver substantially overrated against the various dollars, all of which were rated at 5s. The crown, on the basis of its silver content and not on its legal sterling value, should have been rated at 5s. 5.25d. rather than at 6s. if the American dollar was worth 5s. The other silver coins listed in the 1845 Blue Books were not legal tender except for the French crowns, and it is not certain at what rates they were current. Under the 1786 currency act, the French crowns were legal tender at 5s. 6d.; the 5-franc piece had been legal tender from 1821 to 1826 at 5s. and the pistareen had been popularly rated at 10d. in 1828. If the old French crowns minted between 1726 and 1793 circulated at 5s. 6d. they were undervalued by 8d. to 9d. against the British crown. However, they were at least 50 years old and wear may have reduced them to a rough equality. (Ten years earlier they had been considered the cheapest coin in which to pay a debt.)[22] The 5-franc piece at 5s. was undervalued about 2d. against the crown.

The end result of the currency act of 1844, combined with the effects of earlier currency acts, was to make the new eagle by far the cheapest gold coin and British silver the cheapest silver coins.

In 1850 another attempt was made to correct the ratings of the coins. A bill was passed which raised the rate of the sovereign to £1 4s. 4d. without changing the rates at which other coins were received. Although the act correctly rated the pre-1834 eagle in terms of the sovereign, it upset the relationship between the sovereign and British silver. As a result the home government refused to confirm the bill.

In the same session an act was passed limiting the legal currency of aliquot parts of silver coins other than those of Great Britain, Ireland and the United States to 5s. The act was evidently aimed at preventing an influx of devalued Spanish and Latin American silver from the United States and was similar to 13 and 14 Victoria, C.9, passed in Canada.

Towards a common currency with Canada

The two acts may have been prepared in concert, for in 1850 representatives of New Brunswick and Canada began to consult on the possibility of adopting a common currency. At a meeting in Toronto in 1851, Canada, Nova Scotia and New Brunswick agreed to work towards a common currency, preferably a decimal currency. A year later the New Brunswick legislature passed an act which rated the sovereign at £1 4s. 4d. currency and the new U.S. eagle weighing 258 grains at £2 10s. (see Table 28). Other British and American gold coins minted before 1852 which were multiples or fractions of sovereigns or eagles were, if not less than 2 grains light, to be legal tender in proportion. One halfpence was to be deducted for every quarter-grain that gold coins fell short of their legal weight. In payments of £50 or more gold could be weighed, allowing 94s. 10d. per ounce for British gold and 93s. per ounce for American gold. British silver was rated as nearly in proportion to the sovereign as possible.

Provision was made for the issuance of provincial gold or silver coinage at the rate of £1 4s. 4d. currency to £1 sterling. The legal tender status of silver was limited to payments of £2 10s. The act provided for the optional use of dollars and cents in accounts with $4.86⅔ currency equal to £1 sterling. The currency acts of 1786, 1818, 1835 and 1844 were repealed, and as a result all non-British silver lost its legal tender status, although it continued to circulate until the 1860s.[23]

178

The act came into effect 1 October 1852; a similar Canadian act, 16 Victoria C.158, came into effect 1 August 1854. As a result, Canadian and New Brunswick currency were compatible, and both could be converted easily into American currency. The change provided a strong impetus towards the complete adoption of decimal currency, and in 1860 legislation provided that all accounts submitted to the provincial government would be in dollars and cents, although a second column could show the values in pounds, shillings and pence. The ratings for legal tender coins established in 1852 were not changed, although in future they would normally be expressed in dollars and cents, with the eagle equal to $10.00 and the sovereign equal to $4.86⅔. In proportion the crown would be worth $1.216, the shilling 24.3¢, and the English penny 2¢. The pound currency would be equal to $4.00 or 400 cents; under the old system £1 currency contained 240 pence. The act came into force 1 November 1860.

15 Victoria had provided for the issue of a provincial gold or silver coinage. The provision was not acted on although the clause was used as a justification for an issue of provincial copper tokens in 1854. The decimal currency act of 1860 also provided for a new subsidiary coinage of silver, which was to be legal tender to $10.00, and copper or bronze to be legal tender to 20¢. In June 1860 the lieutenant-governor requested that $10,000 in bronze 1¢ pieces, $5,000 in silver 5¢, $15,000 in silver 10¢ and $30,000 in silver 20¢ pieces be minted for the colony. The bronze cents were put in circulation in 1861 and the silver coins in 1862. The British treasury had been reluctant to authorize the 10¢ and 20¢ pieces on the grounds that similar coins had proven unacceptable in Canada, but there seems to have been no difficulty in circulating the coins in New Brunswick. In 1864 an additional issue of $30,000 in 20¢, $10,000 in 10¢, $5,000 in 5¢ and $10,000 in 1¢ pieces was made.

Table 28 Ratings Established by 15 Victoria, C.85, 1852, New Brunswick

	Weight (grains)	Rating (£/s./d.)	Purity	Precious Metal Content (grains)	Grains per Shilling	In Effect Until
Sovereign	123.27	1/4/4	.9166	113.0	4.64	1860
U.S. Eagle, post-1834	258.0	2/10/0	.900	232.2	4.64	1860
Crown	(436.36)	6/1	.925	403.63	66.35	1860
Half-Crown	(218.18)	3/0.5	.925	201.82	66.35	1860
Shilling	(87.27)	1/2.5	.925	80.7	66.77	1860
Sixpence	(43.64)	7.25	.925	40.37	66.82	1860

( ) - weights taken from Chalmers or other sources (see Table 5)

Changes in par value

With the conversion to a decimal system New Brunswick adjusted the par of exchange between its currency and sterling. From 1786 to 1861 Halifax currency, as used in New Brunswick, had been converted to sterling by subtracting one-tenth of the currency value and converted from sterling by adding one-ninth of the sterling value. This system had been reasonably accurate so long as the dollar was, in fact, worth 4s. 6d. sterling and was rated at 5s. currency and so long as the dollar was the principal coin in circulation. The ratio became less accurate after the period of currency reform in the 1820s which resulted in the American eagle and its parts becoming the dominant coins in New Brunswick. The old eagle was worth about £2 3s. 9.66d. sterling compared to the sovereign but in currency was rated at £2 10s., an increase on its sterling value of about 14% rather than the 11% prescribed by custom. After 1834 when the new eagle quickly replaced the old eagle, the difference between the sterling value of the eagle and its currency value increased to 21.7%. In effect currency had been devalued by about 10% but the old, and now fictitious, par value of £111.11 currency to £100 sterling was retained until 1861. To allow for the difference, sterling exchange always bore a premium of about 10% after 1826. Beginning in 1862 the Blue Books began to refer to the par of exchange as a 21.66% advance on sterling instead of 11%. Even this change seems anachronistic for it was based on pounds, shillings and pence, and it seems probable that when most New Brunswickers converted from sterling to currency they would also have converted from sterling pounds, shillings and pence to dollars and cents and not to currency pounds, shillings and pence.

The currency acts of 1852 and 1860 brought New Brunswick currency into agreement with the currency of the Province of Canada and there were only minor adjustments after Confederation. In 1871 New Brunswick's bronze and silver coins were made legal tender along with the copper and silver issued by Canada. Dominion notes, formerly provincial notes, were made payable in Saint John, as well as in Toronto, Montreal and Halifax in 1868, and in 1870 banks in all the provinces were brought under common legislation.

Table 29 Bank-Notes in Circulation in New Brunswick, 1820 – 67. (Expressed in local currency)[24]

Year	Bank of New Brunswick	Charlotte County Bank	Commercial Bank	Central Bank	City Bank
1820	Opened	–	–	–	–
1821	£ 9,837 Ma	–	–	–	–
1822	–	–	–	–	–
1823	–	–	–	–	–
1824	–	–	–	–	–
1825	–	Chartered	–	–	–
1826	–	–	–	–	–
1827	–	–	–	–	–
1828	–	–	–	–	–
1829	–	–	–	–	–
1830	–	–	–	–	–
1831	–	–	–	–	–
1832	70,106 O	£17,992 S	–	–	–
1833	–	–	–	–	–
1834	53,597 Ja	–	Chartered	Chartered	–
1835	–	–	–	–	Chartered
1836	50,809 Ma	17,512 A	£ 61,641 O	£ 51,260D	£ 23,360 O
1837	–	16,616 A	63,444 O	45,978D	33,105 N
1838	16,129 Ja	–	86,981 O	43,216D	25,171 N
1839	20,865 Ja	–	109,687 O	30,915D	–
1840	37,303 Ja	–	94,284 O	25,653D	Absorbed by
1841	30,345 Ja	–	82,302 O	18,067D	the Bank of
1842	20,625 Ja	–	28,106 O	12,771D	Nova Scotia
1843	8,623 Ja	5,385 Ma	18,257 S	16,206D	–
1844	8,854 Ja	6,413 Ma	40,448 S	27,443D	–
1845	24,265 Ja	10,437 Ma	70,361 O	40,989D	–
1846	38,880 Ja	11,664 Ma	78,641 O	38,571D	–
1847	43,918 Ja	9,268 O	75,279 A	43,637D	–
1848	45,746 Ja	6,594 O	53,850 O	31,870D	–
1849	36,863 Ja	5,595 O	53,454 O	30,206D	–
1850	46,913 Ja	6,384 O	73,021 O	38,909D	–
1851	50,730 Ja	6,132 O	115,656 O	58,299D	–
1852	59,485 Ja	11,356 O	134,149 O	70,184D	–
1853	72,134 Ja	14,510	–	108,980D	–
1854	92,734 Ja	15,372 O	–	127,319D	–
1855	93,623 Ja	11,420 O	–	78,051D	–
1856	71,619 Ja	–	116,154 O	–	–
1857	–	19,115 O	109,717 A	58,727D	–
1858	62,645 Ja	17,443 O	58,449 D	28,692D	–
1859	64,853 Ja	–	69,938 D	31,103D	–
1860	83,685 Ja	–	$346,640 D	$225,555D	–
1861	$ 302,512 Ja	–	–	215,334Ja	–
1862	269,034 Ja	–	263,964 M	153,698Ja	–
1863	284,160 Ja	–	254,809 F	Failed	–
1864	373,876 Ja	–	409,511 F	–	–
1865	322,757 Ja	Failed	323,829 D	–	–
1866	361,417 Ja	–	–	–	–

Ja=January F=February M=March A=April Ma=May J=June Ju=July

Table 29 (Continued)   Bank-Notes in Circulation in New Brunswick, 1820 – 67. (Expressed in local currency)

Year	Saint Stephen's Bank	Bank of British North America	Westmore-land Bank	Peoples Bank	Estimates of total circu-lation from the Blue Book
1820	–	–	–	–	–
1821	–	–	–	–	–
1822	–	–	–	–	£45,000
1823	–	–	–	–	45,000
1824	–	–	–	–	45,000
1825	–	–	–	–	45,000
1826	–	–	–	–	45,000
1827	–	–	–	–	53,000
1828	–	–	–	–	53,000
1829	–	–	–	–	53,000
1830	–	–	–	–	53,000
1831	–	–	–	–	53,000
1832	–	–	–	–	85,000
1833	–	–	–	–	89,000
1834	–	–	–	–	110,000
1835	–	–	–	–	200,000
1836	Chartered	–	–	–	350,000
1837	£11,440	Branch	–	–	350,000
1838	11,232 Ju	established	–	–	350,000
1839	10,122 Ju	–	–	–	350,000
1840	12,864 Ju	–	–	–	350,000
1841	13,094 Ja	–	–	–	350,000
1842	10,423 Ja	–	–	–	110,000
1843	8,678 Ja	–	–	–	172,300
1844	12,122 Ja	–	–	–	80,000
1845	14,150 Ja	–	–	–	225,000
1846	19,762 Ja	–	–	–	249,390
1847	20,862 Ja	–	–	–	256,000
1848	19,107 Ja	–	–	–	198,000
1849	17,181 Ja	–	–	–	170,400
1850	17,252 Ja	–	–	–	204,000
1851	21,181 Ja	–	–	–	200,000
1852	30,746 Ja	–	–	–	330,000
1853	40,385 Ja	–	–	–	400,000
1854	56,265 Ja	–	Chartered	–	645,145
1855	51,895 Ja	£ 30,042 Ja	26,374 Ja	–	473,162
1856	36,171 Ja	–	26,374 Ja	–	404,380
1857	31,069 Ju	–	31,484 Ju	–	283,390
1858	27,417 Ja	–	23,795 Ja	–	254,980
1859	40,039 Ja	–	22,542 Ja	–	313,246
1860	46,357 Ju	–	34,750 Ja	–	300,000
1861	$ 181,883 Ja	–	$ 118,619 Ja	–	320,000
1862	134,313 Ja	–	96,968 Ja	–	300,000
1863	92,651 Ja	–	109,029 Ja	–	310,000
1864	143,973 Ja	–	108,775 Ja	Chartered	400,000
1865	155,448 Ju	–	90,108 Ja	60,980 F	–
1866	160,178 Ja	–	89,712 Ja	99,157 F	–

Au=August S=September O=October N=November D=December

Chapter Five

Prince Edward Island

Sample of coins in Prince Edward Island, c.1815

guinea, 1798

Bank of England dollar, 1804

Bank of England 3s. piece, 1814

"holey" dollar

plug from holey dollar

British penny, 1807

Like New Brunswick, Prince Edward Island (also known as Ile St. Jean) fell between the jurisdictions of Canada and Ile Royale, although the influence of Louisbourg was probably greater than that of Quebec. In any case the population of the Island was so small when it was taken by the British in 1758 that it is doubtful that it had any circulating currency. In 1763 the Island was formally annexed to the government of Nova Scotia but after only six years a separate government was established on the Island. Presumably during the brief period when it was a part of Nova Scotia it followed the Halifax currency standard. The lack of legal currency standard evidently did not pose many problems for the Islanders. In 1770 the Executive Council considered establishing a par of exchange, for Island currency against sterling but deferred the decision and did not return to the problem until 1785. In that year the legislature, in an act establishing provincial duties, stated that "all rates, duties and imports before mentioned shall be paid in lawful money of this Island (being at the rate of 5 shillings per Spanish milled dollar)".[1] This brief mention was apparently the only definition of Island currency rates until an order of the Executive Council established ratings for several coins in 1813.

During the years before the War of 1812 coins were in short supply in the Island. In 1786 Lieutenant-Governor Patterson recommended that, in view of the hardship caused by the shortage of specie, Island produce such as fish, grain and lumber should be made legal tender to a limited extent within the Island. Nothing was done at the time but in 1795 a bill was introduced in the legislature which would have made wheat legal tender. The bill did not become law.

By 1790 the conditions which had prompted Patterson's suggestions had not improved, and the lieutenant-governor recommended that the province issue treasury bills designed to serve as currency. The legislature authorized the issue of £500 worth of notes in 1s., 1s. 3d., 2s. 6d., 5s., 10s., £1, and £2 denominations. The notes did not bear interest nor were they redeemable on demand; however, they were to be withdrawn and redeemed after three years. The notes were to be legal tender for all duties payable at the provincial treasury. In his speech from the throne in 1792 the lieutenant-governor remarked that the bills would soon become due and that some provision must be made to redeem them. He also remarked that the bills had not been a success and that the colony still suffered from a shortage of circulating medium. He suggested that the colony might follow the lead of some West Indian colonies and mark Spanish dollars and their parts. The marked coins would be legal tender in the Island and their export would be forbidden. Although the proposal was not acted on at the time, a very similar procedure was followed in issuing the "holey" dollar in 1813.

In the absence of an adequate supply of specie much of the business of the Island was done by barter. The Executive Council minutes of 1806 contain an application by a Mr. Power, who had been collecting debts in the Island and had to take payment in produce, for a licence to export the produce collected.[2]

Currency regulations

By 1813, when Lieutenant-Governor Smith arrived in the colony, it was still almost entirely without a circulating medium although the lieutenant-governor believed there were substantial hoards of British and Spanish coin on the Island. To bring out the coin and to attract other coin, the Executive Council in 1813 adopted several measures relating to currency. First the council established a rate at which the provincial treasury would receive the principal coins and tokens circulating in the Island (see Table 30).

On the surface the rating was a rather rough adaptation of the Halifax currency system by which sterling values were increased by 11% to obtain the currency value. However, the Bank of England tokens were overvalued in sterling and consequently were overvalued in the currency rating. The tokens had first been introduced in England when the Bank of England suspended specie payments in 1797. The first issue of Bank of England dollars was simply Spanish dollars with the British sterling hallmark stamped on the neck of the Spanish king. (The hallmark consisted of the head of George III, and the stamping led to the witticism "The Bank, to make its coin pass/Stamped the head of a fool on the neck of an ass.'') These were first issued at 4s. 9d. sterling although they were only worth from 4s. 4.5d. to 4s. 5.75d. In 1804 their nominal value was increased to 5s. and in 1812 to 5s. 6d. The counterstamped dollars could easily be counterfeited, and to avoid this problem dollars issued after 1804 were overstamped as 5s. pieces. These pieces were also revalued at 5s. 6d. in 1812. The 1s. 6d. and 3s. tokens were minted from melted-down Spanish dollars and were rated in proportion to the dollar valued at 5s. 6d. sterling.[3] In rating the Bank of England dollar the Prince Edward Island council took 5s. 6d. as its true sterling value and raised it to the nearest convenient sum, 6s., which approximated an increase of one-ninth. The same was done with the tokens. As a result the Bank of England dollars and tokens were valued about one-third above their sterling value while true dollars and British gold were only valued one-ninth above their sterling value.

Table 30 Ratings Established by Order in Council of 22 September 1813, Prince Edward Island

	Weight (grains)	Rating (£/s./d.)	Purity	Precious Metal Content (grains)	Grains Per Shilling	In Effect Until
Guinea	(129.4)	1/3/4	.9166	118.6	5.06	1849
Half-Guinea	(64.7)	11/8	.9166	59.3	5.08	1849
Bank of England Dollar and 5s. piece	(417.6)	6/0	.903	377.0	62.83	1849
Bank of England 3s. token	–	3/4	–	–	–	–
Bank of England 1s.6d. token	–	1/8	–	–	–	–
Dollars	(417.6)	5/0	.903	377.0	75.40	1849

( ) - weight taken from Chalmers or other sources (see Table 5)

The "holey" dollar

Perhaps the government realized that dollars could not circulate in competition with the overvalued tokens, for in the same order-in-council it directed that 1,000 Spanish dollars should have a circular hole punched out of them. The resulting doughnut was to circulate at 5s. currency and the plug at 1s. currency. The two parts would be worth 6s., the same amount as the Bank of England dollars. In addition the coins' mutilated condition would restrict their export from the colony.

The "holey" dollar, while ingenious, was not successful. It was too easily counterfeited and in 1814 was withdrawn from circulation. However, some of the counterfeits were accepted and continued to circulate until about 1824. The Bank of England dollars were not accepted at the treasury after 1816, but they (or 5s. tokens) continued to have some currency in the island until at least 1829. The smaller tokens continued to be generally accepted until at least 1847.

As a third measure to increase the circulating medium the council directed that warrants on the provincial treasury for sums of £5 or more, except for balance warrants, should be issued in denominations of £5 or multiples of £5. In effect they formed a paper currency and were eagerly sought by those with payments to make at the treasury. Warrants evidently continued to circulate until the issue of formal treasury notes in 1825 made them redundant.

In spite of these expedients coin remained in short supply. In 1818 the island merchants petitioned for a remission of the royal quit rents on the grounds that there was insufficient specie in the province to pay them.[4] During the 1820s the Blue Books estimated the total amount of coin circulating, hoarded, or in the treasury at between £7,000 and £11,000 for a population approaching 25,000 people. According to a report of 1828, the coin in circulation consisted of "Bank of England tokens issued during the late war, six shillings and three and four penny pieces, the old smooth shillings and half crowns, some French silver and Island Treasury notes".[5] A few doubloons also circulated. British silver and Spanish dollars could only be had at a premium of about 7%. Bills of exchange on England brought a 20% premium.

The treasury notes referred to had been issued in 1825 to supplement the meagre coin supply. 5 George IV, C.18 authorized the issue of £5,000 in treasury notes in £5, £2, and £1 denominations. The notes were to be issued from the treasury in payment of warrants and were to be received at the treasury and by the collectors of impost at face value. The notes did not bear interest but after 31 December 1825 they were payable in gold or silver at the treasury. If they could not be

191

redeemed they could be exchanged for interest-bearing certificates.

Initially the notes were quite successful, and in response to a petition from the merchant community[6] a second session of the legislature in 1825 authorized the issue of an additional £5,800, but by 1830 only £2,890 worth of notes had actually been put in circulation. In 1830 and 1831 two additional issues totalling £6,000 were approved, and by the end of 1831 the total actually issued had reached £11,780. Two years later a fifth issue was authorized and put in circulation, bringing the total outstanding to £16,780 (see Table 33).

Currency depreciation

The rapid expansion of the paper currency, unsupported by anything except the island's slender revenues, caused concern as to its soundness. Defenders of the notes pointed out that they were payable in gold or silver or could be exchanged for interest-bearing certificates and took the fact that no one had ever exchanged any of the notes as an evidence of their soundness. Their detractors pointed out that the procedure for funding notes was so cumbersome as to make the notes inconvertible.[7] Some also argued that Prince Edward Island currency had begun to depreciate almost immediately after the first introduction of the notes in 1825. T.H. Haviland, Colonial Secretary in 1847 and Provincial Treasurer from 1830 to 1839, testified before a currency commission in 1847 that the Spanish dollar, which for many years had been valued at 5s. currency rose to 5s. 6d.currency in 1826 or 1827.[8] His testimony is not supported by the information in the Blue Books which show that, with the exception of 1831, the dollar was customarily rated at 5s. currency until at least 1835. Also, a draft bill to establish legal ratings for various coins in 1829 indicates that 5s. had been the customary rating for the dollar for the previous 20 years. The explanation of the discrepancy may be found in Lieutenant-Governor Ready's comment in 1828 that British money could only be obtained at a premium of about 7% and that Spanish dollars generally did not circulate.[9] The rate quoted in the Blue Books may be regarded as the customary par of exchange while Haviland's figure of 5s. 6d. was the market exchange rate. More striking evidence of the difference

192

between the customary par and the market rate is to be found in a comparison of the par for various coins quoted in the 1835 Blue Books with the rate paid in provincial treasury notes for the same coins as reported in a letter to the Halifax *Nova Scotian*. If payments were made in treasury notes a premium of 44% was charged on the purchase of sovereigns, 25% on doubloons, 30% on dollars and 5% on the 3-shilling Bank of England tokens.[10]

Of necessity the government and the general population adjusted to the steady devaluation of the currency. According to T.H. Haviland the customary rating of the dollar was increased to 6s. in 1833 and in 1836 the merchants of Charlottetown, in reaction to a shortage of change, agreed to accept the shilling at 1s. 6d. currency and the sixpence at 9d.[11] This was apparently an increase from the prevailing rate of 1s. 3d. and 7.5d. rather than from the official rate of 1s. and 6d. The increase did not specifically apply to other British silver or gold but they were affected. Some observers believed that the value of British coinage fluctuated in relation to the rates on bills of exchange on England. From 1836 to 1848 sterling bills on England traded at about a 30% premium which, added to the par of one-ninth, amounted to a 44% difference between sterling and currency. To have remained in circulation the sovereign would have had to pass for at least £1 8s. 10.5d. currency; in fact, testimony before the 1847 commission on currency indicates that between 1844 and 1847 the sovereign rose in trading from 29s. to 30s. currency. In the same period the doubloon rose from £4 10s. to £4 12s.; the latter value was a 48% advance on its sterling value.

Withdrawal of treasury notes

The treasury note issue of 1833 was authorized by 3 William IV, C.13. Section 3 of the act provided for the retirement of the notes over a five-year period but before any notes had been withdrawn the legislature passed a second act, which suspended their retirement for one year. Colonial Office officials were alarmed by the dramatic increase in the colony's debt from 1825 to 1833 and immediately upon hearing of the issue of £5,000 worth of treasury notes in 1833 they instructed the lieutenant-governor that only in cases of extreme urgency was he to assent to any further increase in the debt without prior approval from London.

The Colonial Office also demanded that the colony retire the treasury notes issued in 1833 as originally planned.[12] As a result, by 1840 the value of treasury notes in circulation had been reduced to £11,500 currency, a level which was maintained until Confederation. The reduction did not, however, involve a reduction in the provincial debt for as the notes were withdrawn they were replaced by warrants on the treasury. Like the ordinances in Canada before 1760 the warrants served as a secondary paper currency. They were not as convenient as the warrants issued between 1813 and 1825 in multiples of £5 because they were not in standard denominations. However, they were interest bearing. According to the currency commission of 1847 the warrants circulated with little more difficulty than the treasury notes, although like the notes they were at a discount. Warrants were introduced into circulation more rapidly than treasury notes were withdrawn so that by 1840, when the value of treasury notes in circulation had been reduced from £16,500 to £11,500, over £10,000 worth of warrants were outstanding for a net increase of about £5,000 in the provincial debt. The home government was aware that its intentions were being circumvented but did nothing and the value of warrants outstanding continued to grow until by 1846 over £30,000 in warrants were outstanding.

Interestingly the continued increase in the value of treasury notes and warrants outstanding did not cause a continued depreciation of the island currency. The letter in the Halifax *Nova Scotian*, already referred to, indicated that in 1835 a dollar was worth 6s. 6d. in treasury notes and a £1 Nova Scotia treasury note was worth £1 5s. in Prince Edward Island notes. In 1845 the lieutenant-governor reported that the dollar was worth 6s. and the Nova Scotia note was worth £1 4s..[13] The major depreciation evidently took place before 1835; perhaps the growth in the island's economy in the 1840s justified the increased circulation.

Although their interest-bearing feature made the warrants more attractive than they would otherwise have been, it also made them a more expensive way to finance debt than the interest-free treasury notes. In 1845 the legislature requested permission to issue an additional £10,000 in treasury notes which would be used to retire warrants. The measure was opposed by some island residents, and the Colonial Office refused to sanction the measure and demanded an explanation of the over £26,000 in treasury warrants in circulation. Undeterred by this rebuff the assembly proposed a similar measure the next year raising the proposed issue to £15,000; however, it was unable to get the Legislative Council's support for a joint address on the subject.

In 1848, following a report by a commission on the currency and warnings by the Colonial Office that if nothing was done the issue of any further treasury notes or warrants would be forbidden, the legislature undertook to reform the currency. As a first step it proposed to eliminate the warrants by new issues of treasury notes which would be payable in cash on demand. However, the council and the assembly were unable to agree on the ratio of specie in the reserve fund to notes outstanding. The session also considered a legal rating system for foreign coins. Here the stumbling block was the conversion of rents which were stated in sterling to currency. Traditionally the rents had been payable in currency by the addition of one-ninth to the sterling value. Tenants wished to keep this conversion ratio while the landlords wished to have rents paid on the basis of the new exchange rate which would have involved the addition of one-half to the sterling value of the rent.

The question of currency was given more urgency by court decisions in 1848 which held that the Spanish dollar was legal tender in Prince Edward Island at 5s. in spite of the fact that both public officials and private citizens had been accepting it at 6s. or more for at least 10 years. Even the rating at 6s. was conservative for reports in the Prince Edward Island *Examiner* indicate that dollars brought from 6s. to 6s. 7d. on the open market.[14]

A new rating system for coins

In 1849, by ignoring the question of rents and of reserve funds for treasury notes, the Legislative Council and House of Assembly were able to reach agreement on a rating system for coins (see Table 31). The sovereign, doubloon, eagle, British silver, French 5-franc piece and United States, Peru, Mexico and Central American dollars and their parts were made full legal

195

tender at about a 50% advance on their sterling value. Pence and halfpence current in the United Kingdom, Nova Scotia, New Brunswick and Canada were legal tender to a limit of 18d.

Table 31 Ratings Established by 12 Victoria, C.24, 1849, Prince Edward Island

	Weight (grains)	Rating (£/s./d.)	Purity	Precious Metal Content (grains)	Grains Per Shilling	In Effect Until
Sovereign	123.27	1/10/0	.9166	113.0	3.77	1871
Doubloon	415.0	4/16/0	.825	342.38	3.57	1871
Eagle	258.0	3/0/0	.9	232.2	3.87	1871
Crown	(436.36)	7/6	.925	403.63	53.82	1871
Half-Crown	(218.18)	3/9	.925	201.82	53.82	1871
Shilling	(87.7)	1/6	.925	80.7	53.80	1871
U.S. Dollars	412.0	6/3	.900	370.8	59.33	1870
Peru Dollars	412.0	6/3	.903	372.04	59.33	1870
Mexican Dollars	412.0	6/3	.903	372.04	59.53	1870
Central Amer. Dollars	412.0	6/3	.8964	369.32	59.09	1870
5 Francs	(385.8)	5/6	.900	347.2	63.13	1870
Half-Dollar	–	3/0	–	–	–	1870
Quarter-Dollar	–	1/6	–	–	–	1870
Eighth-Dollar	–	0/9	–	–	–	1870

( ) - weight taken from Chalmers or other sources (see Table 5)

Silver to gold price ratio 15.46:1
Crown to sovereign price ratio 15.08:1

The act created a number of anomalies as a result of inequitable ratings. Doubloons and British silver were both overvalued, but by 1850 the doubloon was a comparatively rare coin in Prince Edward Island and the overrating does not seem to have attracted any new supplies. All dollars were undervalued against British silver. Although the act set a minimum weight of 412 grains for all dollars, Latin American coins generally weighed about 416 grains compared to 412.5 grains for United States dollars. Latin American dollars were also marginally purer than American dollars. As a result the Latin American dollars sometimes brought a premium. The eagle was also undervalued in relation to the sovereign and sometimes brought a slight premium. The rating of the American dollar at 6s. 3d. with the eagle at 60s. must also have caused some problems since 10 dollars would be worth 2s. 6d. more than an eagle. A similar anomaly in Canada in the 1840s had led to the export of eagles and the import of dollars. There is no evidence that this happened in Prince Edward Island; perhaps the premium on the eagle made up for the difference. The fractions of the dollar were undervalued in proportion to the dollar. Although this might have caused some problems initially in keeping change in circulation, the problem would have been corrected in the early 1850s when both Latin American and American fractional silver currency was devalued and became token currency.

The overall result of the currency act of 1849 was to make British coinage, especially silver, the dominant coinage in the island, with dollars and American gold in a secondary role. However, coin of any type formed only a small part of the island's circulation. The Blue Books for the 1850s estimate the value of coin in the colony at from £20,000 to £30,000 compared with £11,500 in treasury notes, £20,000 to £150,000 in out-of-province bank-notes and £6,000 to £51,000 in Prince Edward Island bank-notes. In addition some £10,000 to £30,000 in treasury warrants were normally outstanding (see Table 33).

The passing of the currency act provided the occasion for adjusting the par of exchange between Prince Edward Island currency and sterling. The customary conversion factor of one-ninth had been unrealistic since 1835 and probably since the 1820s. The difference had been allowed for in trade by charging a premium of about 30% on sterling exchange. Beginning in 1848 the Blue Books began to convert money of account from sterling to currency by the addition of one-half instead of one-ninth and from currency to sterling by subtracting one-third instead of one-tenth. In spite of this change in accounting procedures the Blue Books continued to use the old basis in reporting exchange rates; thus sterling exchange continued to bear a premium of about, 30 – 35%, plus one-ninth for conversion to currency, until Confederation.

The legislature had only been able to reach agreement on the currency act by ignoring the question of rents and treasury notes, but it returned to these issues in 1851. The currency act of 1849 had specifically exempted rents from the effects of the change in the rating system. In 1851 the legislature sought to make the one-ninth conversion factor legally binding for rents but the home government refused to give royal assent for the legislation. In 1854, when it became apparent that landlords might, through court decisions, obtain payment of their rents in currency using a conversion factor of one-half, the legislature passed a modified version of the 1851 act which gained royal assent. Under 17 Victoria, C.6, all rents and leases which were stated in sterling were to be paid in currency with the addition of one-ninth so long as Prince Edward Island currency did not depreciate beyond the standard of £1 sterling, £1 10s. currency.

The problem of treasury notes and warrants proved a more difficult issue. In 1851 the British treasury urged that the colony make a concerted effort to reduce the value of warrants in circulation and to replace small-denomination warrants with larger denominations. Fortunately for the island the early 1850s were prosperous, and the government was able to reduce the outstanding warrants from over £30,000 in 1850 to about £11,000 in 1854, partly through payments from the provincial revenues and partly through the sale of £10,000 in debentures which bore interest at 5% compared to the 6% on warrants. The province proposed to eliminate the remaining warrants by the issue of additional treasury notes on a similar basis to the proposed issue of 1845. Once again the home government refused to agree to a further issue of treasury notes and suggested that a private note-issuing bank would be preferable to note issues by the government.[15]

Chartered banks

Whether this suggestion was taken as a directive is not clear but within months of its receipt the legislature had passed an act incorporating the Bank of Prince Edward Island. However, the act of incorporation did not conform to the guidelines for bank charters set out by the British government and it was not confirmed. A revised act, passed in 1855, was confirmed and the Bank of Prince Edward Island began business in 1855 or 1856. It was the only bank in the island until 1863 although many notes from banks in Nova Scotia and New Brunswick circulated freely. In 1863 the Union Bank of Prince Edward Island

and the Farmer's Bank of Rustico were incorporated, and in 1865 the Summerside Bank was incorporated.

All of the bank charters had similar provisions based on the Colonial Office guidelines, which included the requirements that notes be paid in specie and that no notes for less than 5s. be issued. Bank-notes quickly became the dominant form of circulating currency in the colony: by 1860, Bank of Prince Edward Island notes in circulation equalled the estimated circulation of all other notes (exclusive of treasury warrants) and coin (see Table 33).

The Bank of Prince Edward Island's act of incorporation included a clause prohibiting the unauthorized issuance of circulation of bank-notes. Prior to 1855 there had been little need to control private issues. Only a few private notes of the type known in Canada as bons had been issued in Prince Edward Island. A publisher, James (or Henry) Hasyard, had printed some 2s. 6d. notes payable in treasury notes in 1836. A Mr. Fitzpatrick had issued notes of the same denomination but printed on leather at about the same time, but the both issues were so soundly denounced at a public meeting in 1836 that they were withdrawn from circulation. Perhaps more important than public indignation was a law of 1836 prohibiting the issue of promissory notes for less than £5 which were intended to circulate. Samuel Cunard's notes also circulated in the island, at least among the merchant community. The notes were eagerly sought in Charlottetown where they brought a premium of 15% over provincial treasury notes because the Cunard notes could be used to make remittances to Halifax. A bill was introduced in the assembly in 1839 which would have prohibited the circulation of all private notes but it was defeated in the Legislative Council largely because it was believed to be aimed specifically at Cunard who was a large landowner in the island.[16]

Although the island was not greatly troubled by private paper money it *was* troubled by the importation of large numbers of spurious copper coins. In 1842 the legislature attempted to deal with the problem by providing for an issue of provincial copper coinage. The act was disallowed on the grounds of the royal prerogative and because it had made no provision for compensating holders of the spurious coin. In defending the act the lieutenant-governor admitted that there had been no popular demand for it and implied that there was no great

199

dissatisfaction with the spurious coin.[17] The currency act of 1849 provided that copper coins current in the United Kingdom, Nova Scotia, New Brunswick and Canada should also be legal tender in Prince Edward Island, but the act does not seem to have had much practical effect. The Blue Books through the 1850s and 1860s continued to report that most of the copper in circulation was spurious.

Following the currency reforms of 1849 – 53 there was relatively little change in currency legislation until the 1870s. In 1864 a limit of £6 currency was put on the legal tender value of silver in any single payment. A year later a revenue act declared that in converting prices on invoices, American dollars should be rated at 6s. currency. This ruling apparently conflicted with the rating of 6s. 3d. established in 1849, but as the 1849 act related principally to coin and the revenue act to money of account the conflict probably had few practical consequences.

The value of outstanding treasury warrants had been reduced to £10,663 currency in 1856 but by 1869 almost £70,000 worth were in circulation; in the same period the value of provincial debentures increased from £10,000 to £80,000. Although it is not clear whether the warrants continued to serve as currency, the rapid growth of the provincial debt would have been inflationary unless it was matched by an equally rapid growth in the provincial economy. The fact that the exchange rate remained stable from 1855 to 1870 is an indication that the growth in the provincial debt was justified.

Adoption of decimal currency.

By 1870, Prince Edward Island was the only one of the British North American colonies not to have adopted decimal currency. As most of its trade was with Canada and the United States the legislature passed a decimal currency act in 1871; the actual conversion to decimal currency was made in stages between December 1871 and February 1872. The dollar of 100 cents was made the unit of account with the sovereign legal tender at $4.866 and the crown at $1.20, 1.5 cents less than its sterling value in relation to the sovereign but more than its intrinsic value. Other British silver was rated in proportion to the crown. The U.S. dollar, in gold, was rated at $1.00 or $10.00 for the eagle.

The U.S. silver dollar had been demonetized in 1870 along with other foreign silver and was not made legal tender in 1871 although the Mexican and Spanish dollars were. Spanish and Mexican doubloons and French 20-franc gold pieces and 5-franc silver pieces were also made legal tender. Canadian silver was to be legal tender at its face value. The old Prince Edward Island currency was to be converted to decimal currency at the rate of $3.244 per £1 currency (see Table 32).

The rating overvalued British silver both against gold and against other silver. To prevent an influx of silver the subsequent session of the legislature put a $10.00 limit on payments in British and Canadian silver and a 25-cent limit on payments in copper coins. In fact there was little danger of an influx of British silver. The act left the smaller coins at awkward amounts: 48¢ for the florin, 24¢ for the shilling and 12¢ for the sixpence. To avoid the nuisance of accepting them at these rates or the loss of accepting them at even amounts the Bank of Prince Edward Island exported the coins and imported Canadian silver in their place. In 1872 the legislature demonetized all foreign silver and specified that the eagle minted after 1 July 1834 and weighing at least 258 grains should be legal tender for $10.00 with its parts in proportion.

The decimal currency act provided for the reissue of treasury notes in dollars and cents and for the issue of a provincial copper coinage. One million bronze cents were procured in England and were put into circulation in 1872.[18] At the same time the old copper coinage was withdrawn at the rate of 16 cents per shilling currency. About £1,854 currency was withdrawn; of this, roughly 80% by value was in the form of tokens and 12% was provincial pence and halfpence, presumably from the other British North American colonies. The remainder was British and French coins.

Prince Edward Island entered Confederation in 1873 but it was not until 1876 that dominion notes were made legal tender in the island and not until 1881 that the provisions of the uniform currency act of 1871 were extended to it.

Table 32 Ratings Established by 34 Victoria, C.5, 1871 Prince Edward Island

	Weight (grains)	Rating ($)	Purity	Precious Metal Content (grains)	Grains per Dollar
Sovereign	(123.27)	4.86̂	.9166	113.0	23.22
Eagle	(258.0)	10.00	.900	232.2	23.22
Spanish Doubloon	(417.6)	16.00	.875	365.4	22.84
Mexican Doubloon (1832)	(416.20)	15.40	.872	362.93	23.57
20-franc piece	(99.55)	3.80	.900	89.60	23.58
Crown	(436.36)	1.20	.925	403.63	336.36
Half-Crown	(218.18)	.60	.925	201.82	336.37
Shilling	(87.3)	.24	.925	80.7	336.33
Sixpence	(43.64)	.12	.925	40.37	336.39
Spanish Dollar	(417.6)	1.00	.903	377.0	377.00
Mexican Dollar (1843)	(416.66)	1.00	.902	375.83	375.83
5-franc piece	(385.80)	.90	.900	347.2	385.80

( ) - weight taken from Chalmers or other sources (see Table 5)

Canadian silver at face value
Silver to gold ratio 15.24:1
British silver to gold ratio 14.4:1

Table 33 Treasury Notes, Treasury Warrants, Bank-Notes and Coin in Circulation in Prince Edward Island, 1825–1871 (Expressed in local currency)[19]

Year	Coin (£)	Total Treasury Notes (£)	£5	£2	£1	10s.	5s.	Treasury Warrants (£)
1825		1,400	–	–	–	–		–
1826	–	2,890	450	750	1,150	540	–	–
1827	–	–	–	–	–	–		–
1828	–	2,890	450	750	1,150	540	–	–
1829	7,000	2,890	450	750	1,150	540	–	–
1830	7,000	5,890	450	750	2,650	2,040	–	
1831	7,000	11,780	1,160	1,660	4,160	3,800	500	–
1832	7,000	11,780	1,160	1,660	4,160	3,800	500	–
1833	7,000	16,780	2,660	3,660	5,160	4,300	1000	–
1834	7,000	16,780	2,660	3,660	5,160	4,300	1000	–
1835	–	15,780	2,520	3,606	4,854	4,032	768	–
1836	–	14,780	2,350	3,396	4,534	3,732	768	1,110
1837	–	13,780	2,255	3,234	4,324	3,390	667	5,094

Table 33   (Continued) Treasury Notes, Treasury Warrants, Bank-Notes and Coin in Circulation in Prince Edward Island, 1825–1871 (Expressed in local currency)

Year	Coin (£)	Total Treasury Notes (£)	£5	£2	£1	10s.	5s.	Treasury Warrants (£)
				Number of Treasury Notes by Denomination				
1838		–	12,780	2,155	8,628	3,904	3,078	617
1839	–	11,500	–	–	–	–	–	7,115
1840	–	11,500	–	–	–	–	–	10,081
1841	–	11,500	–	–	–	–	–	12,208
1842	–	11,500	–	–	–	–	–	14,345
1843	–	11,500	–	–	–	–	–	16,947
1844	15,000	11,500	–	–	–	–	–	21,277
1845	14,500	11,500	–	–	–	–	–	26,223
1846	14,500	11,500	–	–	–	–	–	30,200

* Figures which were given in sterling in the Blue Books have been converted to currency by multiplying by 1.1111 to 1849; after 1849 sterling was converted by multiplying by 1.5

Coin and Notes in Circulation

Year	Coin (£)	Treasury Notes (£)	Treasury Warrants (£)	Out of Province Bank-Notes (£)	U.S. Bank-Notes (£)
1847	20,000	11,650	29,307	10,000	–
1848	20,000	11,350	30,293	10,000	–
1849	20,000	11,350	–	10,000	–
1850	20,000	11,500	30,664	20,000	–
1851	30,000	11,500	–	20,000	–
1852	30,000	11,500	13,436	20,000	–
1853	–	11,500	12,109	100,000	–
1854	–	11,500	11,416	150,000	–
1855	–	11,500	10,808	150,000	–
1856	–	11,500	10,663	135,000	–
1857	–	11,500	22,687	90,000	–
1858	30,000	11,500	30,594	22,500	600
1859	30,000	11,500	27,733	22,500	900
1860	24,000	11,500	29,488	15,000	300
1861	15,000	11,500	–	6,000	300
1862	18,000	11,500	44,123	6,000	600
1863	18,000	11,500	57,033	16,500	750
1864	18,750	11,500	49,185	16,500	750
1865	15,000	11,500	56,381	15,000	1,500
1866	13,500	11,500	56,137	12,000	2,250
1867	13,500	11,500	59,658	12,000	2,000

Table 33 (Continued)

Year	Coin (£)	Treasury Notes (£)	Treasury Warrants (£)	Out of Province Bank-Notes (£)	U.S. Bank-Notes (£)
1868	33,000	11,500	63,138	6,000	2,000
1869	22,500	11,500	69,513	5,000	2,000
1870	33,000	11,500	63,606	6,000	2,000
1871	75,000	11,500	39,741	3,000	2,000
1872	–	11,500	22,045	–	–

Bank-Notes in Circulation

Year	Bank of P.E.I. (£)	Union Bank (£)	Bank of Rustico (£)	Summersite Bank (£)	Merchants Bank of P.E.I. (£)
1847	–	–	–	–	–
1848	–	–	–	–	–
1849	–	–	–	–	–
1850	–	–	–	–	–
1851	–	–	–	–	–
1852	–	–	–	–	–
1853	–	–	–	–	–
1854	–	–	–	–	–
1855	–	–	–	–	–
1856	8,999 S	–	–	–	–
1857	34,047 S	–	–	–	–
1858	32,945 M	–	–	–	–
1859	33,537 M	–	–	–	–
1860	–	–	–	–	–
1861	29,200 S	–	–	–	–
1862	29,298 S	–	–	–	–
1863	46,987 S	–	–	–	–
1864	38,027 S	28,656 N	–	–	–
1865	36,020 M	–	–	–	–
1866	24,877 O	36,322 M	4,351 A	2,437 F	–
1867	19,380 S	24,000 B	2,528 O	10,545 Au	–
1868	31,765 M	27,981 M	4,869 B	15,947 F	–
1869	33,209 M	28,480 M	5,000 B	16,202 F	–
1870	33,900 S	31,765 B	4,869 B	14,161 Au	–
1871	54,585 M	50,918 M	2,734 A	13,644 B	11,138 B

Ja=January; F=February; M=March; A=April; Ma=May; J=June;
Ju=July; Au=August; S=September; O=October; N=November;
D=December; B=Blue Books, date uncertain

204

Chapter Six

Newfoundland

$10.00 Union Bank of Newfoundland note

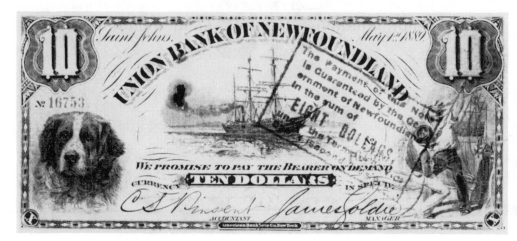

note counterstamped by the Government of Newfoundland

actual size: 180 mm x 81 mm

The early history of Newfoundland's currency is even less well known than that of other Canadian colonies. The island was claimed for England in 1497 by John Cabot but for nearly 200 years the English government actively discouraged settlement on the island, preferring to maintain it as a summer base for the fishing fleet. In addition to the English fleet, those of France, Spain and Portugal regularly visited Newfoundland. The French maintained territorial claims and settlements on the island until the Treaty of Utrecht in 1713. From 1713 to 1904 they had special (and in theory exclusive) fishing privileges on the north and west shore of the island. They also held, and hold, the small colony of St. Pierre and Miquelon off the south shore.

The presence of the fleets of four nations in the waters surrounding Newfoundland probably resulted in coins of several nations being present in the area in the sixteenth and seventeenth centuries but the lack of permanent settlements may be taken as an indication that very little coin actually circulated.

In spite of the efforts of the English government to discourage settlement the island had a permanent population of about 2,000 in 1650, which grew to 8,000 a century later. In 1697 a British garrison was established at St. John's and this probably led to the first introduction of substantial sums of coin, for the garrison was paid in cash, at least when supplies could be obtained from England. This coin does not seem to have circulated very far in the colony, as the reports on the fishery which were submitted annually during the first three-quarters of the eighteenth century indicate that employees in the fishery were paid in fish, in train oil, in bills of exchange, in provisions, or in liquor. New England traders who brought provisions to the island were also paid in oil or in fish, although at least one report stated they were paid partly in cash.[1]

The supplies of coin sent out to pay the troops were evidently both irregular and insufficient to meet the needs of the colony, for when Governor Waldegrave brought out £6,000 in silver and £1,000 in copper coin in 1798 it was treated as a great event. When supplies of coin failed, the troops, like the civilian population, were paid in small bills drawn on the local merchants. These bills were only redeemable in goods or in other bills drawn on England. It seems probable that the bills circulated to some extent; in addition, by the end of the eighteenth century many of the local merchants had resorted to the issue of private paper money similar to the bons of Canada. E. Chappell, who visited St. John's in 1814, reported that private notes issued in denominations ranging from 5s. to £5 formed the principal circulating medium in the island, although British coins and Spanish dollars also circulated.[2]

Establishment of a currency system

Governor Waldegrave's arrival in 1798 sparked the first known discussion of currency in Newfoundland. His advisers predicted that the coin he had imported would be quickly exported as remittances and suggested that the importation would have to be repeated annually. The St. John's magistrates suggested that the best solution to the currency problem would be to have a special token coinage minted for the colony which would not be exported. Although the governor recommended the idea to the Colonial Office nothing was done.

Newfoundland does not seem to have adopted an inflated local currency of accounts as a means of attracting coin to the colony, although all other North American colonies had done so by 1800. In the spring of 1798, before the governor arrived with a supply of coin, the paymaster of the Royal Newfoundland Regiment attempted to raïse money by the sale of bills of exchange on the regiment's London agent. He received only two replies to his advertisement. One was an offer to supply £100 in dollars at a premium of 5%, the other was an offer of £500 worth of dollars if he would take the dollars at the rate of 5s.[3] In effect the second offer would have involved accepting the Halifax currency standard and the paymaster refused it.

The fact that the offer was made may indicate that in some cases an inflated currency of account was accepted in practice. Certainly the concept was not unfamiliar to Newfoundlanders, and in 1811, faced with a continuing shortage of coin, Governor Duckworth "recommended" to merchants that they accept the

Spanish dollar at 5s. and the English stamped dollar or Bank of England tokens at 5s. 6d. At the same time the officer commanding the forces directed that army officials should pay and take dollars and tokens at the recommended rate.[4]

The new rating seems to have been generally accepted and evidently brought dollars into circulation, for in 1817 the governor stated that dollars were the only coin circulating in the island with the exception of a few bank tokens. He also implied that the increase in the rating of the dollar had ended the practice of circulating bills of exchange and private paper money;[5] this suggestion disagrees with the report by E. Chappell in 1814 that private paper formed the principal circulating medium in Newfoundland.

The increased value applied only to the dollar and to bank tokens. Until at least 1825 British coinage continued to be received at its face value; as a result it can hardly have circulated in competition with the overvalued dollar. The 1823 Blue Books indicate that old half-crowns, shillings, sixpences, two-penny and one-penny pieces were the only coins in circulation besides dollars and half-dollars. Because only the dollar circulated at an enhanced value islanders did not consider that they had adopted the Halifax currency system. They considered 5s. to be the sterling value of the dollar and kept their accounts in sterling.[6]

The British attempt to put sterling money into circulation throughout the empire was resisted by the assemblies in most of the British North American colonies but in Newfoundland, which did not have an assembly, the attempt met with some initial success. The government accepted the imperial valuation of the dollar at 4s. 4d. sterling and kept its accounts on the basis of a sterling dollar. The army, which from 1811 to 1823 had been paid in dollars rated at 5s. and from 1823 to 1825 in dollars rated at 2d. less, was also paid at the new rate. However, the general public continued to accept the dollar at 5s. and gradually began to take British coins at an enhanced value as well. By 1842 the sovereign typically passed for £1 3s. 4d., the shilling for 1s. 2d. and the sixpence for 7d.[7] Two separate currency systems developed: Newfoundland currency, generally used by the public, and Newfoundland sterling used in government accounts. £115.38 Newfoundland currency was equal to £100 Newfoundland sterling or British sterling. In 1825 Newfoundland sterling and British sterling were identical;

however, when the dollar was revalued at only 4s. 2d. sterling in 1838 the Newfoundland government continued to value it at 4s. 4d., and as a result £104 Newfoundland sterling was equal to £100 British sterling. The devaluation of the dollar also affected the relative values of Newfoundland currency and British sterling, but the traditional conversion ratio was maintained until Newfoundland adopted decimal currency in 1863.

Although the Newfoundland government adopted sterling money in its accounts the attempt to introduce British coin into general circulation was a failure. The British government provided an initial supply of £5,000 in coin in 1825, and £5,000 in 1826 and 1828. All of the new British coin was quickly collected by merchants who preferred to remit it to England rather than pay the standard 3% premium on government bills of exchange. Whether the export of coin was stopped when the premium on bills of exchange was cut in half is not known. However, throughout the 1830s the British government imported about £6,200 sterling per year from Nova Scotia for the "military chest" or the "public service" in Newfoundland.[8] The necessity for these imports, which were made in dollars and in British coin, suggests that there was a continuing shortage of silver in the colony and this may have been the result of continuing remittances to Britain.

A rating for coins

In 1837 the Bank of British North America opened a branch in St. John's and began to issue its notes and sell exchange. Its exchange dealings led to disputes over the correct value of the dollar, and in 1838 the legislature passed a bill reaffirming the rating of Spanish and Latin American, but not United States, dollars at 4s. 4d. sterling. The bill was received in England shortly after the British government had reduced the sterling rating of the dollar from 4s. 4d. to 4s. 2d. As a result it was not confirmed.

The failure of the bill did not greatly affect practical aspects of currency in Newfoundland. Two currency systems, Newfoundland sterling with the dollar at 4s. 4d., and Newfoundland currency with the dollar at 5s., continued to operate. Bonnycastle, writing in 1842, reported that Spanish and South American dollars, Spanish half- and quarter-dollars, American half-dollars, and a multitude of foreign coins from the old Spanish piastre down to the American dime were in use. Bank of England 3s. and 1s. 6d. tokens circulated at face value and British gold and silver circulated at an advance of about one-sixth; the sovereign was usually accepted at £1 3s. 4d. currency, the shilling at 1s. 2d. and the sixpence at 7d. although the rate fluctuated depending on the exchange. A great variety of copper money also circulated, most of it as halfpence. Only the British penny and the Guiana stiver circulated as pennies. In addition to legitimate copper coin, merchants' tokens also circulated. Some were issued by local businessmen such as I. and S. Rutherford of St. John's and Harbour Grace; many others came from Prince Edward Island, New Brunswick and Nova Scotia.[9]

In 1844, in an effort to control the spurious copper, the assembly provided for the purchase of £1,000 worth of pence and halfpence which would circulate at one-fourteenth and one twenty-eighth of the shilling sterling each. The importation of other copper coin except legal copper of Great Britain was to be forbidden. The British treasury considered that the effect of the act would be to exclude British silver and copper from circulation and recommended that it not be confirmed.[10]

A year later the colonial government attempted a more complete reform of Newfoundland currency and drafted a law which would have codified the existing system of Newfoundland currency (see Table 34). The par of exchange was established at £115 7s. 8d. with the dollar rated at 5s. currency, the sovereign at £1 4s. and the doubloon at £3 16s. 9.6d. British silver was rated in proportion to the sovereign. The draft also provided for the importation of a new copper coinage. The proposed act did not win the approval of the home government, largely because it involved the formal introduction of a currency of account other than sterling. It was not until 1854 that Newfoundland finally passed a currency law; however, it seems probable that the ratings proposed in the draft legislation were used after 1845. If they were, British silver should have driven the Spanish dollar out of circulation; however, Spanish and Mexican dollars were reported to be the principal circulating medium until the mid-1850s when they largely disappeared.[11]

Table 34   Proposed Ratings in Draft Legislation, Newfoundland, 1845

	Weight (grains)	Rating (£/s./d.)	Purity	Precious Metal Content (grains)	Grains per Shilling
Sovereign	(123.27)	1/4/0	.9166	113.0	4.71
Doubloon	(417.6)	3/16/9.6	.875	365.4	4.76
Dollar	(417.6)	5/0	.903	377.0	75.40
Crown	(436.36)	6/0	.925	403.64	67.27
Shilling	(87.3)	1/2.4	.925	80.7	67.25
Sixpence	(43.64)	7.2	.925	40.37	67.29

( ) - weights taken from Chalmers or other sources (see Table 5)

Parts in proportion.
Silver to gold ratio 14.65:1.

Colonial paper currency

In the same period in which it was attempting to establish a legal tender in coin, Newfoundland introduced the concept of a colonial paper currency. In 1834 the legislature, finding that a hoped-for imperial subsidy was not forthcoming and that newly imposed colonial duties could not be collected until 1835, authorized the issue of £5,600 in treasury notes. The notes were intended as a temporary measure until revenue from colonial duties became sufficient for the government's needs. Only £4,400 worth of the notes were issued. By the fall of 1835 all but £1,800 worth had been redeemed and the governor expressed his confidence that the notes could be withdrawn by year end.[12]

No further issue of treasury notes was approved until 1846, although it may be argued that the debentures issued to secure a loan for £10,500 in 1838 formed a currency. However, since the lowest denomination was £25 it seems unlikely that the debentures circulated to any extent. The issue of treasury notes in 1846 was also in large denominations: 500 £10 notes, 200£25 notes, and 200£50 notes. The notes were to be issued from the treasury, at the discretion of the recipient, and were to be received at the treasury on the same basis as silver. They could be reissued by the governor during a two-year period or redeemed in silver after notice. The notes bore interest at 5%. It is unlikely that any of these notes were put into circulation, for in 1847 the home government authorized a loan of £20,000 from commissariat and agreed to take the treasury notes as security.[13]

A third issue of treasury notes was authorized in 1850, and approximately £2,000 worth were issued before the act was disallowed because it did not have a suspending clause and did not provide for the redemption of the notes. The legislature immediately passed a second act which provided for the issue of £10, £5, and £1 notes to a total value of £20,000. The notes were to be payable on demand in Spanish or Mexican dollars at the rate of $4.00 to the pound currency. A fund equal to one-third of the notes outstanding was set aside for their redemption. The notes, which did not bear interest, were to be issued from the treasury as equal amounts of the provincial debt were discharged. They were receivable by both the treasury and the other collectors of revenue and could be reissued for a period of 10 years.

The act was confirmed and about £7,800 worth of notes were issued. The colony found that it could not keep the notes in circulation in competition with private bank-notes, which could be issued in smaller denominations, and in 1855 it provided for the replacement of the original issue with £1, 10s., and 5s. notes. The same act prohibited the issue of notes of less than £1 by banks doing business on the island. The home government had only confirmed the original act of 1851 under pressure from the colony, and initially it refused to confirm the 1855 act. In general it opposed the issue of small-denomination paper money, and in particular it opposed the new act because it discriminated against the private banks. After two years' discussion the home government once again gave in and the act was confirmed. However, for some unknown reason the colonial government decided not to issue the small treasury notes and, in fact, called in all of its treasury notes by the end of 1857.[14] The Newfoundland government did not issue paper money again until after 1900.

The growth of private banks.

One of the reasons for the withdrawal of treasury notes may have been the growth of private banking in Newfoundland. A savings bank had been established under the auspices of the colonial government in 1834, and a group of local merchants planned the formation of a local bank of issue in 1837, but the idea evidently fell through when the Bank of British North America opened a branch in St. John's in 1837. Little is known of the bank's operations in Newfoundland although it did issue its notes in the colony from at least 1841[15].

A second attempt was made to organize a local bank in 1844. An act of incorporation was passed by the legislature, and the necessary capital was subscribed but the bank failed to open. A third attempt was more successful. The Union Bank of Newfoundland began business as an unincorporated bank early in 1854 and applied for a charter later that year. The charter was quickly granted by the legislature, but confirmation of the act was delayed for two years until an amendment was passed bringing the charter in line with standard provisions for all banks in the empire. These provisions included payment of notes on demand in specie, double liability for stockholders and forfeiture of the charter for a suspension of payments of more than 60 days. The act did not include a minimum denomination for notes issued but the treasury note act of 1855 limited all banks to notes of £1 or more.

The Union Bank quickly assumed a dominant role in Newfoundland banking. In 1857 the St. John's branch of the Bank of British North America was closed and the Union Bank took responsibility for its notes. In 1858 a second bank, the Commercial Bank of Newfoundland, opened but it did not seriously challenge the Union Bank's lead.

Together the two banks usually had about £200,000 to £250,000 of paper currency in circulation; two-thirds of this belonged to the Union Bank. The value of coin in circulation in the years 1855 to 1900 ranged from £80,000 to £125,000. Both the figures for coin and paper in circulation are deceptively low measures of economic activity in Newfoundland, for barter continued to be an important factor in exchange throughout the nineteenth century.

In the early 1840s various merchants began to import copper tokens into the colony. The colonial legislature attempted

214

to control copper coinage by legislation in 1844 and 1845, but both bills were disallowed by the home government. By 1851 spurious copper had become such a nuisance that the legislature made a third attempt and passed a bill which authorized the governor to spend £500 in the purchase of copper penny and halfpenny tokens which would be made legal tender for sums of up to one shilling. Once the new tokens were in circulation the importation of any copper tokens would be prohibited. The act did not prohibit the circulation of copper tokens already in Newfoundland; it was assumed that the existence of legal tender tokens would drive the spurious copper out of existence. The British treasury objected to the powers given the governor and council in designing the tokens, but it might have accepted the act if the entire question of British North American currency had not been under review at the time. As it was, the treasury recommended that no action be taken until a definite decision was made on the form which British North American currency was to take and the act was not confirmed.

Currency legislation

The question of a legal currency came up again in 1853 when the Bank of British North America began to refuse to accept sovereigns at 24s. currency, the commonly accepted rate, or to import them for circulation. Instead it imported silver which was overvalued in the colony to pay its notes. In 1853 the assembly passed a bill which would have made the sovereign legal tender at 24s. currency, but because of a disagreement with the Legislative Council the bill was not passed into law. However in 1854 a currency law was passed which made the sovereign legal tender for 24s., with all British silver legal tender in proportion to a limit of 48s. The duration of the act was limited to one year and thence to the end of the next session. In transmitting the act to London Governor Hamilton threw some light on the state of Newfoundland currency prior to 1854:

> Before the act was passed there was no law or legal usage or custom in this colony which defined the value in our local currency at which British gold and silver coins should be taken. Debts payable in currency were by legal cus-

215

tom or usage redeemable in dollars only, and sovereigns and shillings were not – in the absence of express agreement – a legal tender for any debt or at any currency value; and to render the acceptance of British coins compulsory as a sufficient tender for such currency debt, this act was passed.[16]

In 1856 the 1854 currency act was extended for one year and at the same time a broader currency law was introduced (See Table 35). The 1856 law retained the rating of the sovereign at £1 4s. with British silver as legal tender in proportion to a limit of £2 10s.. or $10.00. American eagles minted between 1834 and 1852 were made a legal tender at £2 9s. 3d. with their fractions and multiples in proportion. U.S. silver was not made legal tender (unless it was considered a fraction of the gold eagle), but this did not prevent American fractional silver from forming an important part of Newfoundland's circulation in subsequent years[17]. Doubloons containing at least 363 grains of pure gold, Peruvian, Mexican, Columbian and old Spanish dollars containing at least 363 grains of pure silver, and 5-, 2-, and 1-franc pieces were also made legal tender. British and American gold which was not more than 2 grains under its legal weight continued to be legal tender with one-half penny currency deducted for every quarter-grain lacking. In payments of over £50, British and American gold could be weighed, allowing 93s. 6d.per ounce troy for British gold and 91s. 7.5d. for U.S. gold. The act also provided for the striking of gold, silver, and copper colonial coins and for the prohibition of the circulation of spurious copper. Copper coins were made legal tender to a limit of 1s.

The act contained a suspending clause and did not come into effect immediately. When it was referred to the British Treasury for comments a treasury officer pointed out that the average weight of pure gold in the doubloon was 362 grains, not 363 and that even at 362 grains the doubloon remained undervalued. He also pointed out that Canada and New Brunswick had recently adopted compatible currency systems in which the sovereign was equal to £1 4s. 4d. and the eagle £2 10s. The treasury refused to recommend confirmation of the act until the Newfoundland government had considered the advisability of adopting the same rating system as Canada. The Newfoundland government responded that the disadvantages of upsetting existing agreements and devaluing Newfoundland currency outweighed any advantages which might be gained by having a common rating system with Canada and New Brunswick. With the reluctant assent of the treasury the home government confirmed the currency act in 1857.

In 1858 the legislature made some minor amendments to the act. An officer of the Union Bank had complained that only pre-1852 U.S. gold coins were legal tender but that it was difficult to obtain the earlier coins. Post-1852 gold coins could only be made legal tender after having been assayed, but this could not be done in Newfoundland. To evade the problem the currency act was amended so that all double eagles containing 464 grains, eagles containing 232 grains and half-eagles containing 116 grains of pure gold were legal tender. At the same time the minimum pure gold content of the doubloon was lowered to 362 grains.

Table 35   Ratings Established by 19 Victoria, C.11, 1856, Newfoundland

	Weight (grains)	Rating (£/s./d.)	Purity	Precious Metal Content (grains)	Grains per Shilling
Sovereign	123.27	£1/4/0	.9166	113	4.71
Eagle, post-1834	258.0	2/9/3	.900	232.2[1]	4.67
Doubloon	415.0	3/16/9	–	363[2]	4.73
Crown	(436.36)	6/0	.925	403.63	67.27
Shilling	(87.3)	1/2.5	.925	80.7	66.77
Sixpence	(43.64)	7.25	.925	40.37	66.81
Peruvian Dollar	416.0	5/0	–	373.0	74.6
Mexican Dollar	416.0	5/0	–	373.0	74.6
Columbian Dollar	416.0	5/0	–	373.0	74.6
Spanish Dollar	416.0	5/0	–	373.0	74.6
5 franc piece	(385.80)	4/7	.900	347.2	75.75

( ) - weight taken from Chalmers or other sources (see Table 5)

Silver to gold ratio based on crown and sovereign 14.25:1
[1]Reduced to 232 grains in 1858
[2]Reduced to 362 grains in 1858

In commenting on the act the attorney-general of Newfoundland remarked that prior to 1854 Mexican and Spanish dollars had formed the principal circulating medium in

Newfoundland, but that since then, foreign demand for silver had drawn them off.[18] It seems equally likely that the undervaluing of the dollar against both gold and British silver had helped to drive dollars out of the island. Assuming that the world silver-to-gold market price ratio in 1856 was 15.38:1, the dollar should have been valued at 5s. 1.8d. instead of 5s. As a result of this undervaluation, dollars had almost completely disappeared from circulation by the end of the decade. Parts of the dollars, particularly American halves and quarters which since 1852 had been a token currency and overvalued in terms of their silver content, were not affected in the same way. Banks imported American change and it became quite common in the early 1860s. There was also some circulation of the Spanish shilling, presumably the quarter-dollar. British silver was overvalued in comparison to gold: in terms of the relative value of silver and gold the crown should have been rated at about 5s. 7d. instead of 6s. Its limitation as a form of legal tender to payments of £2 10s. or less prevented it from driving gold out of circulation and British gold, with smaller quantities of American gold, remained as part of Newfoundland's currency. Paper money was also becoming increasingly important; the Blue Books for 1860 reported that the two banks had £177,303 in notes in circulation compared to an estimated £80,000 to £100,000 in coin.

The formal adoption of the new currency rating system did not eliminate the differences among Newfoundland currency, Newfoundland sterling and British sterling. The differences led to legal problems in settling of debts, and in 1862 the legislature passed an act defining the terms "British Sterling", "Sterling" and "Pounds, Shillings and Pence". The preamble to the bill outlined some of the history of the problem:

> Whereas since the establishment of a Legislature in this Island in the year 1832, all Grants of the Legislature, Debentures, and Interest thereon, Customs Bonds and Salaries, have been paid in Local Sterling, in dollars at Four Shillings and Four Pence Sterling, each, or its equivalent in Current Money, at the rate of One Hundred and Fifteen Pounds Seven Shillings and Eight Pence and Four Thirteenths of a Penny Currency, for every One Hundred Pounds Sterling granted, except the reserved Salaries, and

the Pensions of the two Retired Judges of the Supreme Court, which have been paid in British Sterling, in dollars at Four Shillings and two Pence Sterling each, or its equivalent in Current Money of One Hundred and Twenty Pounds Currency for every One Hundred Pounds Sterling.[19]

The act made legal what the preamble described as the customary practice since 1832, thereby institutionalizing two separate monies of account, sterling and Newfoundland sterling, and two separate ratings for the dollar, 4s. 2d. sterling and 4s. 4d. Newfoundland sterling, in government accounts. Outside the government the general public was required by the currency act of 1856 to receive coins at a third rate and presumably kept its accounts on the same basis. A final complication arose from the fact that after the British government reduced the sterling value of the dollar to 4s. 2d. in 1838 the true par between Newfoundland currency and British sterling was £120 currency to £100 sterling. This ratio formed the basis for rating British coins in the 1854 and 1856 currency acts, but the old ratio, £115.38 currency to £100 sterling continued to be the generally accepted means of converting currency to sterling until at least 1863. In consequence commercial sterling exchange from the 1840s on was almost never below par and usually bore a nominal premium of from 2% to 7% .[20]

Introduction of decimal currency

Almost immediately after the defining act of 1862 established three separate monies of account in Newfoundland, the whole system was abandoned and decimal currency adopted. In 1863 a decimal currency act provided for the rating of all coins in dollars and cents, but did not significantly change the relative values of coins (See Table 36). Dollars, formerly valued at 5s. or 1.2 times their sterling value of 4s. 2d. were made equal to $1.00 and other coins were rated in proportion: the sovereign at $4.80 the eagle at $9.85, and the doubloon at $15.35. Sovereigns, eagles and doubloons were made unlimited legal tender. Multiples and parts of sovereigns and eagles were also made legal tender to any amount. Dollars containing at least 373 grains of pure silver and their parts were made legal tender in payments up to $10.00 as was British silver which was rated in proportion to the sovereign. British pence and halfpence continued to be legal tender to a limit of 25¢ and the governor-in-council was given authority to have copper or bronze cents and half-cents struck. When the new cents were introduced all other copper coin, with the exception of British pence and halfpence, was to be taken out of circulation and its holders compensated at 50% of its current value. The act authorized Her Majesty to have special gold and silver coins struck for the colony. Gold coins made legal tender by the act lost their status if they wanted more than two grains of the weight assigned by the act. In payments of more than £50, British and American gold coins could be weighed and $18.695 allowed per ounce troy for British coins and $18.325625 per ounce troy for American coins. Existing liabilities were to be converted to the new currency at the following rates:

> £1 currency = 20s. currency = $4.00
> £1 Newfoundland sterling = 23s. .9231d. currency = $4.61
> £1 Sterling = 24s. currency = $4.80

In future the term "pound" was to mean $4.00 and the term "pound sterling" was to mean $4.80. The act contained a suspending clause and did not come into effect until 2 January 1865[21].

The act provided that lall public accounts in future were to be kept in dollars and cents and by its provisions encouraged, but did not make mandatory, the keeping of private accounts in dollars and cents. From the evidence of the Blue Books it appears that the government did keep its accounts in decimal currency after 1865, but that the general public continued to use pounds, shillings and pence. The two local banks did not issue notes in dollar denominations until the early 1880s and it was not until the currency act was revised in 1887 that the use of the term "pound currency" was dropped. In explaining that 1887 act the attorney-general commented that although the decimal system was established by law it had not met with general acceptance. The currency act of 1887 was designed to encourage the "speedy adoption by the general public" of the decimal system of accounts.[22].

Table 36   Ratings Established by 26 Victoria, C.18, 1863, Newfoundland

	Weight (grains)	Rating ($)	Purity	Precious Metal Content (grains)	Grains Per Shilling	In Effect Until
Sovereign	123.27	4.80	.9166	113.0	23.54	1895
Eagle	258.0	9.85	.900	232.2	23.57	1895
Doubloon	–	15.35	–	362.0	23.58	1887
Crown	(436.36)	1.20	.925	403.63	336.36	1895
Shilling	(87.3)	.24	.925	80.7	336.25	1895
Sixpence	(43.64)	.12	.925	40.37	336.42	1895
Dollar	416.0	1.00	–	373.0	373.00	1887

(American, Peruvian, Mexican, Columbian, old Spanish)

These rates came into force 2 January 1865.
( ) - weights taken from Chalmers or other sources (see Table 5)

Local coinage and paper money

The currency act of 1863 provided for the issue of a local coinage and the following year the governor ordered 240,000 copper 1¢ pieces, 80,000 silver 5¢ pieces, 80,000 10¢ pieces, 100,000 25¢ pieces and 10,000 $2.00 gold pieces from the Royal Mint (see Table 37). The coins were put in circulation in 1865 and with further issues, including a 50¢ piece first issued in 1870, must have formed a substantial part of the metallic currency. How common the other coins which were made legal tender in 1863 remained is not known, with the exception of the silver dollars. Spanish and Spanish-American dollars were uncommon as early as 1860, although some subsidiary Spanish coins as well as subsidiary United States silver remained common. By 1880, dollars and their parts were reported to be depreciated and rare; by 1882 the banks were refusing to accept dollars except at a discount. United States dollars evidently were taken at 93¢ and Spanish and Spanish American dollars at 80¢. In 1887 dollars and their parts were demonetized. At the same time the doubloon, which must have been quite rare for many years, was demonetized.[23].

In spite of what appear to have been substantial and regular issues of special Newfoundland coinage as well as issues by the local banks there may have been a shortage of currency in the island, for, after 1875 private paper money began to appear in the colony. One of the earliest firms to issue private notes was the Betts Cove Mining Company, which issued notes in denominations ranging from 10¢ to $20.00 in payment of wages. The Reid Contracting Company, the principal contractors for the Newfoundland railway, also issued private notes in payment of wages and after 1894 Bowring Brothers began to issue wage notes as well. Bowring's notes were only payable in goods at the company's stores; other notes were also payable at company stores but whether in goods or cash is not clear. In consequence of the limitations of their redemption, it is doubtful if any of the private notes circulated far beyond the community in which they were issued.

Table 37   Newfoundland Coinage Issued After 1863

Denomination	Weight (grains)	Rating ($)	Purity	Precious Metal Content (grains)	Grains per Dollar
$2 gold piece	(51.36)	2.00	.917	47.10	23.55
50¢ piece	(181.82)	.50	.925	168.18	336.37
20¢ piece	(72.73)	.20	.925	67.28	336.38
10¢ piece	(36.35)	.10	.925	33.63	336.31
5¢ piece	(18.18)	.05	.925	16.82	336.31

( ) - weight taken from Chalmers or other sources (see Table 5)

A 25¢ piece was authorized in 1887 but was not issued until 1917.

Bank failures

The Commercial and Union Banks remained the only banks in the colony until they failed in December 1894. The banks had substantial deposits and their notes provided the principal circulation in the island; as a result their failure caused widespread commercial distress. In order to keep the banks' notes in circulation the government passed two acts in 1895 guaranteeing the redemption of the Union Bank notes at the rate of 80 cents on the dollar and the Commercial Bank notes at 20 cents on the dollar in 1897. Until they were redeemed they were to be counterstamped and circulated at the reduced rate; the Union Bank $2.00 note at $1.60 and the Commercial Bank $2.00 note at 40 cents and so on.

The affairs of the banks were wound up and they did not reopen. Within a few months of the failure three Canadian banks, the Bank of Montreal, the Bank of Nova Scotia and the Halifax Banking Company, opened branches in Newfoundland.[24]

Newfoundland's currency legislation of 1863 had been based on the assumption of a silver dollar worth 5s. or 1.2 times its theoretical sterling value of 4s. 2d. Four dollars equalled £1 currency, and the sovereign was made equal to 1.2 times the pound currency or $4.80 currency. The American eagle was then rated on the basis of its gold content in comparison to the sovereign, with the result that it was made equal to $9.85, although in the United States it would purchase 10 silver dollars. Canadian currency, on the other hand, had been based not on the silver dollar but on the gold dollar, or more specifically on the eagle, which was worth $10.00 in both American and Canadian currency. The sovereign was rated at $4.866 Canadian currency on the basis of its value relative to the eagle. The net result of these different approaches was that the Newfoundland dollar was worth about $1.014 in Canadian currency. This difference made it inconvenient for the Canadian banks to circulate their notes in Newfoundland. To facilitate their circulation Newfoundland currency was made compatible with that of Canada in 1895 (see Table 38).

The value of the sovereign was raised to $4.866 Newfoundland currency and its parts and British silver were raised in value accordingly. The eagle was rated at $10.00 currency. No other substantial changes were made to the legislation of 1863 and 1887. Canadian coins or bank-notes did not become legal tender in Newfoundland, but as there was no difference in the value of the Canadian and Newfoundland dollar there would have been little impediment to their circulation prior to the entry of Newfoundland into Confederation in 1949.

Table 38 Ratings Established by 58 Victoria, C.4, 1895 Newfoundland.

	Weight (grains)	Rating ($)	Purity	Precious Metal Content (grains)	Grains per Dollar
Sovereign	123.27	4.8666	.9166	113.0	23.22
Eagle	258.	10.00	.900	232.2	23.22
Crown	(436.36)	1.2166	.925	403.63	331.77
Shilling	(87.3)	.2433	.925	80.7	331.69
Sixpence	(43.64)	.1217	.925	40.37	331.72

( ) - weights taken from Chalmers or other sources (see Table 5)

Chapter Seven

Western Canada

Hudson's Bay Company notes for 1s. and £1 sterling

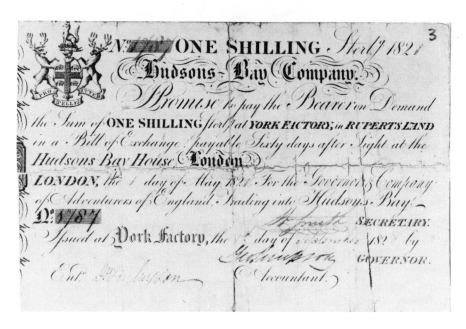

1s. note

actual size: 187 mm x 123 mm

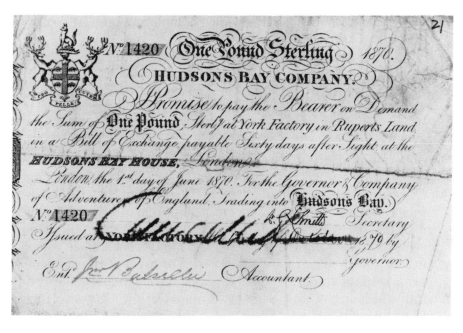

£1 note

actual size: 207 mm x 140 mm

The modern history of Western Canada began with the grant of the Hudson Bay watershed (thereafter known as Rupert's Land) to the Hudson's Bay Company in 1670. Under the terms of the grant Rupert's Land was made a proprietary colony to be governed by the Hudson's Bay Company which in return received a trade monopoly in the area.

The grant was not recognized by France, and until the final loss of Canada in 1763 the French contested the possession of the territory. In this contest the French had the upper hand. Their fur-trade posts on the Red and Saskatchewan River cut the Hudson's Bay Company posts on the shores of Hudson and James Bay off from much of their hinterland. After the transfer of Canada to Britain, traders based in Montreal continued to dominate the western interior in defiance of the Hudson's Bay Company's monopoly until the company began to establish inland posts in the 1770s. The two competing interests rapidly explored to the north and west of the area beyond Lake Winnipeg reaching the Arctic Ocean via the Mackenzie River in 1791 and the Pacific Ocean in 1793. Throughout the years of expansion the traders from Montreal, who eventually coalesced into the North West Company, dominated the Hudson's Bay Company, but when as a result of ruinous competition the two firms merged in 1821 it was under the name of the Hudson's Bay Company.

Although the Hudson's Bay Company charter implicitly gave it the right to issue money in Rupert's Land, this right was not exercised in the first 150 years of its existence. Indeed, prior to the last half of the nineteenth century, neither coin or paper money played a significant role in the economy of western Canada. Most business transactions were effected through barter, with goods such as furs exchanged directly for trade goods such as guns, cloth, or kettles. Very often the exchange also involved the extension of credit: fur traders frequently advanced goods to Indian trappers in the fall and did not receive furs in payment until the following spring. Often debts were carried on the books from year to year and occasionally from generation to generation. Fur trade account books made use of variety of moneys of account but real money, that is coin or paper money, was a rarity in the trade. The Hudson's Bay Company's principal accounts were kept in sterling money of account, those of its rivals from Montreal were kept in livres and sols before 1763 and in whatever form of Halifax, York or New England currency was in use at Montreal after that date. Surviving accounts of the North West Company from the first decades of the nineteeth century were kept principally in Halifax currency but within the overall accounting system a few entries were made in York currency and substantial numbers of entries were made in sterling and in livres. Many of the accounts of expeditions to the Columbia River in this period were kept in dollars and cents. The company also used a special currency known as North West or Grand Portage currency in which the livre was rated at 12 to the pound Halifax currency. Although little is known of this currency it seems to have been used principally in the accounts of employees at or west of Grand Portage and Fort William. In dealing with the Indians the trading companies did not use real money; furs were exchanged directly for trade goods. Any credits or debits in trade were accounted for in the companies' books. Hudson's Bay Company employees in Rupert's Land were also paid through bookkeeping entries. Since there were few persons who were neither Indians nor employees of one of the fur trading companies in the west prior to the nineteenth century there was no need for real money.

"Made beaver"

Although the company used sterling as the unit of account in its principal accounts and in its dealings with most Europeans in Rupert's Land, it developed a special commodity money of account for use in dealing with natives. The unit of account was the "made beaver", which was equal in value to a prime male beaver pelt. Other skins and produce were valued in terms of the made beaver. For example, about 1820 one made beaver was worth two cub beaver or two prime marten or one red or two white fox or eight pounds of goose feathers.[1] The scale of values could be varied to reflect changes in the relative market value of pelts. The system was used principally for accounting purposes and the skins themselves were the only "real money" which corresponded to the money of account until the 1860s or 1870s when the company introduced copper tokens in denominations of one made beaver and fractions of one made beaver in the Eastmain District. Similar tokens were also used in the interior of British Columbia and in the north. The last issue was made in the Northwest Territories in 1946.[2]

The Selkirk Settlement and H.B.C. notes

The establishment of a small agricultural settlement on the Red River by Lord Selkirk in 1812 introduced a new element into western Canada. In its early years the colony was dependent on the goodwill of the Hudson's Bay Company, but as it grew more self-sufficient its interests diverged from those of the company. One of the earlier manifestations of this divergence involved currency. The settlers probably brought a small amount of cash with them but this proved inadequate and the company's traditional method of dealing with all accounts through book entries and transfers proved too cumbersome for the more complex requirements of an agricultural settlement. In response to the demand for a more flexible currency system at Red River the company decided to introduce its own paper money. In 1820 and 1821 it forwarded 2,000 £1 sterling notes, 4000 5s. notes and 4000 1s. notes to York Factory. The new Governor, George Simpson, believed the notes were unnecessary and delayed their introduction, but in 1825 some of the £1 notes were issued and over the next few years the 5s. and 1s. notes were gradually put into circulation. Most of them must have been in circulation by the early 1830s, for in 1832 a second issue of notes was made; this was followed by eight more issues between 1837 and 1870. The final issue, dated Fort Garry rather than York Factory, included £5 and £10 notes.[3]

The notes were issued in payment of the company's debts or in the purchase of bills of exchange on London and were received at company stores in payment of purchases. Notes were redeemable at York Factory in 60-day bills of exchange on London; in practice the company usually would redeem them at Red River where most of them circulated rather than at York Factory, which was almost 1,000 kilometres from the settlement.

The notes were generally acceptable and popular in the vicinity of the Red River settlement. However, as early as 1845 some company officials began to doubt the wisdom of issuing them. Governor Simpson complained that free traders collected the notes and redeemed them for bills of exchange on London which they used to finance their trade in competition with the company. To prevent this he suggested that the notes should be made redeemable in goods at Red River rather than in bills. Alexander Christie, the Chief Factor at Fort Garry, threatened to withdraw all the notes if the public did not stop aiding the free traders. He discounted bills by 5% if notes were cashed in Red River instead of York Factory. The governor and council in London disagreed with his measures and directed that notes should continue to be redeemed in bills of exchange at Red River. They also directed that in some cases notes might be issued in return for bills of exchange on London but if this was done at a season when the bills could not be remitted to London a discount of 6% or more should be charged. It may have been this last provision which Governor Simpson referred to in a letter in which he described the abuse of the company's notes prior to 1853:

> There existed moreover a very injudicious system of making advances to parties known to have funds in England, not in goods yielding a fair profit, but in paper money, which was commonly at once converted into drafts on London. These advances were repaid by bills of exchange given in the settlement of accounts *at the end* of the outfit often 11 and nearly 12 months after the advances had been made, so that by the time those bills could be remitted and reached maturity, a heavy loss of interest occurred, on an average 15 to 18 months.[4]

Perhaps more important than the loss of interest, the system could be used by free traders who were in opposition to the company to finance their operations.

To prevent this the governor ordered the withdrawal of the notes in 1853, and in 1854 ordered that all bills of exchange accepted by the company be discounted 5%. The result was that not only did the paper currency disappear from circulation but the colony's supply of coin was exported. Simpson viewed the export of coin as a conspiracy by the local merchants to force him to reintroduce the paper currency, but it is equally probable that the premium of 5% on bills of exchange made it cheaper to export coin to settle debts than to purchase bills. Whatever the reason the company was forced to relent and return the paper money to circulation. The terms for bills of exchange were also made easier although exactly what was done is not clear. It seems most likely that the company attempted to keep its bills of exchange out of the hands of its trading opponents but sold them to others at or near par.[5]

In 1862 Governor Dallas made a second attempt to reduce the number of notes in circulation by ordering that in future the company not issue its own notes in payment for local produce. In spite of this the notes remained in circulation until the 1870s when the introduction of Canadian money rendered them unnecessary and they were withdrawn.

In addition to Hudson's Bay Company notes some coin circulated in the Red River settlement. A small amount may have been brought by the earliest settlers but it cannot have remained in circulation for long. In 1834 the governor reported that the colony required a unit of currency smaller than the shilling and requested that some penny tokens, not exceeding one-half ounce in weight, be sent to the colony. From the weight specified it is clear that Simpson was requesting a shipment of commercial copper tokens but the following year J. Hargrave reported the receipt of £50 worth of "British copper coins".[6] If Hargrave was not using the term "coin" loosely, then it was legal tender coin and not commercial tokens which were shipped to Red River.

Trade with St. Paul, Minnesota, which began on a regular basis in the 1840s, may also have introduced some coin into the colony, although depending on the balance of trade it might also have drawn coin out of the colony. The latter possibility would have been mitigated by the Hudson's Bay Company policy of redeeming its paper in bills of exchange on England at par.

The arrival of 347 men of the Sixth Regiment in the autumn of 1846 resulted in a major increment in the area's coin supply. During the next two years the troops pumped £15,000 into the local economy. Most of this without doubt went to the Hudson's Bay Company and had no effect on the local circulation, but one local merchant, Andrew McDermot, received £1,400 in gold from the troops during their two-year stay.[7] The Sixth Regiment was replaced by a small body of pensioners, about 140 men, who were in turn succeeded by a detachment of Royal Canadian Rifles from 1857 to 1861. Both of these units would have had some impact on the economy at Red River.

How great the circulation was in Red River in the 1850s is not known. A record of notes issued and cancelled indicates that in 1856–57 there were £5,221 10s.sterling in company notes outstanding; this does not of course include the coin which may have circulated in the colony. Between 1857 and 1871 a further £16,500 worth of notes was put in circulation but it is not clear how many were withdrawn in the same period. Alexander Ross, writing in 1856, estimated the total circulation at £5,000 but at the same time stated "Scarcely a shilling is seen afloat."[8]

During the late 1850s and the 1860s the isolation of the Red River settlement was rapidly broken down. The old line of communication with Britain through Hudson Bay was gradually abandoned and a new route through the United States was developed. The new orientation presumably put some American currency including treasury notes or "greenbacks" into circulation. In the 1860s settlers from eastern Canada probably introduced some of the new Canadian coins, Canadian bank-notes and tokens into circulation.

In spite of the increasing influence of jurisdictions where decimal currency prevailed, sterling remained the dominant money of account in Red River until Manitoba was admitted to Confederation in 1870. Decimal currency was occasionally used with the £1 sterling informally valued at $5.00.[9] With the passing of the Uniform Currency Act of 1871 decimal currency legally replaced sterling as the money of account. The Hudson's Bay Company did not formally convert all of its accounts in the Northern Department to decimal currency until June 1873 although some local accounts at Red River had been kept in decimal currency for several years.[10] Dominion notes had circulated in Manitoba from at least 1870, and as early as 1872 the 25¢ notes were reported to be so common in Winnipeg as to constitute a nuisance but the various acts relating to them were not extended to Manitoba until 1876.[11]

Private banks and the growth of a cash economy

Prior to Confederation there were no banks in Rupert's Land, although the Hudson's Bay Company performed many banking functions: issuing money, buying and selling exchange and, at least in the case of its employees, taking deposits. Other private firms probably provided some banking services as well. In 1870 the Winnipeg firm, McArthur and Martin, began to advertise that it dealt in exchange and currency, and in 1871 two groups gave notice that they would apply for bank charters. Neither of these banks materialized, but in 1873 A. McMicken began to advertise his services as a private banker.[12] The fact that he gave the Merchant's Bank of Canada as a reference may indicate that he acted as its agent. Other private bankers such as Alloway and Champion, and Gordon, Adamson and Company soon entered the field. In 1875 the Ontario Bank opened a branch or agency in the city; it was followed by the Merchant's Bank of Canada and the Bank of Montreal.

With the introduction of Hudson's Bay Company notes in the 1820s the Red River Settlement had begun to move slowly towards a money economy, but the remainder of Rupert's Land was scarcely affected by the changes until after 1870. John Palliser, who travelled widely throughout Rupert's Land south of the Saskatchewan River between 1857 and 1861, asserted that all payments in the country were made in kind. John M. Jones, an American prospector who travelled across the prairies on his way to the Fraser gold fields in 1858 agreed that money was very rare but not unknown and remarked of inhabitants of the prairies "When they get a sight of a shilling they are willing to part with almost anything to gain possession of it."[13] After the transfer of the territory to Canada in 1870 the increasing activity of government agents, police, surveyors, Indian agents and finally railway contractors introduced dominion notes and bank-notes into the society.

How rapidly this change occurred is not clear but it seems to have been well underway by 1880. As early as 1875, policemen in the Fort Walsh and Fort Macleod area were paid in dominion notes. The notes, principally in 25¢ and $1 and $2 denominations, were supplied by I.G. Baker and Company of Fort Benton. The activities of this and other American firms probably introduced a substantial amount of American money into the southwestern prairies as well; accounts of the police force with I.G. Baker and Company in 1874 and 1875 contain a number of orders on Baker and Company to pay residents of the territories in American funds.[14] Baker and Company also issued their own trade tokens; how common these were is not known.

Police wages between 1873 and 1885 amounted to about $1.5 million. It seems reasonable to assume that a large part of this would have entered into circulation in the territory. Similarly police expenditures for supplies and services must have put cash into circulation in the northwest. In 1874 virtually none of the force's expenditures were made in the northwest, but by 1884–85 payments of about $120,000 out of a total budget of about $366,000, excluding pay, were made to territorial firms or individuals.

The increasing activity of the Indian Department also put cash into circulation. The initial treaty payments, beginning with Treaty No. 1 in 1871 were quite probably the first occasions on which many Indians had to deal with cash. By 1877 all of the southern and central prairies had been ceded by treaty. Between 1877 and 1885 the annual annuity payments in the treaty areas 4,6 and 7 amounted to about $120,000 per year. These payments were normally made in dominion notes which went almost directly into the hands of local merchants.

The construction of the Canadian Pacific Railway across the prairies during the years 1880–83 must also have put a great deal of cash into circulation. The construction crews and (presumably) the local suppliers were paid in cash. Moreover, the construction of the railway was followed by a substantial influx of settlers who would have been familiar with a money economy and by the establishment (or growth) of several new commercial centres. By 1885 *Henderson's Manitoba and the North-West Territories Directory* listed bankers in Battleford (Alex Macdonald), Calgary (Lafferty and Smith), Edmonton (McDonald and Co.), Qu'Appelle (S.H. Carswell) and Regina (Bank of Montreal). It is unlikely that anyone living on the prairies was unfamiliar with money by 1885. This is not to say that barter and credit had disappeared, but it was no longer the sole or even the dominant means of exchange as it had been fifteen years earlier.

The west coast

The Hudson's Bay Company grant of 1670 did not include the Pacific watershed, what is now British Columbia. The coast was explored in the eighteenth century by Spanish, Russian, British and American expeditions. From the landward side Canadian fur traders and American government expeditions explored the interior between 1793 and 1812. By the end of the War of 1812 the North West Company had gained effective control of the trade in the interior as well as of the only settlement on the coast, Fort George, at the mouth of the Columbia River.

With the union of the North West Company and the Hudson's Bay Company in 1821 this control passed to the Hudson's Bay Company which was given an exclusive licence to trade in the area beyond Rupert's Land. The licence applied only to British subjects; the Americans and British had agreed in 1818 to a joint occupation of the territory. This continued until 1846, but with the exception of the lower Columbia Valley, the Hudson's Bay Company dominated the trade. Its trading licence was renewed in1838 for 21 years. In 1849 the licence was revoked insofar as it applied to the new colony of Vancouver Island, and in 1858 it was cancelled and the new colony of British Columbia created.

Little is known of currency west of the Rockies before the 1850s. Doubtless the crews of the various exploring and trading expeditions introduced some coins into the area in the eighteenth century but there was no circulating coinage. The natives had a form of wampum, *hiaqua,* which retained some currency in the interior as late as 1850. Shortly before its absorption by the Hudson's Bay Company, the North West Company issued some copper made beaver tokens. These were used on the west coast, since about 50 of them have been discovered in the Columbia Basin.[15] Some of the North West Company's accounts for the Columbia Department were kept in dollars and cents although its main accounts were kept in Halifax currency. In general the fur trade relied on barter and the debt system until mid-century. However, the American settlers who occupied the Oregon country in the 1840s almost certainly brought American currency with them. In 1846 the governor and council of the Hudson's Bay Company provided that when Mexican dollars were accepted at posts west of the mountains they should be valued at 3s. 9d. sterling and United States dollars at 1d. to 1.5d. less.[16] Such a low rate may have been designed to discourage the use of coin in the area. The discovery of gold in California and in Oregon also put gold, some of it in the form of coins produced by private mints, into circulation. By 1849 when the Hudson's Bay Company abandoned Fort Vancouver as the depot for the Columbia district, gold was a more important item of trade than furs.[17]

Early currency legislation

At Victoria, the capital of the new colony of Vancouver Island, coin remained uncommon until 1858: virtually all of the white inhabitants of the colony were employees of the Hudson's Bay Company who were paid with credits at the company store. The discovery of gold on the Fraser River in 1857 brought a rush of new settlers, many of them Americans from California who brought American gold coinage with them. Dollars quickly became the unit of exchange in private transactions, although the colonial government continued to use sterling until 1 January 1863 when the Vancouver Island Decimal Currency Act came into effect. The act provided that all public accounts should be kept in dollars and cents. The post-1837 eagle was made legal tender at $10.00 with its parts and multiples in proportion. American 50¢, 25¢ and 10¢ pieces were also legal tender at face value. All coins which were legal tender in the United Kingdom were made legal tender on Vancouver Island with the sovereign rated at $4.85 and its parts in proportion. All silver was limited as legal tender to payments of $10.00 or less. British silver was to be rated in proportion to the sovereign and the Blue Books for 1863 showed the half-crown circulating at 60.6¢, the florin at 48.5¢, the shilling at 24.3¢ and the sixpence at 12.5¢. The ratings were evidently found inconvenient for the following year the Blue Books show the half-crown rated at 50¢; the florin at 37.5¢ and the shilling at 25¢.

Nothing is known of currency on the mainland prior to the formation of the colony of British Columbia save that the Hudson's Bay Company kept its accounts in sterling. The new colonial government continued the practice. Private accounts were kept in dollars and cents, as they were on the island. Before 1865 there was no legally established par of exchange between dollars and pounds, but in practice the pound was valued at $5.00, the florin at 50¢ and the shilling at 25¢.

Supply of coinage

Until 1861, currency of any sort was in short supply and frequently brought a premium; in 1861 Governor Douglas estimated that premium at 5%. The shortage of coin in a gold mining area created a paradox reported in the Victoria *Colonist* in November 1861; although more than a million dollars worth of gold dust had been brought to Victoria in the previous month very little had been sold because there was no coin available to pay for it.[18]

Gold dust was sold as a commodity and to some extent functioned as a currency. Following the establishment of an assay office in New Westminster in 1860 ingots of unrefined gold may also have served as currency. However, the ingots were too large for general use, and because of a dispute over whether to use decimal or sterling denominations they were not inscribed with their monetary value. Until April 1861 they were not even marked with their weight and purity.

In 1859 Governor Douglas requested that the British government forward a supply of British coin to alleviate the shortage of small change in the colony, and in 1860 40,000 florins, 40,000 shillings, 32,000 sixpenny pieces and 8,000 threepenny pieces were shipped to the colony. As a more permanent measure to relieve the shortage of coin, the colonial government sought and received permission to establish a mint at New Westminster. Coining machinery was purchased and installed in 1862 and a few gold $10 and $20 specimen coins were produced but for reasons which are not clear the mint never went into regular operation. The most probable reason for the failure of the mint to begin operation is that an increase in the colony's circulation plus the unexpectedly high costs of operating the mint made it unnecessary.

A number of factors in addition to the shipment of coin from Britain in 1861 combined to increase the circulation of the colony after 1861. To assist in financing the construction of roads to the interior the government began to issue promissory or treasury notes to contractors early in 1862; some notes may also have been issued in 1861. Little is known about the issue, but it seems probable that a maximum value of $45,000 in $5, $10 and $25 denominations was put into circulation. The notes were issued to road contractors in payment of subsidies and were redeemable on demand at the provincial treasury. By November 1862 all but £100 worth of the notes had been withdrawn from circulation.

Banks were another factor in the increased circulation of the colony, or rather in the two colonies of British Columbia and Vancouver Island, for it is difficult to keep the currency affairs of the two separate. In addition to importing coin the banks began to issue their own notes. The Bank of British North America began to issue $1, $2, $5, $10 and $20 notes shortly after it established a branch in Victoria in 1859. The Bank of British Columbia opened for business in both Victoria and New Westminster in the autumn of 1862 and began to issue its notes in $1, $5 and $20 denominations. Two private banks, Wells, Fargo and Company, and Macdonald and Company also had offices in Victoria. As early as 1861 Macdonald and Company issued $1, $5 and $10 notes; it is not known if Wells Fargo and Company issued any notes.[19]

How adequate the circulating medium was in the two colonies by 1861 is hard to tell. According to Dr. Helmecken, gold coin was plentiful and there was no further problem about currency. According to the Victoria correspondent of the *Alta California*, writing in October 1861, "the scarcity of coin is notorious". The British Columbia Blue Books for 1861 indicate that the variety of coin was sufficient even if the quantity was not. British and Australian sovereigns and halves as well as American gold $20, $10, $5, $3, $2.50 and $1 pieces were in circulation. The silver circulation consisted of florins, shillings, six, four- and three-penny pieces, United States 50¢, 25¢ and 10¢ pieces and Mexican, Peruvian and Bolivian dollars and halves. (The Mexican and Peruvian coins were disappearing from circulation by 1862.) Copper coin did not circulate; the provincial treasurer explained that in British Columbia "poverty is unknown and...the habits of the people and their prosperity induce a positive disregard of fractions under a 5 cent (or about 2.5d) piece."[20] The disregard for small change continued for at least another 20 years. In 1880 D.M. Gordon reported:

Copper currency is unknown, the smallest coin being a "bit" that is the English sixpence, whose nearest equivalent is the ten cent piece. The hotel clerk smiles when you offer him three Canadian cents in payment of a three cent stamp, and suggests that he does not keep a museum of curiosities, while it is said that the presence in church of Canadians from the older provinces can sometimes be detected by the discovery of copper coins in the collection.[21]

The Blue Books indicate that there was no paper money in circulation prior to 1863 – 64 but since it is known that the colony put its own notes in circulation in 1862 and that banks based in Victoria had issued notes as early as 1859 it seems probable that the Blue Books only reported what was officially accepted as a circulating medium.

Ratings for coins in British Columbia

British Columbia did not have any currency law until 1865. As noted earlier the government kept its accounts in sterling and the general public kept accounts in decimal currency. There was no official par of exchange but the public generally accepted the sovereign at $5.00 and it appears that for a time the government used the same rate. In applying for a supply of British coins in 1859 the Provincial Treasurer, Captain Gossett, reasoned that the principal coins could be assimilated to a decimal system. Since the florin, worth 2s., or one-tenth of a pound, was generally valued at 50¢ on the Pacific coast, the sovereign could be valued at $5.00. He also proposed the minting of a new coin equal to one-hundredth of a sovereign or 5¢ to complete the system. At about the same time Captain Parsons of the Royal Engineers proposed paying the engineers stationed in British Columbia in U.S. coin at the rate of 4s. per dollar, equivalent to $5.00 per sovereign and the same rate as had already been adopted by the Royal Navy in paying crews on the station.[22]

The home government's response to Gossett's proposal pointed out the fallacy of equating American and British coinage on the basis of the silver florin, which was a token coin, rather than on the basis of gold coins. In fact, the treasury recommended that British Columbia's currency be assimilated to that of Canada. In response to Captain Parson's proposal, the treasury observed that the crown would lose approximately 2.5% on every dollar issued at 4s. and ordered that in paying the troops the eagle should be valued at £2 1s. sterling and the half-eagle at £10s. 6d. Governor Douglas replied that these directions would be followed in paying the troops.[23] The same course seems to have been followed by the provincial government for in 1862 the Blue Book gave the exchange rate as $4.87 and in 1863 and 1864 as $4.85.

The general public continued to accept the sovereign at $5.00 until at least the end of 1862. The overvaluation may have driven other gold out of the colony: a report in the *Columbian* on 22 November 1862 stated that the sovereign was almost the only gold in circulation.[24] The report is at odds with the currency reports in the Blue Books which continue to show American gold in circulation.

In March 1865 the British Columbia legislature passed a decimal currency act. The act, evidently modelled on that of Vancouver Island, declared that public accounts were to be kept in dollars and cents and that the sovereign was to be legal tender at $4.85 and the eagle at $10.00 with their parts in proportion. American 50¢, 25¢ and 10¢ pieces and British silver were legal tender to $10.00. Unlike the Vancouver Island act the British Columbia act specified the rates at which British silver was to pass. British silver was rated on the basis of £1 sterling being equal to $5.00 rather than $4.85. The crown was rated at $1.25, the half-crown at $0.625, the florin at $0.50, the shilling at $0.25, the six-penny piece at $0.125 and the three-penny piece at $0.06. The act came into effect 1 January 1866.

Evidently the conversion ratio based on the pound at $4.85 proved inconvenient for the payment of sums expressed in sterling in areas such as the interior, where only decimal currency circulated. In April 1866 the colony adopted the following conversion ratio for the payment of fines, fees, customs, duties, etc. which were expressed in sterling:[25]

½d. sterling equals 1¢
1d. sterling equals 2¢
1s. or 1s. ½d. sterling equals 25¢
2s. or 2s. 1d. sterling equals 50¢
4s. or 4s. 2d. sterling equals $1.00

6s. or 6s. 3d. sterling equals $1.50
8s. or 8s. 4d. sterling equals $2.00
£1 sterling equals $5.00

The result was that American coins could have two sterling values depending on the purpose for which they were used.

In November 1866 the colonies of Vancouver Island and British Columbia were united under the name of British Columbia and in 1867 a decimal currency act for the combined colonies was passed. The new act reiterated the British Columbia act of 1865, which had been based on the Vancouver Island act of 1862. Consequently there was little change in the currency system of either colony. The 1867 act did, however, incorporate the British Columbia currency conversion act of 1866, mentioned above, and extended it to Vancouver Island. It also made the U.S. silver dollar legal tender to $10.00. Finally, for a reason which has not been explained, it neglected to make the florin, "the commonest of our coins", legal tender.[26] The florin continued to circulate, usually at 50 cents, but on the island it was sometimes taken at 37.5 cents.

British Columbia joined Confederation on 19 July 1871 and consequently the Canadian uniform currency act which came into effect eighteen days earlier did not apply to it. As a result the old act remained in force. How common Canadian notes and bills were in British Columbia before the completion of the railway is not known. In the debate on the bill to extend the various dominion note acts to British Columbia in 1876, Mr. Thompson (Cariboo) commented that there were very few $1 and $2 notes in the province, especially in the interior. Towards the end of the decade, when the province experienced a silver currency shortage, it imported American coins rather than Canadian ones. In 1881 the Canadian government made plans to ship $100,000 in Canadian silver to British Columbia, but before the money could be put into circulation legally the uniform currency act had to be extended to the province.

Banking in British Columbia

Between 1859 and 1863 four banks, two with royal charters (the Bank of British North America and the Bank of British Columbia) and two private banks (Macdonald and Company and Wells Fargo and Company) established branches in Victoria and on the mainland (see Table 39). The banks were unregulated by law in either colony and engaged in a rapid

242

expansion of the money supply. Following a robbery the private bank of Macdonald and Company failed in October 1864.[27]

Even before the failure, British Columbia had moved to regulate the banks. In May of 1864 it passed a comprehensive banking law which prohibited the issue of unauthorized bank notes or of notes for less than 4s. 2d. sterling or $1.00, and made specie payment on demand a requisite. The act also provided regulations for the formation of banks which were similar in concept to those embodied in Canada's free banking act of 1851. Although the home government approved of the act in principle it requested several small changes in the act and until these were included it refused assent to the bill. The governor indicated that a new bill embodying the changes would be brought forward in 1865, but nothing seems to have been done and British Columbia remained without a bank act until it was united with Vancouver Island.

In Vancouver Island the legislature passed two acts dealing with banking in 1864. The first simply provided for the regular publication of bank statements. The second act limited the issue of bank-notes to authorized banks. Unchartered banks which had been issuing notes prior to 1 January 1864 could continue to issue notes only until 1 January 1865. Banks with charters could continue to issue notes afer 1 January 1865. All banks were required to maintain a specie reserve equal to one half of their outstanding notes. The total value of notes in circulation was not to exceed the bank's paid up capital. The two acts were adopted as the banking law of the united colony of British Columbia.

Very little is known of commercial exchange on the west coast. As early as 1846 the Hudson's Bay Company at Fort Vancouver was willing to sell bills of exchange on New York at $5.40 per £1 sterling. The company also provided bills of exchange for its employees who wished to transfer money to London. In the 1860s the principal sources of sterling exchange seem to have been navy bills and bank bills. Sixty-day sterling bank bills, the standard in eastern Canada at this time, typically sold for about $5.00 during the 1860s, a premium of 3% on the legal par of $4.85. Bills on New York generally brought a 6% premium and those on San Francisco brought a 1% premium.[28]

Table 39 Estimates of Money in Circulation in British Columbia and Vancouver Island, 1860–70.
(Taken from the Blue Books)

		British Columbia			Vancouver Island	
Year	Coin	Bank of B.C.	Bank of B.N.A.	Macdonald & Co.	Coin	Bank-notes
1860	–	–	–	–	–	–
1861	–	–	–	–	–	–
1862*	–	–	–	–	–	–
1863	–	–	–	–	$500,000	$ 33,000
1864	–	$150,000	–	Failed	350,000	80,000
1865	–	120,000	–	–	275,000	135,000
1866	–	120,000	$145,000	–	–	–
1867	–	93,963	160,818	–	–	–
1868	–	132,878	158,481	–	–	–
1869	–	100,000	160,000	–	–	–
1870	–	177,997	118,480	–	–	–

*Some government treasury notes were in circulation.

Chapter Eight

Common Threads

Although the history of currency and exchange in the several colonies which came together to form Canada has been dealt with on a colony-by-colony basis, there are many similarities in the story. This is especially true of the six British colonies in eastern Canada: Upper and Lower Canada, New Brunswick, Nova Scotia, Prince Edward Island and Newfoundland, but it is also true of the French colony of Canada which preceded them. The history of currency and exchange in western Canada prior to its union with Canada shares fewer of these common threads. Partly this was the result of physical isolation. Lacking domestic mines of silver and gold the eastern colonies were forced to rely on foreign trade or expenditures by the imperial government to provide themselves with a supply of specie. The colonies typically suffered a trade imbalance with the imperial metropolis, and colonists frequently complained that because coin had to be exported to pay for imports they suffered from a shortage of coin. In attempts to attract additional supplies of coin, all of the eastern colonies adopted special monies of account which gave enhanced values to coins. In French Canada under the system of monnoye du pays coins were rated one-third above their value in France; under the Halifax currency system as it was originally established in the 1760s, coins were rated at one-ninth above their sterling values.

When trade, importation of coin by the imperial power, and the creation of inflated moneys of account failed to provide adequate supplies of specie, most of the colonies resorted to the issue of paper money. In French Canada, excepting Louisbourg, card money and various forms of orders on the treasury were probably the most common form of money in circulation from the 1690s to 1719 and from 1730 to 1760. In Nova Scotia and Prince Edward Island notes on the provincial treasury formed a substantial part of the colonial money supply throughout much of their separate existence. In the territory of Rupert's Land, paper money issued by the proprietary company, the Hudson's Bay Company, played an important role in the economy of the settlement at Red River. The Canadas, New Brunswick, Newfoundland and British Columbia also experimented briefly with government paper money. Following Confederation dominion notes were introduced throughout Canada.

In general the imperial governments resisted the issue of government paper money on the grounds that overissue would lead to devaluation of the currency and/or price inflation. Home governments usually represented the hard-money views of creditors; colonists often favoured the soft-money views of debtors. The home governments' fears of runaway inflation were only partially fulfilled. In the classic case of the paper money of French Canada there was disastrous inflation; however, this case should not be viewed outside of the imperial context of France's decline into bankruptcy. In the case of Nova Scotia and Prince Edward Island, the two British colonies with a long experience of government paper money, devaluation of the currency over the course of colonial history was much less severe. Prince Edward Island currency fell from a par of £111.11 currency per £100 sterling to a par of £150.00 currency. The par for Nova Scotia currency fell from £111.11 to £125 currency. Nova Scotia's devaluation was only slightly worse than that of the colonies which had no long-term experience with government paper money, namely Newfoundland, New Brunswick, and the Province of Canada, where the real par was £121.67 currency. As a counterbalance to the effects of a slightly higher rate of inflation, Nova Scotia, and Prince Edward Island received the benefits of substantial interest-free loans.

In addition to the issue of paper money by governments, private individuals also issued paper money or copper tokens. The practice was most common in the Canadas, where the generic term for private paper money, bons, originated but was not unknown in the other eastern colonies. Typically bons were for small amounts and were intended to overcome a want of small change rather than to provide a full range of currency. In the nineteenth century many private individuals also issued copper penny and halfpenny tokens. The profusion of bons and tokens and their unreliability led to the enactment of laws in the 1830s and 1840s which either banned their issue entirely or restricted their issue to banks.

Banking developed along parallel lines in the Canadas, New Brunswick and Nova Scotia. Banks were established in Lower Canada in 1817, in Upper Canada in 1818, in New Brunswick in 1820, and in Nova Scotia in 1825. Originally the banks were unchartered companies, but within a few years of their formation most were incorporated and brought under regulatory legislation. Under the direction of the Colonial Office banking law was systematized in the 1830s and 1840s so that there were not significant differences from colony to colony. Banks were established in Newfoundland in 1837, in Prince Edward Island in 1855 and in Vancouver Island and British Columbia in 1859 under legislation similar to that in the other provinces. In all the colonies private bank-notes became the dominant circulating medium shortly after banks were established.

When the British colonies adopted Halifax currency in the 1760s and 1770s it was based on the Spanish dollar. The dollar remained the most common coin in the colonies until at least the War of 1812. British guineas, Spanish doubloons, Portuguese Johannes and French crowns and half-crowns also played important, although varying, roles in the different colonies. In the decades following the War of 1812 the rough unity of currency systems which had prevailed prior to the war began to break up. In Nova Scotia changes in ratings drove the dollar out of general circulation and replaced it with the doubloon and its parts. In Lower Canada the overrating of French half-crowns made them the dominant coin. In spite of attempts by the imperial government to introduce British silver into general circulation in the years 1825 – 30 the dollar remained the dominant coin in the other eastern colonies until the late 1840s and early 1850s. The dollar and the doubloon in Nova Scotia and the half-crown in Lower Canada were gradually replaced by American eagles, British silver and eventually Canadian silver. Finally, it should not be forgotten that from the 1830s and 1840s paper money was more common than was coin in all of the colonies with the possible exception of Newfoundland.

In the 1760s when Halifax currency was adopted, the Spanish dollar was, by common agreement, valued at 4s. 6d. sterling. Since in currency the dollar was valued at 5s., there was a difference of one-ninth between sterling and currency. This par was accepted in all the eastern colonies with the exception of Newfoundland. By 1840 the intrinsic value of the silver dollar was about 4s. 2d. sterling or less. The debasement of the silver dollar resulted in an inflation of Halifax currency in relation to sterling money. As a result the old par of £111.11 currency to £100 sterling was no longer a true comparison.

Although the major changes in the true par of exchange took place in the early 1820s it was not until 1837 that Nova Scotia officially adopted a new par of £125 currency to £100 sterling. Other colonies followed gradually: New Brunswick did not finally abandon the old par until 1860 when it completed the transition to decimal currency.

In addition to currency inflation as the result of the declining intrinsic value of the silver dollar, inflation also resulted from the upward revaluations of coins in the 1820s, 1830s and 1840s, the dominance of coins other than the dollar in several colonies, and the widespread use of more-or-less inflated paper currency. Currency inflation as a result of the decline in the intrinsic value of the dollar theoretically affected all of the colonies equally. However, inflation caused by the three other changes resulted in varying rates of currency inflation in different colonies. As a result the unity of the Halifax currency system was broken. Given the fluctuations in commercial exchange rates, changes in the legal rates of coin, changes in the type of coin in circulation and fluctuations in the value of bank notes in circulation it is difficult to determine with certainty what the true par of exchange was after the 1820s; however, par in the Canadas and New Brunswick was about £121.60 currency, in Nova Scotia it was about £125, in Prince Edward Island it was about £150, and in Newfoundland about £120 currency to £100 sterling. A common currency was only restored by the adoption of decimal currency and Confederation.

Although the dollar was the basic coin in most of British North America, from 1760 accounts were generally kept in sterling notation. The increasing importance of trade with the United States in the 1830s and 1840s led to the demand for the adoption of a decimal currency system compatible with the American system. In the 1850s the Province of Canada and New Brunswick adopted decimal currency. Nova Scotia adopted decimal currency in 1860 but on a slightly different basis than Canada and New Brunswick; its currency system was not integrated into the Canadian system until 1871. Newfoundland adopted decimal currency in 1863, but, like Nova Scotia's, its system was not compatible with Canada's and it was not until 1895 that the Newfoundland dollar was made equal to the Canadian dollar. Prince Edward Island adopted a decimal currency act compatible with the Canadian system in 1871. In the west Vancouver Island officially adopted the decimal system in 1863 and British Columbia in 1865; privately decimal currency had been in use since the mid-1850s. In Rupert's Land both official and private accounts were generally kept in sterling until 1870 or 1871.

Appendix A

Commercial Exchange Rates

Much of this book has been devoted to *cambium per mintum*, the exchange of coins and its derivative, the nominal par between monies of account. Less attention has been paid to *cambium per litteras*, the exchange of bills and its derivative, the commercial exchange rate, although in the day-to-day life of government agents, merchants and others involved in exchange dealings the commercial exchange rate was a matter of more importance that the nominal par.

For the historian, commercial exchange rates provide a valuable indicator of the state of international trade and finances and a tool in interpreting historical documentation. In spite of this, very little statistical work has been done on Canadian foreign exchange rates prior to 1900. The two tables presented here are a preliminary attempt to fill this gap for sterling exchange on Britain. Although exchange on the United States (specifically New York) was an important element in Canadian exchange business and often was a major factor in determining exchange rates on Britain, no attempt has been made to prepare Canadian-American exchange rate runs because of a problem in locating adequate sources.

Although sources for sterling exchange on London are more common than sources for rates on New York they are far from complete. Even to assemble the runs presented here it was necessary to draw on 10 major sources and a number of minor sources for the Montreal runs and 7 major sources for the Halifax runs. Different sources often contained information

251

on different types of bills; since the type of bill affected the rate it is necessary to have some knowledge of the sources to use the exchange runs effectively.

Before considering the individual sources it may be useful to review some of the factors which influence bill rates. Essentially there are three technical and two fundamental factors. First, if a bill is purchased in one currency and paid in another there is the conversion factor. Until the adoption of decimal currency Canadian bills on Britain were normally purchased in Halifax currency and paid in sterling. A £100 sterling bill at par cost £111.11 Halifax currency. Because the nominal par was a fixed conversion rate it did not actually affect the true commercial exchange rate. However, its existence creates some problems in interpreting exchange-rate quotations for it is not always clear whether a quotation of, let us say 6% on a sterling bill, includes the currency conversion factor or not. If it does then the bill would have cost 111.11 x 1.06 = £117.78 Halifax currency; if it does not the bill would have cost £106.00 Halifax currency.

A second problem in dealing with the currency conversion factor is that from the 1820s onward the nominal par was no longer an accurate reflection of the true par, which had risen to £120 or £121.67 in Montreal and £125 in Halifax. In spite of this change most but not all exchange rate quotations continued to be based on the old par even after the adoption of decimal currency. As a result what was quoted as a 10% premium in Montreal in the 1850s was only a 0.5% premium and an 8% premium was a 1.5% discount. The true par was a 9.5% premium on the old nominal par. In preparing Tables 40 and 41 I have used the old nominal par as a conversion factor and have avoided the problem of discounts and premiums by quoting rates in pounds currency or dollars per £100 sterling.

Before going on, it may be wise to mention a problem related to the nominal exchange rate which had a strong influence on bill prices. From 1797 to 1821 Britain suspended specie payment and substantially increased its money supply through the issue of irredeemable bank-notes. Sterling floated in relation to other currencies and it generally fell in value compared to those which remained tied to gold or silver. Halifax currency was based primarily on silver and rose in value compared to sterling. Sterling exchange normally traded at a discount from about 1800 to 1815 and when the War of 1812 put pressure on the Canadian money supply sterling fell to a very large discount of 20 – 25%.

The second technical factor which affects bill prices is the term of the bill. Most bills of exchange on London were not paid until 30, 60, 90 or occasionally 120 days after the payee presented them to the drawee. Sight bills, which were paid when prsented, and three-day bills, were uncommon in the early nineteenth century but became more common after the completion of the Atlantic cable in 1866. To the term of the bill one must also add the time required for its transmission from Canada to England; until the middle of the nineteenth century this probably averaged at least a month. During the elapsed time between the purchase of a bill and its payment the drawer of a bill had the use of the payer's money. In recognition of this a discount was allowed on the face value of the bill as an interest payment. For example, assuming an annual interest rate of 5% and a total maturity time of 90 days, a payer might expect to pay £98 15s. 4d. sterling for a £100 sterling bill. The same bill, assuming a total maturity of only 30 days, would cost £99 11s. 9.25d. sterling. Given adequate information on maturities and on interest rates it is possible to adjust for these differences and to create what L.E. Davis and J.R.T. Hughes term a "pure" exchange rate.[1] However, for the historian's purposes a "pure" exchange rate is often not as useful as the simple commercial rate, provided bills of varying maturities are not mixed indiscriminately. Since the major Montreal sources prior to 1816 gave data for 30- or 40-day government bills, and all of the sources save one from 1816 to 1900 gave data for 60-day bank bills, and since a similar clear dividing line can be made in 1848 – 49 for the Nova Scotia data, we have not made any attempt to adjust these rates for the interest factor.

The third technical factor which affects bill prices is quality. Quality is a function of the reliability of the person, firm, or government on whom a bill is drawn. If a payer has doubts as to whether a drawee will actually pay a bill when it is presented to him, he will either refuse to purchase the bill or only purchase it at a discount commensurate with the risk. In general, bills on the British government departments were considered the highest quality bills and sold for a higher price than bills on merchants. After Canadian banks became active in the exchange business, their bills formed a third quality of bill. Until the 1840s, British government 30-day bills were taken as the standard in quoting rates. By 1846, 60-day bank bills had become the standard and government bills were dropped from price quotations. Merchant bills typically had a term of 60 or 90 days; after bank bills became the standard of exchange, 90-day merchant bills were quoted more frequently than were the 60-day variety.

Without extensive statistical work and more complete sources than we have yet discovered it is difficult to determine the price spread between different qualities of bills. Up to the end of the War of 1812 spreads of up to 5% between government bills and private bills were not unknown. After the war the spread seems to have been much smaller. If one allows for the effect of differing terms on bill prices, bank and government bills were almost equal in quality and good merchant bills were discounted from 0.5% to 1.5% below bank and government bills.[2]

A fourth and fundamental influence on bill rates is the gold point. Essentially it is the point at which it becomes cheaper for a debtor to forward gold or other legal tender to his creditor to settle a debt rather than to purchase a bill of exchange for the same purpose. The price of gold or other legal tender, the cost of transportation and insurance and the cost of interest all combine to establish the gold point. In theory the gold point sets precise limits on the price of bills of exchange. In practice, the gold point seems to have been a much more amorphous concept than the theory suggests.[3]

A second fundamental influence on bill prices was supply and demand. On the demand side, sterling bills were purchased to settle debts in Britain. Increases in imports from Britain tended to increase the demand for bills and drive their prices up. Debts in Britain could also be settled by the export of Canadian products such as fish, wheat or timber. Increases in Canadian exports reduced demand for bills and tended to lower the exchange rate. On the supply side, sterling bills were sold by individuals or organizations who had money in Britain and needed to raise money in Canada. Until the middle of the nineteenth century the British government was probably the largest seller of sterling bills in Canada. Increases in its expenditures in Canada, generally in connection with increased military activity, forced it to place more bills on the market. Other things being equal the increase in supply would drive the prices down. If the price of its bills fell too low the British government could import coin from Britain, Bermuda, the West Indies or the United States, therby reducing the need to sell bills. British paymasters and commissariat officers devoted a great deal of effort to managing the sterling exchange rate with a view to keeping it as high and stable as possible. Canadian merchants, who were generally purchasers of exchange, did what they could to keep the rate low.

The effect of supply and demand on the rate of exchange cannot be viewed simply as a function of the British North American balance of payments with Britain. From before the American Revolution, Canadian sterling exchange markets were linked with American sterling exchange markets. If sterling bill prices were substantially lower in Canada than they were in New York or Boston, bills would be purchased in Canada and sent to the United States to be sold at a profit. The interrelationship of the markets tended to cause bill prices to move in tandem in the two markets except when extraordinary events such as war broke the linkage.

Seasonal factors also influenced bill prices. For example, in his study of the U.S. sterling exchange market, A.H. Cole suggested a link between exchange rates and the export of the cotton crop.[4] Because cotton exports were a major source of exchange demands for sterling, exchange fell when the crop went to market in Britain. During the years 1851 - 59 exchange usually reached a seasonal low in January, February and March because although cotton was harvested in the late summer and autumn it did not reach Britain until the following spring. In the latter part of the nineteenth century more cotton was shipped by rail than by water with the result that much of it reached Britain within a few months of being harvested and exchange rates were lowest in the fall and early winter. Because central Canada earned most of its foreign exchange from the export of furs, agricultural products and timber which were exported via the St. Lawrence, it would not be surprising if Canadian sterling exchange also followed a seasonal pattern. In addition much of Canada's foreign exchange was the result of British military expenditures and they probably peaked during the summer months.

In preparing Tables 40 and 41 I have drawn on a number of major and minor sources. Typically each major source covered a discrete period; when price quotations from other sources have been introduced into the run they have been

255

identified with asterisks. In the Montreal series, quotations for the years 1767 to 1782 are from Professor Julian Gwyn's "The Impact of British Military Spending on the Colonial American Money Markets, 1760 - 1783". The rates are taken from the Drummond Papers; the Drummond family, in partnership with other individuals, had contracted with the British government to provide specie in North America. The Drummonds shipped some specie to Canada but most of it was raised locally by the sale of their bills on London. For practical purposes these rates may be considered as rates for government bills although they were for a term of 40 rather than 30 days. There was very little fluctuation in the rates from 1776 to 1782; in fact according to these figures there was no fluctuation at all from 1780 to 1782. This extraordinary stability was the result of management of the exchange market by the Drummonds' agents in Quebec. However, to achieve the stability the agent had to sell bills of exchange on credit. At the end of the war a number of Quebec merchants who had purchased bills on credit failed. As a result the contractors lost £160,000 sterling which constituted a discount from the bills which had been sold at par through the years 1780 - 82.

Most of the quotations for the years 1783 to 1799 are taken from the MG 19, A 2, the Jacobs-Ermatinger estate collection in the Public Archives of Canada. The collection consists of the business and personal records of a number of related individuals and contains information on both private and government bills with various terms.

The collection throws some light on differing methods of quoting exchange rates. For example, an entry in E.W. Grays "Waste Book" for 16 April 1789 records the purchase of a £300 sterling bill at 12% for £336 currency. An entry for 30 October 1792 records a similar purchase of a £300 bill at a 1% advance for £303 sterling which was then converted to £336 13s. 3d. currency.[5] The former method of price quotation was in general use in the Ermatinger papers up to about 1790 - 91; the latter was generally used after 1790 - 91 both in these papers and in other sources.

The papers also contain examples of advance purchase of bills as a form of exchange-rate insurance. From 1799 to 1805 some account books, probably those of F.W. Ermatinger, contain references to bills purchased at a specified rate from one to four months in advance of their delivery date, generally

256

October.[6] By purchasing in advance the payer was able to ensure a known exchange rate at the cost of a certain amount of lost interest. Exchange quotations based on bills purchased in advance of their delivery dates have only been used if no other quotation was available.

In addition to Professor Gwyn's work and the Ermatinger collection I have also made use of rates paid for bills negotiated on the British treasury by the Receiver-General of Quebec during the years 1767 - 87. Probably these bills were for 30- or 40-day terms.

For the years 1799 to 1804, exchange quotations are from the Ermatinger collection and from RG8, 'C' Series "British Military and Naval Records", Volumes 110 - 115 and 320 - 324. The quotations from "C" series are for bills drawn on the paymaster-general in London, the treasury and the Ordnance Department. Bills drawn on different departments did not always bring the same price: before 1812 ordnance officers sold their bills in competition with the commissary-general who negotiated bills on the treasury and the paymaster-general. The government bills were for 30 or 40 days. In some cases they were sold on credit which would have effectively lengthened the term and lowered the rate.

In 1800 the colonial secretary instructed colonial governors to submit monthly reports of current prices for supplies, including gold, silver and exchange, in their respective colonies. From 1805 to 1813 bill prices are from these reports. With a few exceptions the rates quoted are for 30-day government bills. It is not entirely clear whether the information was taken from the actual sales of bills by the deputy commissary-general or whether it was supplied by exchange merchants. A reputable merchant had to certify the rates quoted each month. In at least one case the deputy paymaster-general implied that the firm which certified the exchange rate had been careless or dishonest and had certified a rate ranging from par to a 2% discount when the firm was actually dealing in exchange at 4% and 5% discount.[7]

During the War of 1812 the rates at which 30-day government bills were to be sold or exchanged for army bills was fixed by a commission on the 10th and 24th of each month. These rates, published in the Quebec *Mercury*, have been used for the 1814 - 15 quotations. Whether the posted rates were always adhered to is not known. A similar *caveat* attaches to the rates for the years 1818 to 1820 which are rates set by the Bank of Montreal and recorded in its minute books.

The rates for the years 1821 – 1830 are also Bank of Montreal rates but are from a different source. In 1830 when its charter came up for renewal the bank was obliged to provide detailed information on its exchange dealings over the previous ten years. This information, giving monthly purchases and sales of exchange, was published in the Journals of the Lower Canadian Assembly as Appendix N in 1830. Only the rates at which the bank sold exchange from 1821 to 1830 have been included in Table 40.

The Bank of Montreal bills were normally 60-day bills, as were most bank bills. From 1817 to 1900 all quotations in Table 40 are for 60-day bills with the exception of quotations for the years 1830 – 35 which are for 30-day government bills. As a result, one might expect quotations for the years after 1817 to be marginally lower than the quotations for the earlier period. However, the banks were retailers of bills, purchasing them from the British government or from other sources and reselling them. In the years 1821 – 30 the Bank of Montreal paid, on the average, £120.79 for government bills, £120.25 for private bills and sold its bills at £122.49. There is little doubt that the retail markup more than compensated for the longer term of the bank bills.

Beginning in 1822, colonial governors were required to submit standardized annual statistical reports on their colonies. The reports, or Blue Books, included information on money and exchange in the colony. Often the exchange section only gave an average rate or a range for the year, but the reports from Lower Canada from 1828 to 1839 gave monthly rates for 30-day government bills. The rates were bills sold for Spanish or American dollars and were given in terms of shillings and pence per dollar. For example, a rate of 4s. 0.25d. was equal to a premium of 11.917% on the currency par of £111.11 for a rate of £124.35. Occassionally the Blue Books gave comparative rates for bills purchased with bank-notes and with silver dollars. The premium on bills purchased with notes was generally higher than on bills purchased with silver. This difference should be kept in mind since it is probable that many bank bills were purchased with bank-notes. Finally it must be remembered that until at least 1832 – 33, bills on the British treasury could be purchased with British silver coin at a fixed premium of 1.5%.

258

This rate was about 8% below the average commercial rate for bills during the decade; however, the difference was made up for by a premium on British silver.[8]

In 1841 the legisature conducted a general inquiry into currency and exchange. Among the evidence considered by the inquiry was an account of the exchange brought and sold by the chartered banks, excluding, the Bank of British North America, during the period January 1836 to July 1841. As in the case of the Bank of Montreal data for 1821 – 30 we have used the retail exchange rate obtained from this evidence.[9] Over the 5½-year period the banks purchased exchange at an average rate of £122.29 and sold it at a rate of £124.25. This spread, £1.97 per £100, is almost exactly the same as that on Bank of Montreal exchange purchases and sales in 1821 – 30.

From 1841 to 1900 exchange quotations have been taken from various newspapers, the Montreal *Courier, Witness, Gazette, Pilot, Trade Review, Monetary Times* and *Journal of Commerce.* Generally rates are for the best quality 60-day bank bills sold for cash. From January 1858 rates are given in dollars per £100 sterling with $486.66 as par.

Sources for exchange rates at Halifax are much less comprehensive than those for Montreal. As a result the data in Table 41 provides little more than a sampling of exchange rates at Halifax.

The rates for 1757 – 1783 are from Professor Gwyn's paper "The Impact of British Military Spending on the Colonial American Money Markets, 1760 – 1783". As the rates are either for government bills or for bills drawn by government contractors it is probably that most were for 30 or 40 days.

The quotations for the years 1790 to 1810 are based primarily on bills drawn by the naval commissioner at Halifax on the Navy Board in London. A few quotations in 1805 and 1807 are from prices current sent home by the colonial administrators.[10]

The rates for 1811 – 1815 are from papers of the commissariat officers in Halifax, those for 1820 – 22 are from Halifax Dockyard Records, those for 1827 are from the Blue Books[11] and those for the years 1825 and 1837 – 79 are from the *Nova Scotian,* the *British Colonist* and the *Chronicle.* To December 1848 the rates are for 30-day government bills, after 1849 they are for 60-day bank bills.

The exchange data for Montreal, especially after 1800, is detailed enough to provide a good picture of exchange movements. Essentially, Canadian foreign exchange history can be divided into two periods, 1760 to 1819 and 1820 – 1900, and four subperiods, 1760 – 1810, 1810 – 1819, 1820 – 1857 and 1858 – 1900. During the period 1760 – 1820 sterling exchange fluctuated widely around the nominal par of £111.11 currency per £100 sterling and during the second period it fluctuated within much narrower bounds, around what was to become the new par, £121.67 or $486.66. In Nova Scotia a similar pattern emerged although the new par was established at £125 currency or $500.

The shift from one par to another was sudden. In June of 1819 exchange in Quebec was at the old par; by October of 1822 it reached £125.97. During the 1820s it settled into a new range which, on the basis of average annual rates, seldom fell below £120 or climbed above £124. It is difficult to assign a single cause for this sudden shift in pars. Probably it was a result of a number of converging factors including the decline in the intrinsic value of the commonest coins in British North America, the overvaluation of these coins in relation to sterling coins, the widespread use of bank-notes, changes in British monetary policy, changes in the Canadian balance of payments and the influence of the American exchange market.

Obviously, the decline in the intrinsic value of the principal coins in use, the silver dollar and its parts, the doubloon and its parts, and the French crown and its parts contributed to an upward pressure on sterling exchange over the long term. However, in the case of all three coins the reductions in their official precious metal content had taken place in the latter third of the eighteenth century, fifty years before the sudden surge in sterling exchange rates. Reductions in weight due to wear also lowered their intrinsic value. By the 1830s the dollars in use in central Canada were 0.6% under their mint weight and the French crowns and half-crowns, which had not been minted since 1792, were 2.1% and 8.9% under their mint weight. (see Table 13) However, the reductions in weight as the result of wear were gradual and can hardly have been the sole cause of the sudden shift in exchange rates.

The legal overvaluation of coins in Canada also contributed to upward pressure on sterling exchange. However, in both Upper and Lower Canada the major overvaluation had taken place in 1796 and there were no major revisions made in the ratings of commonly used coins until the late 1820s. In Nova Scotia there may be a direct link between the increase in the rating of the doubloon to £4 in 1819 and the subsequent increase in exchange rates. At £4 the doubloon was overvalued by about 24% against the sovereign, a percentage almost equal to the premium on sterling exchange after 1819.

The widespread use of bank-notes and treasury notes in Canada after 1817 – 19 may also have contributed to the rise in cost of sterling exchange. Bank-notes and treasury notes often traded at a discount to coin. They were not, with the possible exception of some treasury notes, legal tender and could be refused by exchange dealers or taken at a discount. As noted earlier, exchange purchased with notes was generally higher than exchange purchased with coin.

A fourth factor which almost certainly contributed to the increase in sterling exchange prices were the changes in the British monetary system after the Napoleonic wars. The resumption of specie payments between 1816 and 1820 resulted in a rapid increase in the value of the pound sterling and a consequent rise in the price of sterling exchange. Taken alone the resumption of specie payments should merely have brought sterling exchange back to its pre-suspension par of £111.11. However, two other developments contributed to a further decline in the value of Canadian currency and a rise in sterling exchange. First Britain introduced a new silver coinage containing 6.5% less silver and limited its legal tender value to £2. Second, the market price of silver, which during the eighteenth century had hovered around 64s. to 65s. per pound troy fell to about 60s. per pound between 1819 and 1821.[12] As a result of these changes if Canadians made remittances to Britain in British silver for amounts of more than £2 sterling the payments would probably only have been accepted at the market rate of 60s. per pound rather than the mint rate of 62s. per pound. A new crown, nominally worth 5s. sterling would only be worth 4s. 6.5d. on the market. If remittances were made in dollars, which at 64.5s. per pound troy of silver in the eighteenth century had been worth 4s. 6.8d. sterling, the dollars would, at the new market rate of 60s. per pound, be worth only 4s. 3d. sterling. The dilemma could not be avoided by making remittances in gold because gold was rare in Canada and could only be obtained at a premium; in 1828 T. Ridout reported that the Bank of Upper Canada charged premiums of 5% for doubloons and 9% for sovereigns if they were purchased with bank-notes or silver.[13] Increased costs of making remittances in coin was reflected in increased sterling bill prices.

A fifth factor which almost certainly affected Canadian exchange rates was the American market centred in New York. During suspension of payments in Britain sterling had normally been heavily discounted in New York but at the end of the war it rose to a premium and from 1817 to 1820 traded at about par. In 1821 it began to rise. By 1823 sterling exchange carried a premium of about 5.8% and for the next 11 years it sold at an average premium of 8%.[14] This premium was not equal to the premium in Canada, about 9.5%, but it provided the base on which the Canadian premium was maintained. The exact reasons for the premium on the American market are not known but since the American currency system was largely based on silver as was the Canadian system, it is probable that the premium was related to the fall in the price of silver.

Finally, it is possible that the shift in the sterling par of exchange after 1819 was the result of changes in the Canadian (or North American) balance of payments. Unfortunately the study of Canada's balance of payments history has not yet reached a stage where this possibility can be usefully explored.

Within the period 1760 – 1819 it is possible to distinguish two subperiods, 1760 – 1809 and 1810 – 19. From 1760 to 1809 exchange fluctuated widely around the par of £111.11; in the second period, sterling fell to a dramatic discount, averaging only £99.99 for the decade.

Prior to 1800, exchange quotations are generally too scattered (except for the years covered by Professor Gwyn's study) to do more than indicate general trends in exchange history. Before the American Revolution, exchange traded at or slightly below par and during the war, as a result of the management of Drummond's agents, it was at par. It continued at or slightly above par until the decade 1800 – 09 when it fell to an average of £109.12. The decline can probably be attributed to the suspension of specie payments in Britain, and, at least in the first half of the decade to successful Canadian wheat exports which reduced demand for exchanges.[15] In fact it is interesting that sterling exchange stayed as high as it did: in the United States sterling was at a discount of about 30% during the decade and actually rose during the War of 1812. In

Canada sterling exchange fell to a 20% to 25% discount before and during the war. The sharp decline presumably was the result of large military expenditures in Canada at the same time that the war cut off the American market for British bills of exchange, combined with the weakness of sterling. At the end of the war exchange returned to par, and after 1819 rose to a premium.

The period 1820 – 1900 may also be divided into two subperiods, 1820 – 1857 and 1858 – 1900. The dividing line is drawn at the date when the Province of Canada adopted decimal currency. This is an artificial distinction but there was a more substantial distinction. From 1820 to 1857 the average sterling exchange rate was £122.35, slightly over what came to be the new par of £121.67 and after 1858 the average rate was £121.26. More important, exchange fluctuated through a much wider range before 1857 than it did after. Why this happened is not clear although it seems probable that as the exchange market grew larger and more sophisticated, fluctuations would decrease. Similar stabilization in sterling exchange rates occurred in the United States in the last half of the century, particularly after the upheavals of the Civil War.

In addition to long-term variations in sterling exchange rates there were identifiable seasonal fluctuations. Until about 1820 prices normally peaked early in the year and then fell until May or June. They remained relatively low until September and then began to climb until they peaked again in the new year. In general the low period, April through September, coincided with the open season on the St. Lawrence when remittances could be made in goods rather than bills. It was also the period when goods were imported but most imports were on at least six-month credits and no payments had to be made on them until the winter months.

During the years 1820 – 1857 the summer months were also months of lower exchange prices but the differences were so small, given the fairly broad fluctuations in the market that the seasonal variations are not statistically significant. After 1858 seasonal variations once again became statistically significant but the season patterns are different from those for the years 1760 – 1819. Exchange rates peaked in the early summer and fell in the late fall and early winter. Perhaps the explanation for the change is similar to that offered by Cole for changes in the American market. Improved transportation, principally the railroads, and perhaps an extended St. Lawrence shipping season, may have allowed Canadian grain to reach Britain the year it was produced rather than the following year. A more probable explanation is that Canadian market patterns were simply conforming to the New York patterns described by Cole.

Annual average sterling bill prices in pounds currency Montreal and Quebec, 1760-1899

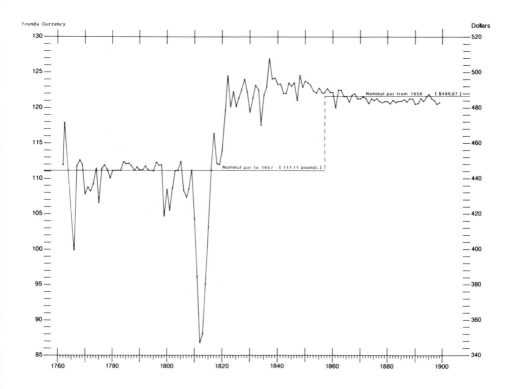

Table 40   Québec and Montreal Prices of Sterling Exchange on London, 1760–1899.

	Jan.	Feb.	Mar.	Apr.	May	June
1760	–	–	–	–	–	–
1761	–	–	–	–	–	–
1762	–	–	–	–	–	111.99
1763	–	117.93	–	–	–	–
1764	–	–	–	–	–	–
1765	–	–	–	–	–	–
1766	–	–	–	–	99.99	–
1767	–	111.00	–	–	Par	112.00
1768	114.00	114.00	114.75	115.00	115.00	112.00
1769	112.00	112.00	113.00	113.00	113.00	113.00
Average	113.00	113.72	113.88	114.00	109.78	112.25
1770	–	107.50	106.50	105.00	105.00	–
1771	–	107.14	107.14	–	107.14	–
1772	–	108.20*	–	108.00	–	104.00
1773	–	107.14	–	–	Par*	107.14
1774	–	Par*	–	–	–	–
1775	113.00	107.50	108.00	108.00	105.50	105.00
1776	–	–	–	–	–	Par
1777	–	–	–	Par	Par	Par
1778	–	–	–	Par	108.00	Par
1779	–	–	–	Par	109.00	106.00
Average	113.00	108.10	107.21	109.06	108.12	107.92
1780	–	Par	Par	Par	Par	Par
1781	Par	Par	Par	Par	Par	Par
1782	Par	Par	Par	Par	Par	Par
1783	–	–	–	–	–	Par*
1784	–	–	–	–	–	Par
1785	–	–	–	111.97*	Par	112.38
1786	115.00[6]	113.00	113.00[6]	–	Par	Par
1787	113.64	111.96	–	Par*	Par	Par
1788	–	Par	Par	–	–	Par
1789	–	Par	–	112.00[6]		112.00
Average	115.22	111.50	111.48	111.40	111.11	111.33
1790	–	Par	–	–	–	–
1791	Par	–	–	–	–	Par
1792	Par	–	–	Par	–	Par
1793	–	–	–	Par	–	–
1794	–	–	–	–	–	–

(Expressed in Halifax currency to 1857 and in dollars from 1858 per £100 Sterling bills on London. Nominal currency par, £111.11. Dollar par, $486.66*)

July	Aug.	Sept.	Oct.	Nov.	Dec.	Average
–	–	–	–	–	–	–
–	–	–	–	–	–	–
–	–	–	–	–	–	111.99
–	–	–	–	–	–	117.93
–	–	–	–	–	–	–
–	–	–	–	–	–	–
–	–	–	–	–	–	99.99
112.00	112.00	112.00	112.00	112.00	112.00	111.79
109.00	109.00	112.00	112.00	112.00	113.00	112.65
112.00	110.00	Par	110.60	111.50	112.00	111.93
111.00	110.33	111.70	111.53	111.83	112.00	111.93
107.21*	104.69*	107.50	111.11*	112.00	Par	107.76
110.00	–	–	110.00	Par	–	108.76
104.00	–	105.00*	117.14[1]	Par	–	108.21
108.00	106.89*	Par	Par	Par	–	109.24
–	108.00	112.00	113.00	113.00	–	111.42
105.00	103.00	100.00	Par	–	–	106.61
Par	Par	Par	Par	113.00	–	111.43
113.00	112.00	112.00	112.50	113.00	–	111.98
Par	–	112.00	113.00	113.00	–	111.33
–	Par	Par	112.00	–	–	110.06
108.68	108.11	109.09	112.21	112.17	111.11	109.52
Par	Par	Par	Par	Par	Par	111.11
Par	Par	Par	Par	Par	Par	111.11
Par	Par	Par	Par	–	–	111.11
–	–	–	–	Par	–	111.11
113.00*	–	–	112.84*	Par	114.00	112.41
–	–	–	113.00	–	–	112.12
111.05	–	–	Par	Par	113.00	112.17
–	Par	–	111.92	Par	112.64	111.75
Par[3]	Par	Par	Par	–	Par	111.11
Par	–	–	111.81	–	–	111.61
111.37	111.11	111.11	111.68	111.11	112.16	111.49
Par	–	–	111.46	Par	Par	111.18
Par	–	–	111.39	Par	–	111.17
Par	–	–	112.22	113.89	–	111.76
–	–	–	111.45	Par[9]	Par[9]	111.19
–	–	–	–	–	–	–

267

Table 40 (Continued)

	Jan.	Feb.	Mar.	Apr.	May	June
1795	–	–	–	–	–	Par
1796	–	112.22	–	–	–	–
1797	–	–	–	–	–	–
1798	112.22[12]	–	–	–	–	–
1799	–	–	–	–	–	–
Average	111.48	111.67	–	111.11	–	111.11
1800	111.48	105.56[9]	105.00[9]	108.33	108.33	108.89
1801	111.11[3]	–	103.61	101.67	101.11[6]	–
1802	–	–	–	104.44[6]	Par	–
1803	–	108.33[3]	–	–	–	–
1804	111.12	–	–	–	–	–
1805	–	–	–	113.89	Par	Par
1806	113.33	113.33*	111.94	–	105.55	105.55
1807	Par	Par	Par	108.33	Par*	105.00
1808	107.78	105.55	106.67	106.67	107.22	105.55
1809	Par^M	Par^M	109.17^M	Par	105.00	–
Average	111.01	109.17	107.92	107.78	107.57	107.22
1810	103.33	104.44	103.33	103.33	105.55	105.55
1811	–	103.89	102.78	102.78	101.39	–
1812	90.28	90.28	90.28	87.50	87.50	87.50
1813	88.88	88.88	88.88	88.88	88.88	87.50
1814	89.44	90.83	90.00	90.42	90.55	90.00
1815	106.94	103.47	107.64	107.64	104.17	91.67
1816	–	–	–	–	–	–
1817	118.40[6]	–	–	–	–	–
1818	114.72	113.33	–	–	–	–
1819	–	109.72	108.89	108.89	–	Par
Average	101.71	100.61	98.83	98.49	96.34	95.56
1820	113.89	113.05	113.33	113.89	112.78	113.05
1821	–	117.78*	–	–	118.33	119.03
1822	123.33	124.58	123.47	124.44	124.44	123.19
1823	125.55	125.55	124.03	118.25	116.80	116.67
1824	120.83	120.83	120.97	121.11	121.11	121.48
1825	122.50	121.11	120.97	121.67	117.78	117.08
1826	122.22	119.25	120.00	120.97	120.14	–
1827	122.78	121.67	122.78	122.22	122.22	121.11
1828	125.55	125.55	125.55	125.55	122.78	122.78
1829	123.19	123.33	122.08	122.50	122.50	121.39
Average	122.20	121.27	121.46	121.18	119.94	119.53

Table 40 (Continued)

July	Aug.	Sept.	Oct.	Nov.	Dec.	Average
–	–	–	–	–	–	111.11
–	–	–	Par	–	112.78	112.30
Par[9]	–	–	113.42[9]	Par	–	111.88
–	–	–	111.74	–	–	111.98
–	104.44[6]	105.00[L]	–	–	–	104.22
111.11	104.44	105.00	111.83	111.67	111.67	111.10
105.56[6]	–	109.44[9]	–	Par[6]	Par	108.48
<u>108.89</u>	<u>109.11</u>	–	103.25	–	–	105.54
–	–	–	107.78[9]	Par	–	108.61
111.11[9]	–	–	111.67	<u>113.33</u>	–	111.11
–	–	–	–	–	–	112.41
113.33	Par	113.33	113.33	113.33	Par	111.12
106.67	106.67	105.55	105.55	–	–	108.24
104.44	104.44	105.55*	102.50	102.50	Par	107.36
107.22	Par	Par	Par	Par	Par	108.52
Par	Par	113.33	115.00	113.33	Par	111.14
108.54	108.93	109.72	108.77	110.83	111.11	109.12
104.44	103.61	102.78	105.55	105.55	–	104.31
–	94.44[6]*	91.67	88.89	88.89	90.29	96.11
84.72	82.50	82.50	83.89	86.11	88.88	86.82
87.50	87.50	87.50	88.33	87.22	87.22	88.10
90.55	94.44	98.89	102.50	105.55	108.33	95.13
93.05	96.67	104.44	107.91	Par	–	103.16
–	–	–	Par*	–	–	111.11
–	–	–	114.44	–	–	116.42
–	–	111.67	110.55	110.55	–	112.16
–	–	–	113.89	115.28	116.11	111.98
92.05	93.19	97.06	102.71	101.28	98.17	99.51
113.89	113.89	115.00	116.67	–	–	113.94
118.89	119.44	119.58	120.28	120.97	122.22	119.61
123.89	124.86	125.00	125.97	125.83	125.42	124.54
118.89	118.89	119.02	119.17	119.02	120.00	120.15
122.22	122.22	122.22	124.30	125.00	125.00	122.27
117.64	119.17	120.28	120.55	121.11	121.67	120.13
–	–	122.22	122.22	122.78	122.78	121.40
121.67	–	121.67	121.67	125.00	125.00	122.58
121.25	–	123.05	123.05	124.44	124.44	124.00
121.67	122.22	122.22	121.67	121.67	122.22	122.22
120.00	120.10	121.03	121.56	122.87	123.19	121.08

Table 40 (Continued)

	Jan.	Feb.	Mar.	Apr.	May	June
1830	121.21	121.21	120.00	120.00	120.00	118.81
1831	117.65	117.65	117.65	118.81	122.45	122.45
1832	123.71*	123.71*	123.08*	123.08*	122.45	122.45
1833	123.08	123.08	124.35	121.83	123.08	122.45
1834	121.21	117.07	115.38	117.65	120.00	114.83
1835	119.40	120.60	121.12	–	121.12	122.20
1836	123.99	124.81	123.68	122.41	121.00	121.51
1837	124.50	124.85	124.94	124.98	125.99	126.63
1838	125.63	123.39	121.40	122.53	123.17	124.17
1839	125.45	124.96	124.11	124.65	123.97	123.54
Average	122.58	122.13	121.57	121.77	122.32	121.90
1840	124.58	124.71	124.54	124.13	123.48	123.36
1841	124.59	124.05	124.39	123.37	123.17	122.78
1842	–	–	–	121.94*	121.67	122.22
1843	–	–	–	–	121.39	121.67
1844	–	–	–	–	122.78	123.33
1845	–	–	–	–	122.50	123.33
1846	121.67	–	–	123.89	124.44	123.33
1847	120.00	120.55	118.89	118.33	120.55	120.55
1848	–	128.89	125.55	125.00	126.11	125.28
1849	123.33	123.89	122.78	120.00	122.22	122.78
Average	122.83	124.42	123.23	122.38	122.83	122.86
1850	–	124.44*	124.44*	123.47*	123.33	123.89
1851	–	–	–	–	–	–
1852	–	–	–	–	122.78	123.05
1853	–	123.33	122.22	122.22	122.22	122.22
1854	122.22	122.22	122.22	121.67	121.67	121.67
1855	122.22	122.22	123.33	123.33	123.33	123.33
1856	121.67	121.67	121.67	122.22	122.22	122.78
1857	122.22	122.22	122.22	122.22	122.22	122.22
Average	122.08	122.68	122.68	122.52	122.54	122.78
1858	491.11	491.11	492.22	491.11	491.11	492.22
1859	491.11	486.11	490.00	490.00	490.00	491.11
1860	491.11	486.11	490.00	490.00	490.00	491.11
1861	477.77	473.33	481.11	483.33	473.33	473.88
1862	492.22	490.55	492.22	490.55	491.11	490.00
1863	492.77	490.55	490.55	492.22	491.11	487.22
1864	489.72	487.77	487.77	483.33	488.61	Par
1865	492.77	486.11	485.00	484.44	–	498.16

Table 40 (Continued)

July	Aug.	Sept.	Oct.	Nov.	Dec.	Average
118.81	120.00	118.23	118.23	118.23	118.23	119.41
123.08	123.08	122.45	122.45	124.35	124.35	121.36
123.08	123.08	122.45	122.05	124.35	124.35	123.15
–	122.45	–	–	121.21	121.21	122.53
114.83	114.83	114.83	120.00	120.00	119.52	117.51
122.45	123.08	123.08	–	–	124.35	121.93
122.92	123.66	122.59	121.90	122.53	124.78	122.98
130.80	129.04	130.02	127.87	125.73	128.44	126.98
125.37	124.25	124.50	124.03	124.87	125.49	124.07
123.99	124.58	124.17	124.55	122.71	123.84	124.21
122.81	122.81	122.48	122.64	122.66	123.46	122.50
121.94	122.18	123.26	122.06	122.62	122.53	123.28
123.56	122.22	122.78	122.78	–	–	123.37
123.33	121.39	121.67	121.67	122.22	–	122.01
121.67	–	122.22	122.78	122.50	–	122.04
123.33	124.03	123.47	123.75	124.03	–	123.53
124.03	123.89	124.03	124.03	122.22	–	122.00
121.67	–	122.78	122.22	121.67	121.11	122.53
–	120.00	122.22	–	124.44	125.55	121.08
124.44	123.33	123.89	122.78	122.22	122.78	124.57
122.78	122.22	123.89	122.78	124.44	123.89	122.92
122.97	122.41	123.02	122.76	122.93	123.19	122.95
123.33.	123.89	123.89	123.75	123.75	123.33	123.77
–	–	123.47	123.61	123.33	–	123.47
122.78	123.33	123.89	123.61	122.78	–	123.17
122.22	122.22	122.22	–	–	–	122.36
122.22	122.22	122.22	122.22	–	122.22	122.00
123.33	123.33	122.78	122.78	121.67	121.67	122.78
122.78	122.22	122.22	122.22	121.67	122.22	122.13
122.22	122.22	121.67	–	120.00	123.89	122.12
122.70	122.78	122.80	123.03	122.20	122.67	122.65
492.22	492.22	491.11	491.66	491.66	491.11	491.57
490.00	491.11	491.11	491.11	485.55	480.00	488.93
490.00	491.11	491.11	491.11	485.55	480.00	488.93
473.88	487.77	485.55	483.33	481.11	485.55	480.00
490.00	488.61	Par	492.22	492.22	492.77	490.76
Par	488.88	490.55	490.00	491.11	488.88	490.04
488.61	485.00	483.33	485.00	485.55	488.33	486.64
486.11	–	487.22	Par	485.00	–	486.94

271

Table 40 (Continued)

	Jan.	Feb.	Mar.	Apr.	May	June
1866	–	481.66	483.05	476.38	486.11	488.88
1867	–	486.94	485.55	485.27	488.33	490.55
1868	490.55	489.72	488.33	487.50	489.55	489.16
1869	487.22	485.55	484.72	483.05	Par	485.83
Average	489.64	486.29	487.54	486.43	487.80	487.98
1870	484.44	485.00	484.44	482.77	486.11	487.22
1871	485.00	487.22	488.33	488.33	489.16	490.00
1872	486.11	485.55	487.22	486.11	487.22	488.61
1873	486.94	487.22	485.00	479.75	482.77	484.72
1874	484.16	484.72	484.16	485.00	487.77	486.11
1875	485.83	485.83	485.83	483.33	483.33	–
1876	486.94	486.11	486.11	486.11	487.22	487.22
1877	483.88	484.72	484.72	486.11	487.77	Par
1878	483.05	483.88	485.00	486.38	485.83	485.55
1879	481.66	485.55	485.55	486.11	486.11	487.22
Average	484.80	485.58	485.64	485.00	486.33	487.04
1880	481.11	482.77	486.11	486.11	485.00	Par
1881	481.66	484.44	483.33	484.44	484.72	483.05
1882	482.22	484.72	486.38	Par	487.22	486.38
1883	482.22	484.16	483.05	485.55	483.88	485.55
1884	485.83	486.94	Par	487.77	487.22	–
1885	481.38	483.33	484.16	486.94	Par	483.05
1886	485.83	Par	487.22	486.11	486.11	486.38
1887	483.88	485.00	484.72	484.72	485.27	484.72
1888	485.83	484.72	486.11	485.83	486.11	486.11
1889	484.72	Par	487.50	Par	487.22	486.38
Average	483.47	484.94	485.53	486.08	485.94	485.37
1890	481.94	482.77	481.66	485.27	483.88	485.00
1891	482.22	485.83	486.11	485.83	484.16	485.00
1892	483.05	485.55	485.27	485.83	485.55	486.94
1893	486.11	486.38	486.38	485.83	485.55	484.72
1894	485.00	485.00	486.94	486.94	487.22	487.22
1895	487.22	488.33	487.22	488.33	487.50	488.05
1896	487.77	486.38	486.11	487.50	487.22	486.38
1897	483.33	484.72	485.83	485.83	485.55	485.27
1898	483.33	483.33	481.66	480.27	480.83	484.44
1899	481.94	483.33	483.61	483.61	485.00	485.27
Average	484.19	485.16	485.08	485.52	485.25	485.83

[1] A quotation in the Ermatinger Estate papers gives a rate of 106.00
*Not taken from the main series.
L For delivery in October.

Table 40 (Continued)

July	Aug.	Sept.	Oct.	Nov.	Dec.	Average
481.94	481.66	479.45	481.66	487.22	Par	483.15
490.27	489.16	488.88	483.05	485.00	486.11	487.19
489.72	488.61	485.27	483.88	487.77	485.83	487.98
486.38	487.77	481.38	485.55	483.88	483.05	485.09
487.15	488.35	486.80	487.10	486.80	486.21	487.34
487.22	487.22	Par	484.44	483.88	483.88	485.27
489.45	488.33	479.45	480.27	483.05	485.00	486.13
488.88	483.33	480.55	483.33	483.88	482.77	485.30
486.94	483.05	482.77	482.22	470.00	481.11	482.71
486.11	486.11	486.11	486.11	486.11	486.11	485.72
–	487.50	483.61	478.88	482.77	485.55	484.25
487.22	487.22	486.94	483.05	480.55	482.22	485.58
486.11	482.77	481.66	481.11	480.55	481.38	483.95
481.66	482.77	480.55	480.00	479.45	481.11	482.94
486.11	481.66	480.55	481.66	480.55	481.11	483.65
486.63	485.00	482.89	482.11	481.08	483.02	484.57
483.88	482.22	481.94	481.94	481.94	–	483.60
483.05	480.83	480.55	480.55	481.11	480.27	482.33
484.44	485.00	484.16	481.11	482.50	482.22	484.42
482.22	483.33	481.66	481.11	481.11	481.38	482.94
480.83	480.83	482.22	481.38	480.00	478.61	483.48
482.77	484.44	482.50	483.05	483.05	484.72	483.84
486.38	482.22	482.77	483.61	482.77	482.22	484.86
481.94	481.38	480.83	481.94	481.38	481.38	483.10
486.11	485.27	484.72	483.05	484.44	484.44	485.23
485.55	484.16	484.16	483.05	481.11	481.11	484.86
483.72	482.97	482.55	482.07	481.94	481.87	483.88
484.44	484.16	480.55	480.83	479.45	479.72	482.37
484.72	483.61	481.66	480.83	480.55	482.50	483.59
486.38	486.38	Par	485.27	483.88	485.27	485.50
481.94	476.66	482.50	482.77	481.66	484.72	483.77
486.38	Par	484.72	Par	486.38	Par	486.32
488.33	488.61	488.05	485.83	487.50	488.05	487.75
486.11	486.11	482.77	481.94	481.11	483.33	485.23
485.27	484.72	483.33	481.66	482.50	482.50	484.21
483.88	483.05	482.77	481.66	482.22	481.66	482.43
484.72	481.38	482.77	480.69	482.77	481.80	483.07
485.22	484.14	483.58	482.82	482.80	483.62	484.44

³ = 30-day bill   ⁹ = 90-day bill
⁶ = 60-day bill   ¹² = 120-day bill
ᴹ = Merchant's Bill
1800–1803 – Underlined quotations are from RG8, "C" Series.

273

Table 41   Halifax Prices of Sterling Exchange on London, 1757–1879

	Jan.	Feb.	Mar.	Apr.	May	June
1750	–	–	–	–	–	–
1751	–	–	–	–	–	–
1752	–	–	–	–	–	–
1753	–	–	–	–	–	–
1754	–	–	–	–	–	–
1755	–	–	–	–	–	–
1756	–	–	–	–	–	–
1757	–	–	–	–	–	–
1758	105.00	–	104.50	–	–	–
1759	103.00	–	102.50	102.50	102.50	102.50
Average	104.00	–	103.50	102.50	102.50	102.50
1760	–	–	102.50	–	–	–
1761	107.50	–	108.00	–	–	–
1762	–	–	112.00	–	–	114.25
1763	–	–	112.50	–	–	110.00
1764	–	–	–	–	110.00	–
1765	–	–	111.81	–	–	110.57
1766	–	–	109.92	–	–	–
1767	–	–	108.75	–	–	–
1768	–	–	110.00	106.50	–	110.43
1769	–	–	110.57	–	–	–
Average	107.50	–	109.56	106.50	110.00	111.31
1770	Par	107.00	107.00	107.00	105.00	Par
1771	–	–	–	–	–	110.00
1772	111.09	111.09	–	–	–	–
1773	–	–	–	–	–	–
1774	–	–	–	–	–	–
1775	–	–	–	–	–	–
1776	–	–	–	–	Par	–
1777	–	Par	Par	–	–	–
1778	112.50	Par	–	–	–	–
1779	106.60	106.60	106.60	106.60	106.60	106.60
Average	110.33	109.38	108.24	106.80	107.57	109.24
1780	106.60	–	106.60	106.60	106.60	105.55
1781	–	–	–	116.66	116.66	–
1782	–	112.50	–	–	–	–
1783	100.00	100.00	100.00	100.00	100.00	100.00

274

(In Halifax Currency to June 1860 and in dollars from July 1860. Per £100 Sterling bills on London. Nominal currency par, £111.11. Dollar par, to June 1871, $5.00; from July 1871, $486.66)

July	Aug.	Sept.	Oct.	Nov.	Dec.	Average
–	–	–	–	–	–	–
–	–	–	–	–	–	–
–	–	–	–	–	–	–
–	–	–	–	–	–	–
–	–	–	–	–	–	–
–	–	–	–	–	–	–
–	–	–	–	–	–	–
105.00	–	–	–	105.00	105.00
–	–	102.50	–	102.50	–	103.65
–	–	–	102.50	102.50	102.50	102.56
105.00	–	102.50	102.50	102.50	103.75	103.13
105.00	105.00	–	–	–	107.50	105.00
–	–	110.00	–	–	112.50	109.50
–	–	–	–	–	–	113.13
–	–	–	–	110.00	111.13	110.91
107.50	–	–	107.14	–	111.13	108.94
–	–	111.13	108.50	–	109.65	110.33
110.00	–	–	110.00	111.43	108.75	110.02
–	–	112.85	110.00	–	–	110.53
110.64	–	–	110.57	–	–	109.63
–	109.11	110.00	107.00	107.00	108.50	108.70
108.29	107.06	111.00	108.87	109.48	109.88	109.67
102.83	104.80	105.00	–	Par	109.07	107.37
110.56	–	–	109.79	110.00	111.09	110.29
–	–	–	–	–	–	111.09
–	–	–	–	–	–	–
–	–	–	–	–	–	–
–	–	–	–	–	100.00	100.00
–	113.33	113.33	–	–	–	112.57
–	–	–	–	112.50	112.50	111.82
–	–	–	–	–	–	111.81
107.70	107.77	107.77	Par	107.77	105.55	107.28
107.03	108.63	108.70	110.45	110.09	107.64	109.03
105.00	103.33	103.33	103.33	104.00	104.00	105.00
Par	Par	Par	113.60	115.55	114.72	113.82
–	105.55	–	–	–	100.00	106.02
100.00	–	–	–	–	100.00	100.00

Table 41 (Continued)

	Jan.	Feb.	Mar.	Apr.	May	June
1784	–	–	–	–	–	–
1785	–	–	–	–	–	–
1786	–	–	–	–	–	–
1787	–	–	–	–	–	–
1788	–	–	–	–	–	–
1789	–	–	–	–	–	–
Average	103.30	106.25	103.30	107.75	107.75	102.78
1790	–	–	–	–	–	–
1791	–	–	–	–	–	–
1792	–	–	–	–	–	–
1793	–	–	–	–	–	–
1794	–	–	–	–	–	–
1795	–	–	–	–	–	–
1796	–	–	–	–	–	–
1797	–	–	–	–	–	–
1798	–	–	–	–	–	–
1799	–	–	–	–	–	–
Average	–	–	–	–	–	–
1800	–	–	–	–	–	–
1801	–	–	–	–	–	–
1802	–	–	–	–	–	–
1803	–	–	–	–	–	–
1804	–	–	–	–	–	–
1805	–	–	Par	–	–	–
1806	–	–	–	–	109.44	–
1807	–	–	–	–	–	–
1808	–	–	Par*	–	Par	–
1809	–	–	–	–	–	108.79
Average	–	–	111.11	–	110.28	108.79
1810	–	–	–	–	109.87	109.64
1811	104.44*	–	–	105.55	105.63	–
1812	96.30	–	–	–	102.22	–
1813	–	–	–	–	91.71	–
1814	–	89.75	91.33	–	94.44	95.39
1815	94.44	101.66	105.00	105.00	108.33	109.55
1816	–	–	–	–	–	–
1817	–	–	–	–	–	–
1818	–	–	–	–	–	–
1819	–	–	–	–	–	–
Average	98.39	95.71	98.17	105.28	102.03	104.86

July	Aug.	Sept.	Oct.	Nov.	Dec.	Average
–	–	–	–	–	–	–
–	–	113.89*	–	113.89*	–	113.89
–	–	–	–	–	–	–
–	–	–	–	–	–	–
–	–	–	–	–	–	–
105.37	106.66	109.44	108.47	111.15	106.24	106.21
–	–	–	–	–	112.78	112.78
–	–	–	–	–	–	–
–	–	–	–	–	–	–
Par	–	–	–	–	–	111.11
–	–	–	–	113.89	–	113.89
–	–	–	–	–	–	–
–	–	–	–	–	–	–
–	–	–	–	–	–	113.89
–	–	–	–	113.89	–	–
–	–	–	108.33	–	–	108.33
111.11	–	–	108.33	113.89	112.78	112.00
–	–	–	–	–	–	–
–	–	–	109.72	–	–	109.72
–	–	–	–	–	–	–
–	–	–	–	–	109.43	109.43
–	–	–	–	109.58	–	109.58
Par	107.77	–	105.55	–	–	108.89
–	–	–	–	–	–	109.44
–	–	–	Par	109.17	Par	110.46
–	–	–	–	–	Par	111.11
–	108.89	–	–	110.82	–	109.50
111.11	108.33	–	108.79	109.86	110.55	109.77
–	–	–	–	–	–	109.76
102.78*	101.11	–	–	91.67*	90.66	100.26
100.00	–	94.44	94.44	–	91.67	96.51
–	–	88.89*	–	–	–	90.30
–	97.22	–	95.19	89.25	–	93.22
–	104.12	Par	–	–	–	104.90
–	–	–	–	–	–	–
–	–	–	–	–	–	–
–	–	–	–	–	–	–
–	–	–	–	–	–	–
101.39	100.82	98.15	94.82	90.46	91.17	99.16

Table 41 (Continued)

	Jan.	Feb.	Mar.	Apr.	May	June
1820	–	–	–	–	–	117.78
1821	–	–	–	–	–	–
1822	125.00	–	–	127.78	–	127.78
1823	–	–	–	–	–	–
1824	–	–	–	–	–	–
1825	125.00	–	120.00	–	122.78[6]	120.55[6]
1826	–	–	–	–	–	–
1827	125.00	125.00	125.00	125.00	124.44	127.78
1828	–	–	–	–	–	–
1829	–	–	–	–	–	–
Average	125.00	125.00	122.50	126.39	123.61	123.47
1830	–	–	–	–	–	–
1831	–	–	–	–	–	–
1832	–	–	–	–	–	–
1833	–	–	–	–	–	–
1834	–	–	–	–	–	–
1835	–	–	–	–	–	–
1836	–	–	–	–	123.89*	125.00
1837	–	–	–	–	–	128.33
1838	130.55	129.44	129.44	129.44	126.11	126.11
1839	126.67	–	126.67	126.67	–	125.55
Average	128.61	129.44	128.06	128.06	125.00	126.25
1840	124.44	126.67	126.67	126.67	–	–
1841	125.55	125.55	–	–	–	128.89
1842	–	–	–	–	–	–
1843	126.11	125.55	125.55	125.55	–	125.55
1844	125.00	–	–	–	–	–
1845	126.67	126.94	126.94	126.94	126.94	126.94
1846	–	–	–	–	–	–
1847	–	–	–	–	–	–
1848	–	–	–	–	–	–
1849	–	–	–	–	125.00	–
Average	125.55	126.18	126.39	126.39	125.97	127.13
1850	–	–	–	–	124.72	–
1851	–	–	–	–	–	–
1852	–	–	–	–	–	–
1853	–	–	–	–	–	–
1854	–	–	–	–	–	–
1855	–	–	–	–	–	–
1856	–	–	–	–	–	–

278

July	Aug.	Sept.	Oct.	Nov.	Dec.	Average
117.78	–	–	–	–	–	117.78
–	–	122.22	–	125.00	–	123.61
127.78	127.78	–	127.78	–	–	127.32
–	–	–	–	–	–	–
–	–	–	–	–	122.22	122.22
–	–	–	–	–	–	122.08
–	–	–	–	–	–	–
127.78	126.67	125.00	125.00	125.00	127.78	125.79
–	–	–	–	–	–	–
–	–	–	–	–	–	–
124.45	127.23	123.50	126.39	125.00	125.00	123.13
–	–	–	–	–	–	–
–	–	–	–	–	–	–
–	–	–	–	–	–	–
–	–	–	–	–	–	–
–	–	–	–	–	–	–
–	–	–	–	–	–	–
125.00*	–	–	–	–	–	124.63
129.72	130.55	130.55	130.55	130.55	130.55	130.11
126.11	126.67	126.11	126.11	126.67	126.39	126.43
126.67	126.67	126.67	126.67	126.67	126.67	126.56
126.88	127.96	127.78	127.78	127.96	127.87	127.18
126.67	126.67	126.67	126.67	126.67	125.00	126.28
128.33	128.33	126.11	126.11	126.67	–	126.94
–	–	–	–	–	–	–
125.55	125.55	125.00	125.00	125.00	125.00	125.40
–	–	–	–	126.11	126.11	125.74
126.94	126.94	126.94	126.94	126.67	126.67	126.87
–	–	–	–	–	–	–
–	–	–	–	–	–	–
126.67	127.22	126.67	126.67	126.67	126.67	126.76
125.00	–	–	–	–	–	125.00
126.62	126.94	126.28	126.68	126.30	125.89	126.18
124.72	–	–	–	–	–	124.72
–	–	–	–	–	–	–
–	–	–	–	–	–	–
–	–	–	–	–	–	–
–	–	–	–	–	–	–
–	–	–	–	–	–	–
–	–	–	–	–	–	–

Table 41 (Continued)

	Jan.	Feb.	Mar.	Apr.	May	June
1857	–	–	–	–	–	–
1858	–	–	–	–	–	–
1859	–	–	–	–	–	–
Average	–	–	–	–	124.72	–
1860	–	–	–	–	–	–
1861	–	–	–	–	–	–
1862	–	–	–	–	–	–
1863	–	–	–	–	–	–
1864	–	–	–	–	–	–
1865	–	–	–	–	–	–
1866	Par	Par	497.78	Par	Par	504.44
1867	502.22	502.22	502.22	502.22	502.22	502.22
1868	502.22	504.44	504.44	504.44	504.44	504.44
1869	Par	502.22	502.22	Par	Par	502.22
Average	501.11	502.22	501.67	501.67	501.67	503.33
1870	502.22	–	–	–	502.22	502.22
1871	502.22	–	502.22	–	–	–
1872	Par	Par	–	–	488.88	–
1873	–	Par	487.77	–	485.55	485.55
1874	483.33	484.44	485.00	485.55	487.77	487.77
1875	486.11	487.77	485.55	Par	487.77	487.77
1876	485.00	487.22	Par	487.50	Par	487.77
1877	484.44	484.44	485.55	485.55	487.77	487.22
1878	482.22	482.22	485.00	487.77	487.22	Par
1879	483.33	485.55	487.22	Par	Par	487.77
Average	484.44	485.62	486.11	486.62	487.29	487.22

*Not taken from the main series
⁶=60-day bills

July	Aug.	Sept.	Oct.	Nov.	Dec.	Average
–	–	–	–	–	–	–
–	–	–	–	–	–	–
–	–	–	–	–	–	–
124.72	–	–	–	–	–	124.72
–	–	–	–	–	–	–
–	–	–	–	–	–	–
–	–	–	–	–	–	–
–	–	–	–	–	–	–
–	–	–	–	–	–	–
–	–	–	502.22	502.11	Par	501.11
504.44	Par	Par	Par	Par	502.22	500.74
502.22	502.22	504.44	502.22	502.22	502.22	502.41
504.44	504.44	502.22	502.22	502.22	501.11	503.42
502.22	502.22	502.22	502.22	502.22	501.11	501.57
503.33	502.22	502.22	501.78	501.55	501.33	501.85
502.22	502.22	–	502.22	502.22	502.22	502.22
–	–	–	–	–	–	502.22
488.88	–	–	484.44	Par	Par	486.98
485.55	487.22	484.44	482.22	480.00	484.44	484.94
Par	487.22	Par	485.55	485.00	Par	485.97
487.77	487.22	485.55	Par	483.88	485.00	486.48
487.77	487.77	Par	484.44	485.55	483.33	486.36
Par	486.11	482.77	482.22	482.22	482.22	484.76
485.55	483.33	485.55	482.77	483.88	482.22	484.53
486.11	481.66	481.66	482.22	483.33	482.22	484.53
486.87	485.79	484.76	483.82	483.82	484.09	485.57

Appendix B

Intrinsic Value of The Silver Dollar

From 1600 to at least 1840 the most common coin in the western hemisphere was the silver dollar, specifically the Spanish or Spanish-American silver dollar. Because of its ubiquity Halifax currency was based on it and changes in the intrinsic value of the dollar affected the value of Halifax currency. (see Table 42)

In a proclamation of 4 December 1704 and an "Act for ascertaining the Rates of foreign Coins in Her Majesty's Plantations in America" of 1707 the British government set out the average weight and sterling value of six types of Spanish dollar. Overall the gross weight was about 420 grains and the pure silver content was about 386 grains. Compared to the shilling, which contained 85.9 grains of silver, the dollars were worth about 4s. 6d. sterling. Although only two of the different types of dollars were worth exactly 4s. 6d. sterling, 4s. 6d. came to be the accepted sterling value of all Spanish dollars and was later applied to Spanish-American and United States dollars. The customary rating of 4s. 6d. sterling was retained until at least 1825 although the pure silver content of the dollar was less than 386 grains from as early as 1728. The decline in the real value of the dollar resulted in an inflation of the colonial currencies based on it. In foreign exchange dealings this inflation was allowed for by charging a premium on sterling exchange.

The correct rating of the dollar became much more complex after 1816 when Britain adopted the gold standard and reduced its silver coinage to a token status. Prior to 1816 the British mint paid 62s. per pound troy of standard silver and minted 62s. from each pound. Thus the intrinsic value of the

282

coins, at the mint price for silver, was equal to their face value. After 1816 the mint continued to pay 62s. per pound of silver but it minted 66s. from each pound and kept 4s. as a minting fee. As a result the intrinsic value of the new British silver was 6% less than its face value at mint prices; a crown, nominally worth 5s. sterling, contained only 4s. 8.3d. worth of silver at the mint price.

The original valuation of the dollar at 4s. 6d. sterling had been based on the mint price of 62s. per standard pound (containing 5,760 grains of standard silver or 5,328 grains of pure silver) for a dollar containing an average of 386.27 grains of pure silver. Based on the mint price, the average dollar of the 1820s containing 372.5 grains of pure silver was worth about 4s.4d. sterling but if one rated the same dollar on the basis of the silver content of the new shilling, 80.7 grains, the dollar was worth 4s. 7.4d.

A further complication in rating the dollar arises from the fact that the mint price for silver was an artificial price. During the eighteenth century when the mint price was set at 62s. per pound of standard silver the market price was about 64s. or 65s. per pound. The difference in price resulted in a scarcity of British silver coinage, as it was melted down and sold as bullion. The difference also meant that although the silver content of dollars in circulation early in the nineteenth century was only about 372.5 grains compared to the 386 grains of the dollars tested in 1704, they were still on the basis of the market price of silver, worth about 4s. 6d. sterling although on the basis of mint price they were only worth 4s. 4d. The difference may be the reason why sterling exchange in Canada remained roughly at the old par of £111.11 throughout the eighteenth century in spite of the declining silver content of the dollar. However, about 1820 the market price of silver fell to 60s. per pound, 2s. below the mint price. At the new market price the dollar was only worth about 4s. 2.3d.

When the British government reduced the sterling value of the dollar from 4s. 6d. to 4s. 4d. in 1825 it based its calculations on the mint price of silver. In 1838, the sterling value of the dollar was further reduced to 4s. 2d. although the silver content of the dollar had not delcined in the years since 1825. The new rating was based on the market price for silver.[1] In 1825 the British government met criticism that the dollar should be evaluated on the basis of a direct comparison with the silver content of the crown and the shilling by pointing out that, unlimited amounts of British silver could be converted to gold by the purchase of bills of exchange at a premium of 3%. This was above British silver's true value at either the mint or the market price. In 1830 a commissariat official put forward the argument that although in law British silver was limited as a legal tender, in practice, the Bank of England and the public received it to any amount.[2] This advantage was not afforded to dollars or other foreign silver.

British North Americans rejected these arguments and evaluated the dollar on the basis of its silver content relative to British silver. They argued that in North America British silver did not enjoy the advantage of unlimited conversion into gold at its face value and that it had to circulate as a true coin, not as a token, in competition with foreign silver. By their reasoning if a new crown containing 403.63 grains of pure silver was worth 5s. sterling then a dollar containing 372.5 grains was worth 4s. 7.33d. sterling.[3]

A further complexity was added to the case after the independent Spanish-American republics and the United States began to issue silver dollars. By the 1830s Spanish-American dollars, particularly Mexican dollars, had generally replaced the old Spanish dollars. After some hesitation it was decided that the Spanish-American dollars were equal to or exceeded, in value the old dollars and could be accepted at the same rate. United States dollars posed a problem because even at their mint weight they were slightly less valuable than the popular Mexican dollars although they were slightly more valuable than old Spanish dollars. Because of the difference U.S. silver dollars were occasionally treated differently from other silver dollars: for example in 1842 the Nova Scotia legislature did not make them legal tender when it made other silver dollars legal tender at 5s. 2.5d. and in 1820 New Brunswick increased the rating of Spanish dollars to 5s. 4d. currency but left the U.S. dollar at 5s.

Table 42   Sterling Value of Silver Dollars, 1700–1848
(Based on the pre-1816 mint price of 85.9 grains of pure silver per shilling or 62s. per pound troy of standard silver)

	Weight (grains)	Purity	Silver Content (grains)	Sterling Value (s./d.)
Mint weight, 1700–28	432.9	.931	394.6	4/7.1
Average weight by assays, 1702–17	419.9	.921	386.27	4/6
Mint weight, 1728–72	417.6	.9166	382.8	4/5.5
Weight by assay, 1765	416.5	.906	377.4	4/4.7
Mint weight, 1772–1848	417.6	.903	377.4	4/4.7
Average weight by assays, 1801–26	416.3	.8947	372.5	4/4
Average weight by assays, 1834, Spanish Dollar	416.0	.8916	370.9	4/3.8
Average weight by assays, 1834, Bolivian Dollar	416.1	.9018	375.25	4/4.4
Average weight by assays, 1834, Central American Dollar	416.4	.8964	373.27	4/4.1
Average weight by assays, 1834, Chilean Dollar	421.6	.9018	380.2	4/5.1
Average weight by assays, 1834, Columbian Dollar	417.17	.9095	379.4	4/5
Average weight by assays, 1834, Mexican Dollar	416.73	.8962	373.47	4/4.2
Average weight by assays, 1834, Peruvian Dollar	413.75	.9024	373.35	4/4.2
Average weight by assays, 1834, Rio la Plata Dollar	412.0	.8958	369.05	4/3.6
Mint Weight, U.S. Dollar, pre–1837	416.0	.8924	371.24	4/3.9
Mint weight, U.S. Dollar, post–1837	412.5	.900	371.25	4/3.9

Appendix C
Army Sterling and Customs Currency

During the Seven Years' War the British army stationed in North America had difficulty rationalizing pay to troops stationed in different colonies with different currency systems and different ratings for the principal coins in circulation. In 1757 the treasury directed that local currency systems should be ignored and that all troops in North America should be paid in coins valued at the same rate. The basic coin was to be the Spanish dollar rated at 4s. 8d. sterling with other silver and gold rated in proportion.[1] The troops were generally paid in dollars rated at 4s. 8d. and most transfers within the army were made at the same rate. Army accounts were usually kept on the same basis. Since the dollar was valued at 4s. 6d. sterling in Britain, army accounts kept in "army sterling" had to be converted to sterling at the rate of £103 14s. 1d. to £100 sterling. In dealing with civilians in North America the army continued to use local currency, usually Halifax currency, in which the dollar was rated at 5s.; £107.14 Halifax was equal to £100 army sterling. Army accountants sometimes converted army sterling to Halifax currency by the additon of one-fourteenth. A more common method of converting from one currency to another was to convert a sum in one currency into dollars at the appropriate rate and then to convert the sum in dollars into the desired currency.

The directive establishing army sterling remained in force in British North America from 1757 to 1825 with the exception of a period from April 1809 to April 1810 when the dollar was valued at 4s. 6d. Newfoundland may have been an exception to this rule; a report in 1824 stated that the dollar was paid at 5s. sterling there.[2] In 1825 the British government attempted to introduce British silver into circulation throughout the empire and as part of its program it directed that in future the dollar would only be accepted at 4s. 4d. sterling. This rating was to apply in both civil and military contexts. As a result, the difference between army sterling and sterling disappeared although the term army sterling continued to be used into the 1850s and army accountants used different conversion factors depending on the coins in use (see Appendix D).

Army sterling was not the only example of a special currency created by a government agency. In 1774 an imperial act, 14 George III, C.88, placed import duties on rum, brandy, molasses and syrup as a means of raising a revenue for the civil government of Quebec. The duties were stated in sterling and the act provided that they could be paid in silver at the rate of 5s. 6d. sterling per ounce of silver, a rate which was slightly above the market price of silver. The act did not specify standard or pure silver but it was generally interpreted as having meant standard silver. At 5s. 6d. per ounce the dollar, the most common silver coin in Canada at the time was believed to be worth about 4s. 8.75d. although at the mint price of 5s. 2d. per ounce it was only valued at 4s. 6d. and, in fact, was only worth about 4s. 4.7d. Beginning in 1775 and extending at least to 1813 the Collector of Customs at Quebec paid over the duties he had collected to the Receiver-General of Canada at the rate of 4s. 8.75d. sterling per dollar, or 5s. 6d. per ounce of silver. However, duties were almost always paid to the collector at the traditional sterling rate of 4s. 6d.per dollar. The difference was pocketed by the collector and quickly became one of the established emoluments of the office. The practice, and the loss which it entailed to the provincial revenue, were known to the government of the province and on at least four separate occasions (in 1777, 1788, 1796 and 1810) the executive council investigated it but was unable to pry the collector loose from his perquisite.[3]

During the War of 1812 most of the customs duties were paid in army bills and the collector attempted to apply the principle of collecting duties at one rate and paying them to the receiver-general at another rate to the bills. The council refused to accept this innovation and was supported by the governor who ordered that the excess previously amassed by the collector be turned over to the receiver-general until orders could be received from London. No response was received from

London and although the collector at Quebec appealed to have the case reopened in 1817 nothing was done. The collectors at St. John's, Quebec, and Coteau du Lac attempted to gain similar emoluments for themselves after 1825 but they were forced to abandon the practice and make restitution to the province in 1829.[4]

The loss of the collector's perquisites in 1814 did not end the use of the 4s. 8.75d. sterling dollar. What seems to have happened is that the merchants became aware of the possibility of paying duties levied under 14 George III, C.88 at this rate instead of 4s. 6d. and began to insist on the more advantageous rate. The practice continued until 1828 when the executive council recommended that customs officers refuse to accept any silver in payment by weight at 5s. 6d. per ounce unless it was standard British silver. At the same time, the imperial government ordered the customs office to refuse any payment in silver except for British coins or dollars rated at 4s. 4d. sterling. Although the Quebec merchants appealed to the treasury for a change in the regulation and eventually sued the collector of customs at Quebec for the money lost as a result of the change, the day of the 4s. 8.75d. sterling dollar was over.

The special customs dollar was also used in Nova Scotia until the War of 1812. Customs duties were normally collected at the rate of 4s. 6d. per dollar and paid over to the province or remitted to Britain at the rate of 5s. 6d. sterling per ounce of standard silver. In 1813 directions were given that dollars and other silver were to be accepted and paid out of the customs house at the rate of 5s. 6d. per ounce. Although there is some contradictory evidence it seems that the new directive was implemented in 1817 and the Nova Scotia customs establishment continued to accept and pay out the dollar at 5s. 6d. sterling per ounce until July 1828 when the rate was reduced to 4s. 4d. sterling per dollar.[5]

Appendix D

Currency Conversion Table

Because of the differences between nominal and real pars, differences among colonies, and differences from one time to another, one must take care in making conversions from one currency to another. Table 43 is intended to simplify conversion at the nominal rate of exchange when conversion is only from one money of account to another. It is not intended for use when actual foreign exchange transactions are involved.

The table is adequate for conversion at the nominal rates from 1760 to 1825. In 1825 the British government began to value the dollar at 4s. 4d. sterling instead of 4s. 6d. The new value was applied to both sterling and army sterling accounts; as a result the difference between sterling and army sterling disappeared. The change also affected the relative value of Halifax currency and sterling. Previously £111.11 Halifax currency had been equal to £100 sterling; this relationship was based on the relative value of the dollar at 5s. currency and 4s. 6d. sterling. On the basis of the new relative values 5s. and 4s. 4d., £115.38 currency was equal to £100 sterling or army sterling. The British government and the army in North America adopted the new conversion ratio with one exception: in Lower Canada the 5 franc piece was legal tender at 4s. 8d. currency. The army accepted it at 4s. sterling; to allow for the use of the franc in their accounts, army accountants sometimes converted currency to sterling at the rate of £116.67 per £100. In November 1838 the British government further reduced the rate at which it would accept the dollar to 4s. 2d. and on the basis of this change army accountants adopted a new conversion ratio of £120 currency per £100 sterling.

The colonial governments and merchants generally ignored the inflationary effect of the decline in the sterling rating of the silver dollar and continued to convert currency to sterling on the basis of the old standard for another decade. In 1836 – 37 Nova Scotia adjusted its nominal par to £125 currency per £100 and in 1848 Prince Edward Island adopted a nominal par of £150 currency per £100 sterling except in the case of rents which were expressed in sterling; they continued to be converted and paid in currency at the old rate. The currency law passed by the Province of Canada in 1841, which came into effect in May 1842, suggested a revision of the nominal par of exchange. On the basis of the sovereign which was valued at £1 4s. 4d. currency the new exchange rate should have been £121.67 currency per £100 sterling and indeed there was a move on the part of bankers, merchants, exchange dealers and the British army to adopt the new rate. The colonial government also adopted the new rate in its accounts when actual foreign exchange trasactions were involved but in simple bookkeeping matters, it generally used the old rate of £111.11 per £100. As a result most of the private sector reverted to the old system and continued to use it until decimal currency was adopted in 1858.[1] The British army used the new rate in its accounts when it was dealing with bank-notes and most coins but adopted different rates for dealing with silver dollars and U.S. eagles. After 1 April 1843 the army issued eagles at the rate of £121.70 currency per £100 sterling on the basis of their rating at £2 10s currency and £2 1s. 1d. sterling. Silver dollars, which were worth 5s. 1d. currency and 4s. 2d. sterling, were issued at £122 currency per £100 sterling. Because they were the most common coin used by the army in the 1840s, £122 per £100 was sometimes given as the currency/army sterling par.[2] The Blue Books from 1842 to 1855 continued to state that £120 currency was equal to £100 army sterling; this was the pre-1842 par based on a dollar worth 5s. currency. There is no evidence that the army actually used this conversion factor in the 1840s, and it seems likely that the compiler of the Blue Books was mistaken.

New Brunswick continued to use the old conversion factor of £111.11 to £100 until it adopted decimal currency in 1860.

In Newfoundland correct practice in converting accounts is uncertain. Until about 1825 accounts were kept in sterling although from 1811 the dollar was valued at 5s. sterling, 6d. above its accepted sterling value in Britain. In 1825 the government began to keep its accounts in sterling based on a 4s. 4d. sterling dollar. It followed this practice until it adopted decimal currency in 1865, even though the British government reduced the rate at which it would accept the dollar to 4s. 2d. sterling in 1838. As a result, from 1838 to 1863, £104 Newfoundland sterling was equal to £100 sterling. In the years 1825 – 1830 the Newfoundland population gradually adopted Newfoundland currency based on the dollar valued at 5s. currency and 4s. 4d. sterling. As a result £115.38 Newfoundland currency was equal to £100 sterling or Newfoundland sterling. When the British government reduced the rating of the dollar to 4s. 2d. in 1838 the true Newfoundland currency/sterling par should have been changed to £120 currency per £100 sterling or £104 Newfoundland sterling but it is not clear that the change was made. Foreign exchange quotations, for example, continued to be made on the basis of £115.38 Newfoundland currency per £100 sterling until at least the 1860s.

The decimal currency acts of the Province of Canada, New Brunswick and Prince Edward Island came into effect January 1858, November 1860, and January 1871. All adopted the United States par of $486.66 to £100 sterling. In July 1860 Nova Scotia began to use decimal currency with a par of $500 to £100 sterling; in July 1871 it was brought within the Canadian currency system with a par of $486.66. Newfoundland's decimal currency act came into effect in January 1865. Par was $480.00 to £100 sterling. After the failure of the Newfoundland banks the difference between Newfoundland and Canadian currency was found to be inconvenient and the Newfoundland par was adjusted to $486.66 as of 7 January 1895.

Table 43   Currency Conversion in British North America

	Dollars	Sterling	Army Sterling	Halifax Currency	Quebec Currency	York Currency	Livres
Dollars	1.0	.2250	.2333	0.25	0.3	0.4	6.0
Sterling	4.4444	1.0	1.0371	1.1111	1.3333	1.7778	26.6664
Army Sterling	4.2857	.9643	1.0	1.0714	1.2857	1.7143	25.7147
Halifax Currency	4.0	.90	.9333	1.0	1.2	1.6	24.0
Quebec Currency	3.3333	.75	.7778	.8333	1.0	1.3333	19.9998
York Currency	2.5	.5625	.5833	.625	0.75	1.0	15.0
Livres	0.1667	.0375	.0389	.0417	0.0500	0.0667	1.0

Example: To convert $11.00 to Quebec currency, multiply $11.00 by .3 to get
£3.30 or £3/6/0 Quebec currency.

From 1825 the conversion rate for army sterling is usually the same as for sterling.
From 1837 £125 Nova Scotia currency = £100 sterling.
From 1848 £150 Prince Edward Island currency = £100 sterling.
From 1825 £115/7/8.3 Newfoundland currency = £100 Newfoundland
  sterling = £100 sterling.
From 1838 £120 Newfoundland currency = £104 Newfoundland sterling =
  £100 sterling.
From 1 January 1858 $486.66 (Canada) = £100 sterling.
From 1 July 1860 to 1 July 1871 $500.00 (Nova Scotia) = £100 sterling.
From 1 November 1860 $486.66 (New Brunswick) = £100 sterling.
From 1 July 1863 to 19 July 1871 (?) $485.000 (Vancouver Island) = £100 sterling.
From 2 January 1865 to 8 January 1895 $480.000 (Newfoundland) =
  £100 sterling.
From 1 January 1866 to 19 July 1871 (?) $485.00 (British Columbia) =
  £100 sterling.
From December 1871 to February 1871 $486.66 (Prince Edward Island) =
  £100 sterling.
From 7 January 1895 $486.66 (Newfoundland) = £100 sterling.

Appendix E
Monetary Weights

Weights in the chapter "New France" are given in French grains; in other chapters weights are given in Troy or English grains.

French Monetary Weights, (*Livre poids du roi* or *livre poids du marc* – From Larousse, *Grand Dictionnaire Universelle,* Volume 6, p. 431)

1 livre	=	2 marcs	=	489.50584 grams
1 marc	=	8 onces	=	244.752923 grams
1 once	=	8 gros	=	30.594115 grams
1 gros	=	3 denier	=	3.824265 grams
1 denier	=	24 grains	=	1.274760 grams
1 grain	=	———	=	.053115 grams

English Monetary Measure (Troy weight). From *Encyclopedia Britannica,* 1974, Volume 18, p. 391 and Volume 23, p. 485

1 pound troy	=	12 ounces	=	373.24175 grams
1 ounce	=	20 pennyweight	=	31.103479 grams
1 pennyweight	=	24 grains	=	1.5551739 grams
1 grain	=	———	=	.0647989 grams

Appendix F

Conversion of Shillings and Pence to Decimal Currency

Shillings	Pence 0	1	2	3	4	5	6	7	8	9	10	11
0		.0042	.0083	.0125	.0167	.0208	.0250	.0292	.0333	.0375	.0417	.0458
1	.0500	.0542	.0583	.0625	.0667	.0708	.0750	.0792	.0833	.0875	.0917	.0958
2	.1000	.1042	.1083	.1125	.1167	.1208	.1250	.1292	.1333	.1375	.1417	.1458
3	.1500	.1542	.1583	.1625	.1667	.1708	.1750	.1792	.1833	.1875	.1917	.1958
4	.2000	.2042	.2083	.2125	.2167	.2208	.2250	.2292	.2333	.2375	.2417	.2458
5	.2500	.2542	.2583	.2625	.2667	.2708	.2750	.2792	.2833	.2875	.2917	.2958
6	.3000	.3042	.3083	.3125	.3167	.3208	.3250	.3292	.3333	.3375	.3417	.3458
7	.3500	.3542	.3583	.3625	.3667	.3708	.3750	.3792	.3833	.3875	.3917	.3958
8	.4000	.4042	.4083	.4125	.4167	.4208	.4250	.4292	.4333	.4375	.4417	.4458
9	.4500	.4542	.4583	.4625	.4667	.4708	.4750	.4792	.4833	.4875	.4917	.4958
10	.5000	.5042	.5083	.5125	.5167	.5208	.5250	.5292	.5333	.5375	.5417	.5458
11	.5500	.5542	.5583	.5625	.5667	.5708	.5750	.5792	.5833	.5875	.5917	.5958
12	.6000	.6042	.6083	.6125	.6167	.6208	.6250	.6292	.6333	.6375	.6417	.6458
13	.6500	.6542	.6583	.6625	.6667	.6708	.6750	.6792	.6833	.6875	.6917	.6958
14	.7000	.7042	.7083	.7125	.7167	.7208	.7250	.7292	.7333	.7375	.7417	.7458
15	.7500	.7542	.7583	.7625	.7667	.7708	.7750	.7792	.7833	.7875	.7917	.7958
16	.8000	.8042	.8083	.8125	.8167	.8208	.8250	.8292	.8333	.8375	.8417	.8458
17	.8500	.8542	.8583	.8625	.8667	.8708	.8750	.8792	.8833	.8875	.8917	.8958
18	.9000	.9042	.9083	.9125	.9167	.9208	.9250	.9292	.9333	.9375	.9417	.9458
19	.9500	.9542	.9583	.9625	.9667	.9708	.9750	.9792	.9833	.9875	.9917	.9958
20	1.0000											

Notes

A preliminary version of this book, with more extensive footnotes is available in Parks Canada's *Microfiche Report Series,* No. 125.

Introduction and Definitions

1. In quoting exchange rates I will use decimalized sterling notation with X amount in currency being equal to £100 sterling. In all other references the traditional sterling notation, pounds (£), shillings (s.) and pence (d.) will be used.
2. Angela Redish, "Why was specie Scarce in Colonial Economies? An analysis of the Canadian Currency, 1796 – 1820," Department of Economics, University of British Columbia, Discussion paper No. 83 – 22, p. 1.
3. *Ibid.,* p. 3.

Chapter One   New France

1. Adam Shortt, *Documents Relatifs à la Monnaie, au Change et aux Finances du Canada sous le Régime Français.* Volume 1 (Ottawa: F. Acland, 1925), p. 3; François Leblanc, *Traite Historique de Monnoies de France* (Amsterdam: Chez Pierre Mortier, 1692), pp. 328 – 9. Weights, purity and ratings of French coins have been taken from Leblanc, Shortt and Dutot, *Reflexions Politique Sur les Finances et le Commerce...*(The Hague: Frères-Vaillant and N. Prevost, 1738). Unless otherwise noted, Shortt's *Documents* is the source for material in this chapter.
2. Leblanc, *Traite Historique,* p. 303; Shortt, *Documents,* Volume 1, pp. 545 and 567.
3. Leblanc, *Traite Historique,* p. 304.
4. R.C. Willey, "A Canadian Numismatic Dictionary" *Canadian Numismatic Journal,* Volume 16, No. 11, November 1971, p. 140 "Sous Marque".
5. "for the risks of the sea". Shortt, *Documents,* pp. 2 – 4.
6. Louise Dechêne, *Habitants et Marchands de Montréal au XVIIᵉ Siècle* (Montréal: Librairie Plon, 1974), p. 131n.
7. The rationale is generally deprecated by theorists who argue that overvaluation of the coinage simply causes prices to rise an equivalent amount thereby nullifying any benefit gained by raising the value of the coinage. Experience of successive revaluations of coins in the Thirteen Colonies also suggested that overvaluation in one colony was often countered by overvaluations in neighbouring colonies.
8. W.J. Eccles, "The Social, Economic and Political Significance of the Military in New France", *Canadian Historical Review,* Volume 52, No. 1, March 1971, p. 3.
9. R.W. McLachlan, "Annals of the Nova Scotia Currency", *Transactions of the Royal Society of Canada,* 1892, Section II, p. 33 states that several specimens of the special coinage have been found in Nova Scotia but only one in Quebec.
10. After 1760 the British government raised money in Quebec by selling bills drawn on the British treasury or other departments, to merchants in Quebec for coin.

The French government used a similar system as early as 1686. Presumably the procedure described here, in which the bills were drawn on the merchants, not on the government, was related to the government's policy of importing goods and selling them to the colonists. These sales would have established credits with the Quebec merchants on whom the government could then draw bills.

11. Beginning with the issues of 1729, card money was issued on playing card stock, not on actual playing cards.

12. "Otherwise it would appear very odd that money which the Treasurer's agent receives at the half of its original value – this same agent should issue at the same time on the basis of its original value, for the expenditures which his Majesty makes." Shortt, *Documents*, Volume 1, pp. 300 – 1.

13. Shortt, *Documents*, Volume 1, pp. 3, 111, 113, 347, 459, 473 – 7, 505, 517, 525, 529 – 33, 553, 557, 561; Leblanc, *Traite Historique*, pp. 305 – 6, 328 – 9; Dutot, *Reflexions*, pp. 20, 28, 111.

14. Alice J.E. Lunn, *Economic Development in New France* (McGill University, Ph.D. thesis, 1942), pp. 396 – 98; Guy Frégault, *Le XVIIIe Siècle Canadien: Études* (Montréal: Collections Constantes, Editions HMH, 1968), p. 297.

15. Lunn, *Economic Development*, p. 397 – 98; Frégault, *XVIIIe Siècle*, pp. 297, 305.

16. Guy Frégault, *La Civilization de la Nouvelle-France, 1713 – 1744* (Montréal: Société des Editions Pascal, 1944), p. 85.

17. Shortt, *Documents*, Vol. 2, p. 659. For an explanation of the various types of paper money in circulation see pp. 605 – 07n, 705 – 07n.

18. *Ibid.*, pp. 615, 625, 657, 659, 669, 751. Lunn, *Economic Development*, pp. 408, 416, 417, 421.

19. Shortt, *Documents*, pp. 657 – 63.

20. This money was issued over a period of 2 years; 50,250 livres in April 1734, 30,000 livres in October 1734, 47,850 livres in May 1735 and the remainder in 1736. It was in 24, 12, 6 and 3 livres and 30, 15 and 7.5 sols denominations.

21. Frégault, *Le XVIIIe Siècle*, pp. 320 – 21.

22. *Ibid.*, p. 324; Shortt, *Documents*, Volume II, pp. 673 – 77, 685 – 89.

23. The home government had sent out 6,000 livres of sols marqués of 27 and 18 denier to supply the need for change in 1732. In 1733, a more substantial shipment of 57,148 livres 18 sols 10 denier was sent to help balance the budget.

24. Shortt, *Documents*, p. 945.

25. Public Archives of Canada (PAC), Annual Report, 1918, Appendix B, *Ordinances and Proclamations of the Règne Militaire*, pp. 3 – 4, 84 – 85; A.L. Burt, *The Old Province of Quebec* (Toronto: McClelland and Stewart, 1968), p. 42.

26. J.-P. Proulx, *Histoire et naufrage des navires Le Saphire, La Marguerite, Le Murinet et l'Auguste* (Ottawa: Parcs Canada, travail inédit, v. 337), pp. 42 – 43.

27. Charles Bradley, *Coins from the Auguste* (Ottawa: Parks Canada, National Historic Parks and Sites: unpublished paper).

Chapter Two   The Province of Quebec, Lower Canada, Upper Canada, The Province of Canada and the Dominion of Canada, 1760 – 1900

1. PAC, Annual Report, 1918, Appendix B, p. 58; F. Ouellet, *Histoire Economique et Sociale du Québec, 1760 – 1850* (Montréal: Fides, 1966), p. 60.

2. PAC, Annual Report, 1918, Appendix B, pp. 3 – 4, 39, 58, 88, 134.

3. The Blue Books were statistical reports submitted annually by the governor of each colony to the Colonial Office.

4. PAC, MG11, CO44, Volume 1, pp. 5 – 8, Ordinance of 14 September 1764. Ouellet, *Histoire*, p. 61. In a petition dated 8 September 1764 some Quebec and Montreal merchants requested the establishment of New England currency because it was similar to French currency. A more numerously signed petition, dated 6 September 1764, requested the retention of Halifax or Quebec currency. PAC, RG4, A1, Volume 11, pp. 4364 – 72.

5. PAC, Annual Report, 1918, Appendix B, p. 39.

6. A. Shortt "The Early History of Canadian Banking", *Journal of the Canadian Bankers Association*, Volume 4, 1896 – 97, pp. 131 and 136; PAC, MG11, Q, Volume 3, pp. 176 – 77, Irving to Lords of Trade, 7 July 1766.

7. The ordinance undervalued gold and overvalued silver. On the basis of the silver and gold content of the shilling and the guinea the ratio was 15.87 to 1. The overall ratio established by the ordinance was 15.31 to 1 and the ratio for the French silver and gold coins was 15.57 to 1. Although the ordinance underrated gold according to the British standard, the British standard did not reflect European market conditions; in 1765 the Hamburg market established a ratio of 14.8 to 1. Hence the official British ratio overvalued gold, and silver coin almost disappeared from England in the eighteenth century. Evidently Canada responded to the British market and not to the European market: gold, which was undervalued in Canada, could be shipped to England, where it was overvalued, to pay Canadian debts. World silver/gold price ratios are taken from tables in J.L. Laughlin *The History of Bimetallism in the United States* (New York: D Appleton and Co., 1895), pp. 220 – 26.

8. PAC, Annual Report, 1913, Appendix E, *Ordinances Made for the Province of Quebec since the Establishment of Civil Government until 1767*, pp. 69 – 70; 5 George III, An ordinance in addition to an ordinance published the fourth day of October last 'For Regulating and Establishing the Currency of this Province", 15 May 1765.

9. Shortt, *Banking*, Volume 4, pp. 136 – 137; PAC, MG11, Q, Volume 8, pp. 171 – 3; Cramahé to —, 17 August 1772. The evidence for the widespread use of bons in central Canada up to the period of the War of 1812 comes almost entirely from contemporary literature. There is little identifiable evidence in contemporary account books or in estate inventories of their use. I am indebted to Professor Douglas McCalla of Trent University for drawing this anomaly to my attention.

10. R.C. Willey, "Proclamation Money in Canada", *Canadian Numismatic Journal*, Volume 21, No. 9, October 1976, p. 373. H.A. Fleming, "Halifax Currency", *Nova Scotia Historical Society Collections*, Volume 20, 1921, p. 122; PAC, Annual Report, 1914, Appendix C, pp. 9 – 10, PAC, MG11, Q, Volume 3, pp. 176 – 77. Irving to Lords of Trade, 7 July 1766.

11. On the other hand a private account in the Lawrence Ermatinger papers dated 12 April 1777 records a loss on a number of half-Johannes, quarter-Johannes, moidores and guineas as a result of the change from Quebec to Halifax currency. Presumably this means that Ermatinger kept his accounts in Quebec currency until it was formally abandoned in 1777. PAC, MG19, A2, Series 3, Volume 66, p. 543.

12. H.A. Innis and A.R.M. Lower, *Selected Documents in Canadian Economic History* (Toronto: University of Toronto Press, 1933); Volume 1, p. 543 – 5.

13. J. Gwyn, "The Impact of British Military Spending on the Colonial American Money Markets, 1760 – 1783", *Canadian Historical Association, Historical Papers*, 1980, p. 83.

14. PAC, MG21, Add MSS 21706, pp. 15 – 17, Treasury to Day, 20 June 1776; *Ibid.*, Add. MSS. 21715, pp. 98 – 102, Haldimand to the Secretary of the Treasury, 27 July 1782.

15. PAC, MG21, Add MSS 21707, fol. 128, Petition from merchants, 1783.
16. A.B. McCullough, "Aaron Hart's Treasure: A Sample of late Eighteenth Century Coinage in Lower Canada", *The Canadian Numismatic Journal*, Volume 28, No. 1, January 1983, pp. 8 – 9.
17. Innis and Lower, *Selected Documents*, Volume 1, pp. 368 – 69.
18. F. duc de la Rochefoucault Liancourt, *Travels through the United States of North America*...(London: R. Philips, 1799), pp. 216 – 17.
19. PAC, MG23, H, I, 1, Volume 3, pp. 5 – 7, McGill to Simcoe, 8 January 1793.
20. PAC, MG11, Q, Volume 280 – 2, pp. 307 – 57, Simcoe to——, 1 September 1794.
21. A. Barton Hepburn, *A History of Currency in the United States*. (New York: Augustus M. Kelley, 1967), p. 87; Shortt, "Banking", Volume 4, 1896 – 97, p. 246; 50 George III, C.4, 1810, Upper Canada; 51 George III, C.10, 1811, Lower Canada.
22. PAC, RGI, E1, Volume 112, State Book E, fol. 149 – 61, 14 April 1788.
23. R.W. McLachlan, "The Copper Currency of the Canadian Banks, 1837 – 57", *Transactions of the Royal Society of Canada*, 1903, Section II, p. 218 – 9; 38 George III, C.67, 1798, Great Britain.
24. PAC, RG8, C-322, p. 171, Hale to Hunter, 3 April 1802; see Table 40 for bill prices.
25. Hugh Gray, *Letters from Canada, Written During a Residence there in the years 1806, 1807, and 1808*...(London: Printed for Longman, Hurst, Rees and Orme, 1809), pp. 105, 186; A.B. McCullough, "Canadian Sterling Bill of Exchange Rates, 1760 – 1899", unpublished paper presented at the 13th Conference on Quantitative Methods in Canadian Economic History, Wilfrid Laurier University, 16 – 17 March 1984, Table 2.
26. R.H. Flemming, "Phyn, Ellice and Company of Schenectady", *Contributions to Canadian Economics*, Volume 4 (Toronto: The University of Toronto Library, published by the Librarian, 1932), p. 30; PAC, MG19, B5, Volume 3, p. 67, Phyn and Ellice to Van Vlick and Son, 30 April 1774; *Ibid.*, p. 179, Phyn and Ellice to Todd, 20 January 1775; John J. McCusker, *Money and Exchange in Europe and America, 1660 – 1775: A Handbook* (Williamsburg: Institute of Early American History and Culture, 1978), p. 232; PAC, MG13, WO34, Volume 198, p. 276, Amherst to Barrow, 15 October 1760; PAC, MG19, A2, Series 1, Volume 1, pp. 108 – 9, Ermatinger to Reade and Yates, 11 January 1772.
27. PAC, RG1, E1, Volume 35, pp. 263 – 70, 287-320, 6 July and 10 July 1812; 52 George III, C.1, 1812, L.C.; PAC MG11, Q, Volume 118, pp. 97 – 99, 6 August 1812.
28. 53 George III, C.3, 1813, L.C.; 54 George III, C.3, 1814, L.C; James Stevenson, "The Circulation of Army Bills with Some Remarks Upon the War of 1812", *Transactions of the Literary and Historical Society of Quebec*, No. 21, 1891 – 92, pp. 55 – 56.
29. Quebec*Mercury*, 29 September 1812; PAC, MG13, WO57, Volume 14, Robinson to Herries, 27 October 1812.
30. PAC, RG8, C-1219, pp. 52 – 53, Prevost to Bathurst, 6 June 1813; PAC, RG8, C-118, pp. 47 – 48, Riall to Drummond, 8 March 1814; William Canniff reports that Quakers in the vicinity of Picton, Prince Edward County, refused to accept army bills in payment for their produce on the grounds that they were "born of war". They would, however, accept gold. *The Settlement of Upper Canada* (Belleville: Mika Silk Screening Limited, 1971) p. 557.
31. PAC, MG30, D101, Volume 8, Scott, Powell and Campbell to Drummond, 10 January 1814.
32. PAC, RG8, C-330, pp. 192 – 95, 1 December 1814; *Ibid.*, pp. 189 – 91, Green to Freer, 29 October 1814; PAC, MG11, Q, Volume 127, pp. 172 – 76, Prevost to Bathurst, 10 March 1814.
33. Hepburn, *History of Currency*, pp. 87 and 129.

34. The charter received by the Bank of Upper Canada at York had been intended for the bank at Kingston which was also known as the Bank of Upper Canada. A special committee of the executive council, which was dominated by York interests, amended the Kingston bank to include a new set of directors and transferred the principal place of business from Kingston to York. The Bank of Upper Canada at Kingston (referred to contemptuously by the promoters at York as the "so-called" or "pretended" Bank of Upper Canada) carried on as a private bank until 1822 when it failed. C.J. Taylor, "The Bank of Upper Canada", Historic Sites and Monuments Board of Canada, Agenda Paper, November 1979.

35. PAC, RG8, C-145, pp. 175 – 76, Routh to Clegg, 27 October 1832.

36. PAC, MG11, Q, Volume 334, pp. 288 – 93, Robinson to Wilmot, 28 January 1823.

37. Merril Denison, *Canada's First Bank: A History of the Bank of Montreal*, Volume 1, (New York: Dodd Mead and Co., 1966 – 67), p. 258; PAC, C047, Volume 142, 1823, Blue Books, U.C.

38. PAC, MG11, Q, Volume 325 – 1, pp. 185 – 86, Maitland to Goulbourn, 7 May 1819.

39. PAC, MG30, D101, Volume 1, Kingston *Gazette*, 9 December 1815.

40. John MacTaggart, *Three Years in Canada: An Account of the Actual State of the Country in 1826 – 7 - 8* (London: H. Colburn, 129), p. 320.

41. Upper Canada, Journals of the Assembly, 1830, Appendix: Report of a Select Committee on The State of the Currency, p. 22.

42. H.S. Chapman, *Thoughts on the Money and Exchange of Lower Canada* (Montreal: Printed at the Gazette Office, 1832), p.7; Robert Chalmers, *A History of Currency in the British Colonies* (London: Printed for H.M. Stationery Office by Eyre and Spottiswoode, 1893), p. 184. The predominance of French silver in circulation in Lower Canada cannot be confirmed by reference to the holdings of banks and other institutions. A survey of the Bank of Montreal and Bank of Quebec vaults in 1828 and 1829 showed that roughly 58% (by number, not value) of the coins in their values were half-dollars, 11.5% were French half-crowns, 10% pistareens, 9% quarter-dollars, 6% dollars, 5% French crowns, with shillings, 5-franc pieces and gold coins making up insignificant proportions of the total. The high proportion of dollars and their parts in bank vaults may merely be an indication that they were held and the overvalued French crowns were put into circulation. Lower Canada, Journals of the Assembly, 1830, Appendix Q.

43. Upper Canada, Journals of the Assembly, 1830, Appendix: Report of a Select Committee on the State of the Currency, p. 29.

44. Denison, *Canada's First Bank*, p. 290.

45. Lower Canada, Journals of the Assembly, 1828 – 29, Appendix Hh, Testimony of B. Holmes.

46. Thomas Fowler, *The Journal of a Tour Through British America to the Falls of Niagara*...(Aberdeen: Lewis Smith, 1832), pp. 201, 210, 213, 220, 254; PAC, RG4, C1, Volume 36, pp. 22964 – 23007, Macaulay to Harrison, 19 December 1840.

47. A. Shortt, "Banking", Volume 9, p. 272; Chalmers, *Currency in the British Colonies*, p. 26.

48. For an analysis of the contradiction between R. Chalmer's point of view and that of the Lower Canadian legislature, see Appendix B.

49. PAC, MG11, C042, Volume 209, fol. 295 – 98, Dalhousie to Bathurst, 19 June 1826, enclosing an address of the Legislative Council.

50. Chalmers, *Currency in the British Colonies*, pp. 184, 193; Lower Canada, Journals of the Assembly, 1830, Appendix Q, Routh to Couper, 1 October 1829.

51. A. Shortt, "Currency and Banking" in *Canada and its Provinces: A History of the Canadian People and Their Institutions*, Volume 4, ed. A. Shortt and A.G. Doughty. (Printed by T.A. Constable at the University of Edinburgh Press, 1913), p. 619; PAC, MG11, Q, Volume 242 – 1, pp. 212 – 16, Buchanan to Grey, 19 May 1837.

52. PAC, RG8, C-145, pp. 175 – 76, Routh to Clegg, 27 October 1832.

53. Shortt, "Banking", Volume 9, 1901 – 02, p. 3; Denison, *Canada's First Bank*, p. 298. The Banque du Peuple issued notes as early as 1839 although it was not incorporated until 1843 under 7 Victoria, C.66.

54. Shortt, "Banking", Volume 9, 1901 – 02, p. 105; R.M. Breckenridge, *The History of Banking in Canada* (Washington: Government Printing Office, 1910), p. 39. The reduction in circulation in Upper Canada occurred during the initial stages of the panic, before the banks suspended. After the banks suspended, circulation increased. A. Redish, "The Economic Crisis of 1837 – 1839 in Upper Canada: Case Study of a Temporary Suspension of Specie Payments", *Explorations in Economic History*, Volume 20, 1983, Figure 1, p. 405.

55. Shortt, "Banking", Volume 9, 1901-02, pp. 107-27.

56. *Ibid.*, p. 19.

57. 10 – 11 George IV, C.5 and 2 Victoria, C.57 in Lower Canada, and 7 William IV, C.13 in Upper Canada limited the right to issue notes to chartered banks.

58. PAC, MG11, CO42, Volume 242, pp. 328 – 34, Aylmer to Goderich, 15 April 1833.

59. Sir Duncan Gibb, "My Early Experiences of Numismatics in Canada", *Canadian Antiquarian and Numismatic Journal* 1874 – 75, pp. 67 – 73.

60. PAC, MG11, Q, Volume 356, pp. 168 – 69, Colborne to Goderich, 9 April 1831; *Ibid.*, Q, Volume 358 – 1, p. 54, Stewart to Hay, 3 August 1831; PAC, RG 5, A1, Volume 118, pp. 66300 – 3, Allan to Rowan, 19 July 1832; *Ibid.*, pp. 66431 – 3, Allan to Rowan, 31 July 1831; PAC, MG30, D101, Volume 9, Kingston *Herald*, 29 August 1832.

61. McLachlan, "Copper Currency", pp. 220 – 21, 236.

62. R.W. McLachlan, "Some Reflections Upon Being Fifty Years a Coin Collector", *Canadian Numismatic Journal*, Volume 6, No. 12, December 1961, pp. 518.

63. In December 1841 the provincial inspector-general instructed customs officials to collect duties payable in sterling at the rate of 17s. 4d. sterling per £1 currency and 4s. 4d. per dollar, an effective rate of £115.38 currency per £100 sterling. These instructions were rendered obsolete by the 1841 currency act. PAC, RG5, C1, Volume 88, pp. 34465 – 68., No. 3487, Macaulay to Harrison, 12 May 1842.

64. PAC, RG8, C-151, pp. 182 – 86; *Ibid.*, pp. 195 – 97, Fidler to Taylor, 12 November 1842; *Ibid.*, p. 308; PAC, RG8, C-343, pp. 187 – 94, Reports of boards on military chests, March 1843; PAC, MG24, D16, Volume 84, 11 June 1846; *Ibid.*, Volume 85, p. 60357, 1 November 1856; Montreal *Gazette*, 14 January 1843, Advertisement for Wm. Gunn's *Exchange Tables*.

65. PAC, RG7, G20, Volume 30, No. 3413, Wickstead to Daly, 6 April 1844; Province of Canada, Journals of the Legislative Assembly 1841 – 50, Public Accounts; see also currency section of the Blue Books, 1844 – 55.

66. PAC, RG4, C1, Volume 36, pp. 22964 – 23007, Macaulay to Harrison, 19 December 1840.

67. PAC, MG30, D101, Volume 10, Kingston *Chronicle*, 7 May 1842.

68. PAC, RG4, C1, Volume 7, pp. 4093 – 99, No. 1118, Petition of merchants of Montreal, 11 March 1840; *Ibid.*, Volume 8, pp. 5225 – 32, No. 1378, Routh, Moffat, McGill to Murdock, 31 March 1840; PAC, MG30, D101, Volume 10, Montreal *Gazette*, 11 June 1840; PAC, RG8, C-1306, pp. 384 – 85, Rowan to Robinson, 20 March 1852; PAC, RG8, C-156, pp. 119 – 23, Robinson to Rowan, 22 March 1852.

69. 4 – 5 Victoria, C.29, 1841, Province of Canada.

70. PAC, RG1, Volume 84, State Book U, pp. 516 – 21, 24 December 1860.

71. Shortt, "Banking", Volume 11, pp. 27 – 30, 323 – 27; S. Turk, "Some Notes on Foreign Exchange in Canada before 1919", File in the Bank of Canada Library.

72. Shortt, "Banking", Volume 11, pp. 217 – 18, 310 – 12; Breckenridge, *History of Banking in Canada*, p. 71.

73. Chalmers, *Currency of the British Colonies*, p. 201. Readers specifically interested in banking and the financial system after 1867 may read E.P. Neufeld, *The Financial System of Canada*, or R. Craig McIvor, *Canadian Monetary, Banking and Financial Development*.

74. C.A. Curtis, "Statistics of Banking", *Statistical Contributions to Canadian Economic History*, ed. K.W. Taylor (Toronto: Macmillan Company of Canada Ltd., 1937), pp. 3 – 4, 20, 92.

75. 34 Victoria, C.4, 1871, Canada; 38 Victoria, C.49, 1874, Canada; 44 Victoria, C.4, 1881, Canada.

76. Army Bills – 52 George III, C.1, 1812 L.C; 53 George III, C.3, 1813, L.C.; 54 George III, C.3, 1814, L.C.; Canada, Journals of the Legislative Assembly, 1816, App B; *Ibid.*, 1817, App. D; *Ibid.*, 1818, App. C. Bank-notes – those marked "B" are from the reports on currency in the Blue Books in PAC, C047. Others are from PAC, MG24, A12, Reel A-533, Nos. 276 – 86; Lower Canada, Journals of the Assembly, 1823 – 4, App. M; *Ibid.*, 1825, App. N; *Ibid.*, 1826; App. I; *Ibid.*, 1827, App. E; *Ibid.*, 1828 – 9. App. K; *Ibid.*, 1830, App. N; *Ibid.*, 1831, App. M; *Ibid.*, 1832, App. U; *Ibid.*, 1834, App. S; *Ibid.*, 1835, App. S; Upper Canada, Journals of the Assembly, 21 Feb. 1823, p. 333; *Ibid.*, 1828, p. 61; *Ibid.*, 1829, p. 67; *Ibid.*, 1830, p. 56; *Ibid.*, 1831, p. 31; *Ibid.*, 1833, p. 118; *Ibid.*, 1833 – 34, pp. 65 – 66; *Ibid.*, 1837, Report on the Monetary System; *Ibid.*, 1836 – 37, p. 128; Province of Canada, Journals of the Assembly, 1841, App. O; *Ibid.*, 1849, App. Z; *Ibid.*, 1849, App. P; *Ibid.*, 1850, App. H; *Ibid.*, 1851, App. I; *Ibid.*, 1852 – 53, App. R; *Ibid.*, 1854, App. EE. Bank-note circulation in central Canada varied by about 15% on a seasonal basis. In Upper Canada in the 1840s circulation was high from October through April with a peak in February. Expansion in circulation was necessary to finance the purchase and transportation of agricultural produce; generally speaking, produce could only be transported overland to shipping centres during the winter when roads were frozen or sledding was possible, hence the peak in circulation in February. In Lower Canada commercial activity was governed by navigation on the St. Lawrence and circulation rose gradually during the summer to a peak in October and then fell off rapidly to a low in January when the river was frozen. The total circulation by month of five Lower Canadian banks, including the Bank of British North America and three Upper Canadian banks, as a percentage of the median circulation in each province, 1841 – 49, is given below. Median in Upper Canada £2,774,000, and in Lower Canada, £5,600,000.

	Lower Canada	Upper Canada
January	96%	102%
February	99	107
March	99	104
April	99	103
May	100	98
June	100	92
July	100	93
August	102	92
September	107	97
October	111	103
November	103	102
December	99	98

Source: Province of Canada, Journals of the Legislative Assembly, 1841, Appendix O.

Chapter Three   Acadia, Ile Royale and Nova Scotia

1. Adam Shortt, *Documents Relatifs à la Monnaie, au Change et aux Finances du Canada sous le Régime Français*, Volume 1 (Ottawa: F. Acland, 1925), pp. 125 – 27, 135.
2. "a great deal of money in Acadia but the inhabitants don't put it in circulation". *Ibid.*, pp. 135 – 37, 204.
3. *Ibid.*, Volume 2, pp. 735 – 47, 795 – 97.
4. C. Moore, "The Other Louisbourg: Trade and Merchant Enterprise in Ile Royale, 1713 – 58", *Histoire Sociale – Social History*, Volume 12, No. 23, May 1979, p. 86.
5. Shortt, *Documents*, Volume 2, p. 811n.
6. Moore, "The Other Louisbourg", pp. 84 – 85.
7. K. Donovan, "Inflation at Louisbourg – 1757" (Unpublished manuscript, Fortress of Louisbourg, National Historic Park, 1980), p. 2.
8. Moore, "The Other Louisbourg", pp. 92 – 93. The government and merchants may have put less formal types of paper money such as acquits or ordonnances into circulation in the colony and some paper money from Canada may have found its way to Louisbourg either directly by way of trade or through the Acadians. Shortt, *Documents*, Volume 2, p. 691n.
9. Shortt, *Documents*, Volume 2, p. 719.
10. P.N. Moogk, "A Pocketful of Change at Louisbourg", *Canadian Numismatic Journal*, Volume 21, No. 3, March 1976, pp. 97 – 104.
11. J.J. McCusker, *Money and Exchange in Europe and America, 1660 – 1775: A Handbook* (Williamsburg: Institute of Early American History and Culture, 1978), pp. 131 – 34 and Table 3.1.
12. Adam Shortt, *Documents Relating to Currency, Exchange and Finance in Nova Scotia with Prefatory Documents* (Ottawa: King's Printer, 1933), pp. 37 – 38.
13. *Ibid.*, pp. 64 – 65, 93.
14. A.M. Macmechan, ed., *Nova Scotia Archives III, Original Minutes of His Majesty's Council at Annapolis Royal, 1720 – 1739* (Halifax: 1908), p. 141.
15. Public Archives of Nova Scotia (PANS), RG1, Volume 20, p. 57, 11 March 1730 – 31; McCusker, *Money and Exchange*, pp. 140 – 41.
16. In 1740, 1 livre was valued at 4s. New England currency; by 1748 1 livre was valued at 6s. 4.8d. Shortt, *Finance, Currency and Exchange in Nova Scotia*, pp. 211, 273.
17. *Ibid.*, p. 234.
18. *Ibid.*, pp. 243 – 45, 249 – 50, 256 – 57.

19. *Ibid.*, pp. 314 – 15, 327 – 28.
20. R. McQuade, "Halifax Currency in Nova Scotia", *Canadian Numismatic Journal*, Volume 21, No. 10, November 1976, pp. 399 – 402; 32 George II, C.7, 1758, N.S., text in PAC, MG11, CO219, Volume 5, ff. 60 – 61.
21. Shortt, *Finance, Currency and Exchange in Nova Scotia*, pp. 295 – 96, 372.
22. *Ibid.*, pp. 320 – 22.
23. PAC, MG11, NSA, Volume 72, pp. 80 – 93, 29 October 1763, State and Condition of Nova Scotia; PAC, MG11, NSA, Volume 77, pp. 214 – 25, Green to Lords of Trade, 24 August 1766; PAC, MG11, NSC, Volume 6, pp. 176, 183, 4 – 6 November 1766.
24. PAC, MG11, NSA, Volume 72, pp. 80 – 93, 29 October 1763, State and Condition of Nova Scotia.
25. PAC, MG11, NSA, Volume 13, pp. 188 – 89, 31 July 1765; PAC, MG11, NSB, Volume 14, p. 26, 8 August 1766; *Ibid.*, p. 149, 1 August 1767.
26. PAC, MG11, NSA, Volume 80, pp. 183 – 210, Lord William Campbell to the Lords of Trade, (1767).
27. PAC, MG11, NSB, Volume 14, pp. 181 – 83, 7 January 1768.
28. PAC, MG11, NSA, Volume 91, pp. 62 – 66, Address of the Assembly to Legge, 22 October 1774.
29. PAC, MG11, CO219, Volume 13, pp. 119 – 21, No. 216; PAC, MG11, CO219, Volume 14, pp. 118 – 19, No. 263; PAC, MG30, D101, Volume 43, Public Records of Nova Scotia, No. 286.
30. PAC, MG11, NSD, Volume 11, pp. 183 – 88, 18 July 1775.
31. Shortt, *Finance, Currency and Exchange*, pp. 307 – 08; PAC, MG11, NSA, Volume 70, pp. 127 – 28, Mauger to Pownall, 5 March 1763; Table 41.
32. PAC, MG11, NSA, Volume 70, pp. 150 – 51, Board of Trade to Belcher, 16 March 1763; *Ibid.*, Volume 72, pp. 124 – 27, Memorial of Mauger to Board of Trade, 8 December 1763; PAC, MG23, I 13, Volume 2.
33. PAC, MG11, NSA, Volume 78, pp. 187 – 93, Joint Address to the King, 22 November 1766; PAC, MG11 NSC, Volume 6, p. 176, 4 November 1766.
34. PAC, MG11, NSA, Volume 99, pp. 52 – 61, Hughes to Germain, c. April 1779.
35. PAC, MG11, NSA, Volume 94, p. 263, Legge to Dartmouth, 27 November 1775; *Ibid.*, pp. 338 – 44, Legge to Dartmouth, 26 December 1775; *Ibid.*, Volume 96, pp. 19 – 20 Knox to Arbuthnot, 11 June 1776.
36. PAC, MG11, NSA, Volume 101, pp. 321 – 27, Hammond to Germaine, 27 November 1781; *Ibid.*, Volume 100, pp. 159 – 64, 173 – 67, McLean to Germain, 13 and 20 November 1780.
37. PAC, MG11, NSC, Volume 12, p. 53, minutes of council, 3 July 1782.
38. PAC, MG11, NSD, Volume 15, p. 98, 29 November 1784; *Ibid.*, p. 182, 14 December 1785.
39. PAC, MG11, NSA, Volume 117, pp. 165 – 170, Wentworth to Dundas, 27 June 1792; *Ibid.*, pp. 225 – 50, Wentworth to Dundas, 25 October 1792.
40. PAC, MG11, CO217, Volume 144, pp. 172 – 73, Wallace to Bathurst, 16 July 1825.
41. PAC, MG11, NSA, Volume 129, pp. 70 – 71, Wentworth to Portland, 10 April 1799.
42. J.S. Martell, *A Documentary History of Provincial Finance and Currency, 1812 – 36*, Bulletin of the Public Archives of Nova Scotia, Volume 2, No. 4, 1941, p. 13; PAC, MG11, NSA, Volume 148, pp. 153 – 54, General Order, 14 November 1811; *The Free Press* (Halifax), 28 February 1825, Plutus to Mr. Ward.
43. PAC, MG40, J2, HAL/A/4B, Inglefield to ———, 13 January 1810.
44. PAC, MG12, Adm. 106, Volume 2028, Inglefield to the Navy Board, 13 January 1811.
45. PAC, MG11, NSA, Volume 159, pp. 144 – 43, Wallace to Dalhousie, 1 July 1818.
46. Nova Scotia, House of Assembly, Journals, p. 184, 23 March 1818.

47. PAC, RG8, C-1337, p. 101, Dalhousie to Bathurst, 18 July 1818; PAC, MG30, D101, Volume 47, Public Records of Nova Scotia, Manuscripts, Volume 228, Document No. 121, Haden to ———, 10 April 1819; *Ibid.*, Haden to Howe, 30 January 1822.

48. PAC, MG11, NSA, Volume 94, pp. 48 - 53, 92 - 101, Legge to Dartmouth, 31 July 1775; PAC, MG11 NSD, Volume 11, pp. 183 - 88, 18 July 1775.

49. PAC, MG30, D101, Volume 46, Acadian *Recorder,* 14 March 1818; 59 George III, C.9, 1819, N.S.

50. PAC, MG30, D101, Volume 47, Halifax *Journal,* 25 November 1822, "A Retailer" to the editor.

51. *Ibid.*, Acadian *Recorder,* 3 January 1824. A. Drapier to Holland and Co.

52. PAC, MG30, D101, Volume 47, Acadian *Recorder,* 16 and 23 September 1820, "Senex" to the editor.

53. V. Ross, *History of the Canadian Bank of Commerce,* Vol. 1, p. 36, provides an illustration of one of these notes in which the denomination is given as 2 dollars.

54. PAC, MG11, CO217, Volume 145, ff. 95 - 99, Forbes to Harrison, 27 February 1825.

55. PAC, MG30, D101, Volume 47, *Free Press* 28 February 1825, Plutus to Mr. Ward.

56. PAC, MG11, CO217, Volume 144, pp. 437 - 44, Wallace to Bathurst, 16 July 1825.

57. PAC, MG30, D101, Volume 48, *Nova Scotian,* 17 February 1829; PAC, MG11, CO221, Volume 43, p. 126 does not confirm the fall in value of the doubloon and it may have been temporary.

58. PAC, MG30, D101, Volume 48, Nova Scotia *Royal Gazette,* 14 April 1830.

59. 28 George III, C.9, 1787, N.S. A correspondent in the *Free Press,* 28 February 1825, stated that crowns, although legally rated at 5s. 6d., seldom passed for more than a dollar.

60. PAC, MG30, D101, Volume 47, *Nova Scotian,* 29 March 1826.

61. 7 George IV, C.19, 1826, N.S.

62. PAC, MG11, CO221, Volume 48, p. 131; *Ibid.*, Volume 49, p. 131; *Nova Scotian,* 22 January 1834, "Public Meeting".

63. 6 William IV, C.41, 1836, N.S.; *Ibid.*, C.32, 1836, N.S.; PAC, MG11, CO221, Volume 50, p. 79.

64. PAC, MG11, CO221, Volume 49, p. 131 and Volume 50, p. 179; 6 William IV, C.41, 1836, N.S.; 2 Victoria, C.37, 1839, N.S.

65. 5 Victoria, C.8, 1842, N.S.; PAC, MG11, CO217, Volume 184, ff. 73 - 74, Johnston and Uniacke to George, 18 July 1843.

66. For an account of the bank war see Ross, *Canadian Bank of Commerce,* p. 83; Martell *Provincial Finance and Currency,* pp. 22-23; PAC, MG30, D101, Volume 48, *Nova Scotian,* 4 December 1833; *Ibid.*, Volume 49, Nova Scotia *Royal Gazette,* 22 January 1834.

67. PAC, MG30, D101, Volume 49, Public Records of Nova Scotia, Volume 240, No. 103, Lawson to Jeffery, 27 May 1834; Nova Scotia, House of Assembly, Journals, 4 December 1834, p. 716; Ross, *Canadian Bank of Commerce,* p.83.

68. Ross, *Canadian Bank of Commerce,* p. 62.

69. W.S. Moorsom, *Letters from Nova Scotia: Comprising the Sketches of a Young Country* (London: H. Colburn and R. Bentley, 1830), pp. 86-88, 291-292.

70. PAC, MG30, D101, Volume 48, Nova Scotia *Royal Gazette,* 19 September 1832.

71. Ross, *Canadian Bank of Commerce,* pp. 76, 476; J.E. Charlton, *Standard Catalogue of Canadian Coins, Tokens and Paper Money,* 26th edition (Toronto: International Publishing Inc., 1978), pp. 250, 274; Bank of Nova Scotia, *History of the Bank of Nova Scotia 1832 - 1900,* p. 64.

72. PAC, MG30, D101, Volume 49, *Nova Scotian,* 10 February 1836; Nova Scotia, House of Assembly, Journals, 11 February 1835, p. 853; *Nova Scotian,* 14 November 1839, Letter from E. Cunard

73. PAC, MG30, D101, Volume 48, *Nova Scotian,* 15 June 1831; *Ibid.,* Public Records of Nova Scotia, Manuscripts, Volume 311, No. 4, Petition of Grand Jury, 20 January 1832.

74. Ross, *Canadian Bank of Commerce,* p. 90; Bank of Nova Scotia, *History of the Bank of Nova Scotia, 1832 – 1900,* p. 47; *Nova Scotian,* 13 September 1837.

75. PAC, MG11, CO221, Volume 72, p. 67; 24 Victoria, C.36, 1861, N.S.

76. Treasury notes, 1812 – 36 – J.S. Martell, *Provincial Finance and Currency,* p. 50; treasury notes 1838 – 66 – Nova Scotia, Journals of the House of Assembly, Reports of the Committee on Public Accounts; Bank of Nova Scotia, 1833 – 67 – *History of the Bank of Nova Scotia, 1832 – 1900;* Halifax Banking Company, 1830, 1832, and 1839 – Ross, *Canadian Bank of Commerce,* p. 60 and McLachlan, "Nova Scotia Currency", p. 35; all other figures are from the Nova Scotia Blue Books, PAC, MG11, CO221.

Chapter Four   New Brunswick

1. PAC, MG23, D2, Volume 4, Whitlock to Winslow, 24 September 1785. A shipment in September 1785 consisted of 1,768 guineas, 4 Johannes, 435 half-Johannes and 1,078 dollars.

2. *Nova Scotian,* 7 March 1833, Mr. Young on currency.

3. See note 1; PAC, MG11, NBA, Volume 3, pp. 34 – 40, Sydney to Carleton, 19 April 1786.

4. (James Pennington), *The Currency of the British Colonies* (London: Her Majesty's Stationery Office, 1848), pp. 91 – 92; Robert Chalmers, *A History of Currency in the British Colonies* (London: Printed for H.M. Stationery Office by Eyre and Spottiswoode, 1893), p. 192. In 1819 a correspondent in the Halifax *Acadian Recorder* reported that in New Brunswick the Louis d'or was received at £1 2s. 6d. and the French pistolle at 18s., English and Portuguese gold was received at 89s. per ounce and Spanish and French gold at 87s. per ounce; that is at the bulk rates which were provided for in the disallowed act. The correspondent also stated that the doubloon was accepted at $17.50 (£4 7s. 6d. currency) by private arrangement but that the legal rate was lower. PAC, MG30, D101, Volume 47, *Acadian Recorder,* 6 March 1819.

5. 47 George III, C.9, 1807, N.B.

6. PAC, MG13, WO57, Volumes 36 and 37, 25 August 1812, 8 May 1813 and 26 August 1814.

7. 58 George III, C.15, 1818, N.B.; PAC, MG30, D101, Volume 54, New Brunswick Executive Council Minutes, 17 July 1818; 59 George III, C.1, 1819, N.B.; 60 George III, C.9, 1820, N.B.

8. Chalmers, *Currency in the British Colonies,* p. 193.

9. Chalmers, *op. cit.*

10. *The City Gazette,* 15 April 1824.

11. A bill repealing 60 George III, C.25, was passed in 1824 but due to an error in the title of the repealing act it did not receive royal assent and a second repealing act was passed in 1826. PAC, MG11, CO188, Volume 33, p. 23, Douglas to Bathurst, 7 March 1826.

12. Lower Canada, Assembly Journals, 1830, Appendix Q, Routh to Couper, 1 October 1829; Chalmers, *Currency in the British Colonies,* p. 193.

13. The differing interpretations of the proper value of British silver are discussed in Appendix B. Essentially they hinge on the British Treasury's treatment of British silver as a token coinage, translatable into gold at a fixed rate and the colonial legislature's treatment of British silver as a true coinage. The repeal of 60 George III, C.25 had been considered in 1824 before the home government's plans had been received in New Brunswick and was motivated by problems resulting from the overvaluation of the Spanish dollar.

14. PAC, MG30, D101, Volume 54, 3 May 1820; *Ibid.*, New Brunswick *Courier*, 30 December 1837, 15 August 1835, 25 March 1843; Charlton, *Standard Catalogue*, 1978, p. 192.

15. Horace A. Flemming, "Halifax Currency", *Nova Scotia Historical Society Collections*, Volume 20, 1921, pp. 128 – 29; *Nova Scotian*, 14 November 1839.

16. Because of restrictions imposed by their charters several banks were unable to issue notes of less than £1 currency in spite of 1 Victoria, C.18, 1837 – 38, N.B. This put them at a disadvantage and in 1853, 16 Victoria, C.27 allowed all banks the privilege of issuing notes under £1.

17. PAC, MG30, D101, Volume 54, *Weekly Observer*, 23 June 1840; *Ibid.*, *Morning News*, 22 June 1840; *Ibid.*, New Brunswick *Courier*, 27 June 1840.

18. PAC, MG11, CO188, Volume 120, pp. 135 – 38, Head to Newcastle, 19 September 1853; PAC, MG9, A1, Volume 63, p. 3104, Robinson to (Wilmot), 27 January 1857; *Acadian Recorder*, 20 September 1862; S.S. Carroll, "New Brunswick Currency" *Canadian Numismatic Journal*, January 1970, Volume 15, No. 1, pp. 12 – 15.

19. PAC, MG30, D101, Volume 54, *Weekly Observer*, 23 June 1840, *Ibid.*, New Brunswick *Courier*, 3 September 1842.

20. PAC, MG11, CO199, Volume 12, No. 179, ff. 42 – 45; PAC, MG11, CO189, Volume 15, pp. 240 – 43, Glenelg to Harvey, 17 August 1838.

21. £3 17s. 9d. was the rating given the doubloon in the act of 1837 which was not confirmed. £3 17s. 6d. was a customary rate reported in the 1826 Blue Books.

22. *Nova Scotian*, 7 March 1833, Mr. Young speaking on the currency.

23. PAC, MG11, CO193, Volume 48, p. 255.

24. Totals are from the Blue Books in PAC, MG11, CO193; the totals probably include out-of-colony notes from banks which did not report to the legislature. The Bank of New Brunswick figure for 1821 is from PAC, MG19, A1, Volume 59, p. 1260. All other figures are from bank reports in the appendices to the Journals of the New Brunswick Assembly.

Chapter Five   Prince Edward Island

1. 25 George III, C.4, 1785, P.E.I.

2. PAC, MG11, CO229, PEI "B", Volume 10, pp. 38 – 39, 21 April 1806.

3. Sir J. Craig, *The Mint: A History of the London Mint from A.D. 287 to 1948* (Cambridge; University Press, 1953, pp. 262 – 263).

4. PAC, MG11, CO226, Volume 34, p. 61, Petition of Prince Edward Island Merchants, 24 January 1818.

5. PAC, MG11, CO226, Volume 45, pp. 389 – 401, Ready to Murray, 30 September 1828 and enclosures.

6. PAC, MG30, D101, Volume 56, P.E.I. *Register*, p. 2, 20 October 1825.

7. PAC, MG11, CO226, Volume 53, ff. 426 – 28, Spearman to Stephen, 8 March 1836; PAC, MG11, CO229, Volume 14, Prince Edward Island, Journal of the Legislative Council, 1847, Appendix 5, p. 300 (hereafter referred to as "Currency Commission").

8. Currency Commission, p. 294, Haviland to the Commission, 23 January 1847.

9. PAC, MG11, CO226, Volume 45, pp. 389 – 94, Ready to Murray, 30 September 1828.

10. *Nova Scotian*, 22 October 1835.

11. Currency Commission, p. 294, Haviland to the Commission, 23 January 1847; *Ibid.*, p. 301, *Ibid.*, p. 303 - 04, Brennan to the Commission, 4 Janauary 1847.
12. PAC, MG11, CO227, Volume 8, ff. 29 - 20, Spring Rice to Young, 22 July 1834; PAC, MG11, CO229, Volume 8, pp. 141 - 42, Spring Rice to Young, 16 October 1834.
13. PAC, MG11, CO226, Volume 68, ff. 294-6, Huntley to Stanley, 26 August 1845.
14. P.E.I., Journals of the House of Assembly, 4 May 1848, pp. 180 - 82; Prince Edward Island *Examiner*, 18 September 1847 and 19 August 1848.
15. Prince Edward Island, Journals of The House of Assembly, 1853, Appendix N, Bannerman to Colonial Secretary, 2 January 1852; *Ibid.*, 1854, Appendix G, Wilson to Merivale, 13 January 1854.
16. PAC, MG11, CO226, Volume 58, ff. 269 - 74, Fitzroy to Russell, 29 November 1839.
17. 5 Victoria, C.20, 1842, P.E.I.; Prince Edward Island, Journal of the Legislative Council, 1843, Appendix 11; PAC, MG11, CO226, Volume 64, ff. 87 - 94, Huntley to Stanley, 11 November 1842.
18. Chalmers *Currency of the British Colonies*, p. 197; Charlton, *Standard Catalogue*, 1978, p. 121, gives a figure of 2,000,000.
19. Treasury notes, coin, out-of-province bank-notes and U.S. notes – PAC, MG11, CO231, Blue Books 1825 - 71; treasury warrants – P.E.I., Journals of the Assembly, Auditor's Reports and Report of the Currency Commission; bank-notes – bank reports in P.E.I., Journals of the Assembly, and Blue Books.

Chapter Six   Newfoundland

1. The reports are in PAC, MG11, CO194. The 1740 report, PAC, MG11, CO194, Volume 24, pp. 195 - 6, mentioned payments in cash to American merchants.
2. E. Chappell, *Voyage to Newfoundland* (1814), p. 245 quoted in C.F. Rowe, "The Coins and Currency of Newfoundland", *Book of Newfoundland*, Volume 4, p. 503.
3. PAC, MG11, CO194, Volume 23, pp. 433 - 6, Darling to Waldegrave, 2 October 1798.
4. PAC, MG11, CO194, Volume 50, pp. 336 - 8, Duckworth to Liverpool, 29 October 1811.
5. PAC, MG11, CO194, Volume 59, pp. 128 - 30, Pickmore to Bathurst, 1 November 1817. A letter from Senex in the Acadian *Recorder*, 14 October 1820, also suggests that the increased rating of the dollar drove the paper out of circulation.
6. PAC, MG11, CO199, Volume 21, p. 102; *Ibid.*, Volume 22, p. 154; *Ibid.*, Volume 23, p. 160; *Nova Scotian*, 10 and 18 May 1826; PAC, MG11, CO194, Volume 76, ff. 359 - 61, Cochrane to Bathurst, 16 December 1828.
7. PAC, MG11, CO194, Volume 78, p. 117, Cochrane to Murray, 29 April 1829; *Ibid.*, Volume 72, pp. 328 - 30, Wannach to Brenton, 6 November 1826; R.H. Bonnycastle, *Newfoundland in 1842*, Volume II, (London: Henry Colburn, 1842), pp. 191 - 92; PAC, MG11, CO194, Volume 70, p. 239, Cochrane to Bathurst, 28 December 1825.
8. PAC, RG8, C-1338, C-1339 and C-1340.
9. Bonnycastle, *Newfoundland in 1842*, pp. 191–92; R.C. Willey, *Newfoundland and Magdalen Island Coinage*, pp. 373–74.
10. 7 Victoria, C.4; 1844, Newfoundland; PAC, MG11, CO194, Volume 123, ff. 107-9, Trevalyan to Stephen, 3 February 1845.
11. Chalmers, *Currency in the British Colonies*, p. 171; PAC, MG11, CO194, Volume 147, ff. 429-60, Darling to Labouchere, 14 June 1856; PAC, MG11, CO199, Volume 54, p. 159.
12. PAC, MG11, CO194, Volume 88, f. 350, Prescott to Spring-Rice, 21 November 1834; *Ibid.*, Volume 91, ff. 38–40, Prescott to Glenelg, 17 September 1835.
13. 9-10 Victoria, C.5, 1846, Newfoundland; PAC, MG11, CO194, Volume 127, ff. 631–36, Le Marchant to Grey, 31 December 1847.

14. 18-19 Victoria, C.12, 1855, Newfoundland; PAC, MG11, CO194, Volume 145, ff. 92-103, Darling to Molesworth, 14 September 1855; PAC, MG11, CO194, Volume 149, ff. 283-91, Wilson to Booth, 30 May 1856; *Ibid.*, Volume 148, ff. 319-26, Darling to Labouchere, 13 September 1856; *Ibid.*, Volume 151, ff. 594-610, Wilson to Merivale, 17 April 1857; *Ibid.*, ff. 612-15, Wilson to Elliott, 4 May 1857; PAC, MG11, CO199, Volume 53.

15. PAC, MG11, CO383, Volume 59, No. 30, An Act for the Establishment of a Savings Bank in Newfoundland. Rowe, "Coins and Currency of Newfoundland", pp. 506-7; PAC, MG11, CO199, Volume 38, Blue Books, 1841.

16. PAC, MG11, CO194, Volume 141, ff. 212-17, Hamilton to Grey, 21 July 1854.

17. PAC, MG11, CO199, Volume 55, f. 159.

18. PAC, MG11, CO194, Volume 147, ff. 429-60, Darling to Labouchere, 14 June 1856.

19. 25 Victoria, C.10, 1862, Newfoundland.

20. PAC, MG11, CO199, Blue Books.

21. 26 Victoria, C.18, 1863, Newfoundland; PAC, MG11, CO199, Volume 61, p. 159.

22. PAC, MG11, CO194, Volume 210, ff. 187-89, Blake to the Colonial Office, 28 September 1887.

23. PAC, MG11, CO199, Volume 76, pp. 83-85; *Ibid.*, Volume 78, p. 171; Chalmers, *Currency in the British Colonies*, pp. 173-74; Consolidated Statutes of Newfoundland, 1892, C.101.

24. A.R. Jamieson, *Chartered Banking in Canada* (Toronto: Ryerson Press, 1955), pp. 31-32; 58 Victoria, C.1 and C.2, 1895, Newfoundland.

Chapter Seven Western Canada

1. W.J. Noxon, *The Diary of Nicholas Garry, Deputy Governor of the Hudson's Bay Company* (Toronto: Canadiana House, 1973), p. 133.

2. R. Craig McIvor, *Canadian Monetary, Banking and Financial Development*, (Toronto: Macmillan and Co., 1961), pp. 86-88; L. Gingras, "Medals and Tokens of the HBC". *The Beaver*, Summer 1968, Outfit 299, pp. 37-43.

3. Larry Gingras, *Paper Money of the Hudson's Bay Company* (Published under the auspices of the Canadian Numismatic Research Society, 1969); R.H. Flemming, *Minutes of Council, Northern Department of Rupert Land 1821-31* (Toronto: The Champlain Society, 1940), pp. 300, 384-85.

4. PAC, MG20, A12/7, f. 463, Simpson to the Governor, 29 June 1855.

5. *Loc. cit.*; Great Britain, *Report from the Select Committee on the Hudson's Bay Company; together with the Proceedings of the Committee, Minutes of Evidence, Appendix and Index* (Shannon; Ireland: Irish University Press Series, Colonies, Canada, 3), Testimony of J. McLaughlin, Questions and Answers Nos. 4969-4973, and of G.O. Corbett, Questions and Answers Nos. 2784-1790.

6. PAC, MG20, D4/100 f. 33, Simpson to Smith, 27 August 1834; *Ibid.*, D4/102, f. 10, Hargrave to Smith, 17 September 1835.

7. D. Gunn and C. Tuttle, *History of Manitoba from the Earliest Settlement*, (Ottawa: 1880), pp. 302-3; A. Ross, *The Red River Settlement: its Rise, Progress and Present Estate* (London: Smith Elder and Co., 1856), pp. 402-3.

8. PAC, MG20, B235/d/230, f. 20; Ross, *The Red River Settlement,* pp. 394-96.

9. The prospectus for the Nor'Wester in 1859 gave the subscription price as $12.00; generally local news and advertisements in the paper gave prices in pounds, shillings and pence but advertisements which originated in Canada or the United States usually used dollars and cents.

10. P. Goldring, "Papers on the Labour System of the Hudson's Bay Company, 1821-1900", *Manuscript Report Series No. 362* (Ottawa: Parks Canada, 1979), P. 21. Accounts in the York Factory district were kept in sterling as late as 1889. PAC, MG20, D25/6, pp. 277-8.

11. *Manitoban,* 12 November 1870, advertisement for exchange; *Manitoban,* 27 April 1872; 39 Victoria C.4, 1876, Canada.
12. *Manitoban,* 12 November 1870, 17 June 1871 and 1 February 1873.
13. Quoted in I. Spry, "The Transition from a Nomadic to a Settled Economy in Western Canada", *Proceedings and Transactions of the Royal Society of Canada,* Fourth Series, Volume 6, June 1968, Section 2, p. 189; Newberry Library, John M. Jones Diary, p. 47, October 1858. I am indebted to Mrs. I. Spry for the reference from the Jones diary.
14. Canada Sessional Papers, 1879, No. 188, Expenditure for the North-West Mounted Police, 1876-7-8, and of all amounts paid to J.G. Baker and Co.
15. D.B. Smith, *The Remiscences of Doctor John Sebastien Helmecken* (Vancouver: University of British Columbia Press, 1975), p. 123; John A. Hussey, *Historic Structure Report, Historical Data, Volume II, Fort Vancouver* (Denver National Parks Service, 1976), p. 60.
16. PAC, MG20, D5/17, ff. 58-66, paragraph 14, Governor to Simpson and Council, 3 April 1846.
17. R.L. Reid, *The Assay Office and Proposed Mint at New Westminster* (British Columbia: King's Printer, 1926), pp. 3 and 30; M.A. Ormsby, *British Columbia: A History* (Toronto: Macmillan of Canada, 1958), p. 93.
18. Reid, *Assay Office,* pp. 44 and 39.
19. Charlton, *Standard Catalogue,* 1978, pp. 226-8, 259, Ross, *History of the Canadian Bank of Commerce,* pp. 258, 272-3.
20. Quoted in Reid, *Assay Office,* p. 31.
21. D.M. Gordon, *Mountain and Prairie: A Journey from Victoria to Winnipeg via Peace River Pass* (Montreal: Dawson Bros., 1880), pp. 12-13.
22. PAC, MG11, CO60, Volume 4, ff. 387-401, Douglas to Bulwer Lytton, 25 May 1859; PAC, RG7, G8C, Volume 7, pp. 152-56, (Colonial Office) to Douglas, 14 March 1859; PAC, MG11, CO64, Volume 1, pp. 164-67.
23. *Op. cit.;* PAC, RG7, G8C, Volume 9, pp. 306-21, Rogers to Douglas, 19 October 1860; *Ibid.,* Volume 7, pp. 152-56, Hamilton to Merivale, 10 March 1859; PAC, MG11, CO60, Volume 4, ff. 531-2, Douglas to Colonial Office, 31 July 1859.
24. Quoted in Reid, *Assay Office,* p.75, *The Columbian,* 22 November 1862.
25. PAC, MG11, CO61, Volume 1, p. 232, Ordinance for Converting Sterling to Decimal Currency; PAC, MG11, CO60, Volume 24, pp. 220-23, Birch to Cardwell, 17 April 1866.
26. PAC, MG11, CO61, Volume 1, pp. 258-59; PAC, MG11, CO60, Volume 29, f. 65, Seymour to Buckingham, 7 September 1867; PAC, MG11, CO64, Volume 10, pp. 166-72.
27. *British Columbian,* 28 September 1864; PAC, MG11, CO64, Volume 5, pp. 146-51.
28. PAC, MG11, CO478, Volumes 1-2, Vancouver Island Blue Books; PAC, MG11, CO64, Volumes 4-8, British Columbia Blue Books.

Appendix A.

1. L.E. Davis and J.R.T. Hughes, "A Dollar Sterling Exchange, 1803-1895", *Economic History Review,* Second Series, XIII (1960-61), pp. 52-78.
2. Between 1821 and 1830 the Bank of Montreal bought government bills at an average rate of £120.79 and merchant's bills at £120.25. Lower Canada, Journals of the Assembly, 1830, Appendix N. See also PAC, RG8, C-322, pp. 206-08, Hale to Hunter, 2 November 1802; PAC, MG13, WO57, Volume 14, Couche to Gordon, 1 January 1811; PAC, MG11, CO47, Volumes 144-45; newspaper market reports.
3. See Davis and Hughes "Dollar Sterling Exchange", pp. 62-64.
4. A.H. Cole, "Seasonal Variations in Sterling Exchange", *Journal of Economic and Business History,* Volume II, 1929-30, pp. 203-218.

5. PAC, MG19, A2, Series 3, Volume 148, p. 280, 16 April 1789; *Ibid.*, Volume 166, 30 October 1792.
6. PAC, MG19, A2, Volume 171, Sundries, 7 September 1799; *Ibid.*, Volume 174, Sundries, 3 June 1805.
7. PAC, RG8, C-322, pp. 151–52, Hale to Green, 13 March 1802.
8. PAC, RG8, C-145, pp. 39–43, Ridout to Routh, 17 February 1832; *Ibid.*, pp. 45–48, Routh to Ridout, 29 February 1832; *Ibid.*, pp. 34–36, Routh to Clegg, 23 March 1832, Volume C-145 contains over 20 reports of bills being sold for British silver, or issued in exchange for services and goods at a premium of 1.5% at the same time that Spanish dollars were being purchased at a rate of about 4s. 0.75d., a premium of 10.7% on the nominal par. No reports have been found after December 1832.
9. Province of Canada, Journals of the Legislative Assembly, 1841, Appendix O.
10. PAC, MG12, Adm. 106, Navy Board Records; PAC, MG40, J2, National Maritime Museum, Greenwich, Halifax Dockyard Records; PAC, MG11, CO217, Volumes 80, pp. 9, 47 and 61; *Ibid.*, Volumes 81, p. 248.
11. PAC, MG13, WO57, Volumes 136–37; PAC, MG40, J2; PAC, MG11, CO221, Volume 42.
12. Craig, *The Mint*, p. 354; Great Britain, Parliamentary Papers, 1831–32, *Report from the Committee of Secrecy on the Bank of England Charter*, Appendix 96 (Irish University Press Reprints).
13. PAC, RG5, A1, Volume 91, pp. 50319–20, Ridout to Gifford, 1 November 1828.
14. Davis and Hughes, "A Dollar Sterling Exchange", Table A-4.
15. PAC, RG8, C-323, p. 22, Hale to Hunter, 3 April 1802.

Appendix B.
1. Chalmers, *Currency in the British Colonies*, pp. 26–27, pp. 424, Treasury Minute of 11 February 1825.
2. PAC, RG4, A1, Volume 299, pp. 19–20, Routh to Couper, 27 January 1830; *Nova Scotian*, 22 March 1826.
3. PAC, MG11, CO42, Volume 209, ff. 295–98, Address of the Legislative Council of Lower Canada to Dalhousie, 18 March 1826; New Brunswick, Assembly Journals, 1 March 1826, Report on Metallic Currency; PAC, MG11, CO188, Volume 33, p. 65, Douglas to Bathurst, 28 March 1826.

Appendix C
1. PAC, MG13, WO34, Volume 44, p. 17v., Treasury Minute of 25 September 1757.
2. PAC, RG8, C-340, pp. 14–24, Memorandum in Kempt to Dalhousie, 24 March 1824.
3. Lower Canada, Journals of the Assembly, 1828–29, Appendices M and Aa; PAC, RG1, E1, Volume 112, ff. 149–61, 14 April 1788; *Ibid.*, Volume 30, ff. 260–68, March 1796; *Ibid.*, Volume 34, pp. 159–66, 10 May 1810.
4. Lower Canada, Journals of the Assembly, 1828–29, Appendix M, Percevall and Scott to Sewell, 28 December 1813 and 15 December 1817; PAC, MG11, CO42, Volume 156, ff. 109–16, Prevost to Bathurst, 18 February 1814; Lower Canada, Journals of the Assembly, 1828–29, Appendix Aa.
5. PAC, MG11, CO217, Volume 139, ff. 190–200, Atcheson to Bathurst, 19 June 1820; *Ibid.*, Volume 148, ff. 53–54, Instructions to customs officers, 20 December 1827; *Ibid.*, ff. 246–52.

Appendix D
1. Montreal *Gazette*, 14 January 1843, Advertisement for William Gunn's *Tables of Exchange*... PAC, RG4, C-1, Volume 101, No. 1375, G. Wickstead to D. Daly, 6 April 1844; Province of Canada, Assembly, Journals, 1841–58, Public Accounts; PAC, MG11, CO47, Volumes 156–72, Blue Books, 1841–56, Currency.
2. PAC, RG8, C-151, pp. 183–84, Departmental Order, 24 June 1842; *Ibid.*, p. 308, General Order, 7 March 1843.

Bibliography

Acadian Recorder.

Acheson, T.W. "The Nature and Structure of York Commerce in the 1820s". *Canadian Historical Review,* Volume 50, 1969, pp. 406–428.

Alexander, James. *A Few Hints on Decimalizing the Currency.* Toronto: Maclear and Co., 1856.

Andrews, Ferdinand H. *Exchange, Stock, Debenture, Interest, Commission and other Commercial Tables.* Quebec: Lovell, 1860.

Balls, H.R. "Quebec, 1763–1774: The Financial Administration". *Canadian Historical Review,* Volume 41, 1960, pp. 203–14.

Bank of Canada. "Pre-Confederation Currency in Canada". *Annual Report,* 1966.

———.*The Story of Canada's Currency,* 1955.

Bank of Nova Scotia. *History of the Bank of Nova Scotia, 1832–1900.*

Becker, J. Richard. *The Decimal Coinage of Nova Scotia, New Brunswick and Prince Edward Island.* Acton, Massachusetts: Beacon Publishing Co., 1975.

Begg, Alexander. *History of the North-West,* Volume 1. Toronto: Hunter Rose and Co., 1894.

Binhamer, H.H. *Money, Banking and the Canadian Financial System.* Toronto: McGraw-Hill Co. of Canada, 1965.

Blake, William. "Observations on the Course of Exchange". In McCulloch, John R. *A Select Collection of Scarce and Valuable Tracts ... on Paper Currency.* London: 1857.

Bonneville, Alphonse. *Encyclopédie Monétaire: ou Nouveau Traite des Monnaies d'Or et d'Argent en Circulation Chez les Divers Peuples du Monde ...* Paris: A. Bonneville, 1849.

Bonnycastle, Sir Richard Henry. *Newfoundland in 1842: A Sequel to "The Canadas in 1841".* London: H. Colburn, 1842.

Bowman, Fred. *A Bibliography of Canadian Numismatics.* Ottawa: Canadian Numismatic Association, 1954.

———.*Decimal Coinage of Canada and Newfoundland,* 1947.

Bradley, Charles. "Coins from *The Auguste*". Work in progress, National Historic Parks and Sites, Parks Canada, Ottawa.

Breckenridge, Roeliff Morton. "The Canadian Banking System, 1817–1890". *Journal of the Canadian Bankers Association* Volume II, 1894–95, pp. 108–196, 267–366, 431–502, 572–660.

———."The History of Banking in Canada". *Publications of the National Monetary Commission,* Volume 9, No. 1. Washington: Government Printing Office, 1910.

———."Paper Currencies of New France". *Journal of Political Economy,* Volume 1, 1893, pp. 406–431.

Breton, P.N. *Illustrated History of Coins and Tokens Relating to Canada.* Montreal: 1894.

Burt, Alfred Leroy. *The Old Province of Quebec.* 2 volumes, with an introduction by H. Neatby. Toronto: McClelland and Stewart, 1968.

Canada, Dominion of. *Canada Sessional Papers,* 1879, No. 188, Expenditures for the North-West Mounted Police, 1876-7-8, and of all amounts paid to J./sic/ G. Baker and Co.

Canada, Lower. Journals of the Assembly, 4 March 1808, p. 228, Report on a Petition to establish a bank.

———.Journals of the Assembly, 1816, Appendix B; 1817, Appendix D; 1818, Appendix C.

———.Journals of the Assembly, 1828-29, Appendix M and Aa.

———.Journals of the Assembly, 1830, Appendix N, Report of a select committee on the application of the Bank of Montreal for a renewal of its charter.

———.Journals of the Assembly, 1830, Appendix Q, Report of a special committee on the currency.

Canada, Province of. Journals of the Legislative Assembly, 1841, Appendix O, Reports of a committee to inquire and report such measures as will most readily equalize the rates of exchange and assimilate the currency throughout the Province.

———.Journals of the Legislative Assembly, 1852-53, Appendix P. Schedule of Despatches Accompanying the Governor General's Message to the Legislative Assembly of 31st August 1852.

Canada, Upper. Journals of the Assembly, 1823, Report of the Banking and Paper Currency Committee.

———.Journals of the Assembly, 1830, Appendix, Report of a Select Committee on the State of the Currency.

———.Journals of the Assembly, 1836, Appendix 72, Report on Currency and Banks.

———.Journals of the Legislative Council, 1837, Appendix A. Second Report of a Select Committee appointed to examine and report upon the measures which it may be most expedient to adopt in consequence of the present commercial difficulties of the province.

———.Journals of the Assembly, 1837-38. Appendix to the 3rd Report on Finance.

Cannan, Edwin, ed. *The Paper Pound of 1797-1821: The Bullion Report of 8 June 1810.* New York: Augustus M. Kelley, 1969.

Carmichael, Neil. *1957 Canadian Coin Catalogue.* Toronto: Carmichael's Stamp and Coin Company, 1956.

Carroll, Sheldon S. "New Brunswick Currency". *Canadian Numismatic Journal,* Volume 15, No. 1, January 1970, pp. 12-15.

Chalmers, Robert. *A History of Currency in the British Colonies.* London: Printed for H.M. Stationery Office by Eyre and Spottiswoode, 1893.

Chapman, Henry Samuel. *Thoughts on the Money and Exchange of Lower Canada.* Montreal: Printed at the Gazette Office, 1832.

Charlton, E.J. *Exchange Tables Reducing Currency into Sterling from a Penny to £5000 Currency, in a Progressive Series of One Quarter Per Centum, from 5 Per Cent. Premium to 14 1/2 Per Cent Premium, and at the Old Par of Exchange ...* Quebec: J. Lovell, 1853.

Charlton, James E. *Standard Catalogue of Canadian Coins, Tokens and Paper Money.* 26th edition. Toronto: Charlton International Publishing Inc., 1978.

———."The Numismatic Treasures of 'Le Chameau'". *Canadian Numismatic Journal,* Volume 21, No. 8, September 1976.

Cole, Arthur H. "Seasonal Variations in Sterling Exchange". *Journal of Economic and Business History,* Volume II, 1929-30, pp. 203-218.

———."Evolution of the Foreign Exchange Market of the United States". *Journal of Economic and Business History,* Volume I, 1928-29, pp. 384-400.

Craig, Isabel. *Economic Conditions in Canada, 1763-83.* M.A. thesis, McGill University, 1937.

Craig, Sir John H.M. *The Mint: A History of the London Mint from A.D. 287 to 1948.* Cambridge: University Press, 1953.

Coppieters, Emmanuel. *English Bank Note Circulation 1694–1954.* Louvain: Institute of Economic and Social Research, The Hague, Martinus Nijhoff, 1955.

Curtis, C.A. "Statistics of Banking". *Statistical Contributions to Canadian Economic History.* Ed. Kenneth W. Taylor. Toronto: The Macmillan Company of Canada, Ltd., 1931.

———."Currency". *Encyclopedia of Canada,* Volume II. Ed. W.S. Wallace. Toronto: University Associates of Canada, 1934–37, pp. 159–67.

Davidson, G.C. *The North West Company.* New York: Russell and Russell, 1967.

Davis, L.E. and Hughes, J.R.T. "A Dollar Sterling Exchange, 1803–1895". *Economic History Review,* Second Series, XIII (1960–61), pp. 52–78.

Dawson, S.E. "Old Colonial Currencies". *Canadian Monthly,* Volume 1, No. 4, April 1872, pp. 326–33.

Dechêne, Louise. *Habitants et Marchands de Montréal au XVIIᵉ Siècle.* Montréal: Librairie Plon, 1974.

Denison, Merrill. *Canada's First Bank: a History of the Bank of Montreal.* 2 volumes. New York: Dodd Mead and Co., 1966–67.

Dewey, Davis Rich. *Financial History of the United States.* 12th ed. New York: Longmans, Green and Co., 1936.

Donovan, Kenneth. *Daily Financial Transactions: Salaries, Wages and the Cost of Purchasing Goods in Louisbourg.* Unpublished manuscript, Fortress of Louisbourg, National Historic Park, 1979.

———.*Inflation at Louisbourg – 1757.* Unpublished Manuscript, Fortress of Louisbourg, National Historic Park, 1980.

(Dutot). *Reflexions Politique Sur les Finances et le Commerce ...* La Haye: Frères-Vaillant et N. Prevost, 1738.

Eccles, William J. "The Social, Economic and Political Significance of the Military in New France". *Canadian Historical Review,* Volume 52, No. 1, March 1971, pp. 1–22.

Einzig, Paul. *The History of Foreign Exchange.* London: Macmillan and Co. Ltd., 1962.

Elliott, James A. *Canadian and Newfoundland Currency.* Toronto: 1954.

Fetter, Frank W. *Development of British Monetary Orthodoxy.* Cambridge, Massachusetts: Harvard University Press, 1965.

Flemming, Horace A. "Halifax Currency". *Nova Scotia Historical Society, Collections,* Volume 20, 1921, pp. 111–137.

Flemming, R. Harvey. "Phyn Ellice and Company of Schenectady". *Contributions to Canadian Economics,* Volume 4, p. 7–41. Toronto: The University Library, published by the Librarian, 1932.

———, Ed. *Minutes of Council, Northern Department of Rupert Land, 1821–31.* Toronto: The Champlain Society, 1940.

Fort Garry *Manitoban.*

Fort Garry *Nor'Wester.*

Fowler, Thomas. *The Journal of a Tour Through British America to the Falls of Niagara ...* Aberdeen: Lewis Smith, 1832.

Frégault, Guy. *La Civilisation de la Nouvelle-France, 1713–1744.* Montréal: Société des Éditions Pascal, 1944.

———.*Le XVIIIᵉ Siècle Canadien; Études.* Montréal: Collections Constantes, Editions HMH, 1968.

Gallatin, Albert. *Considerations on the Currency and Banking Systems of the United States.* Philadelphia: Carey and Lea, 1831.

Gibb, Sir Duncan. "My Early Experiences of Numismatics in Canada". *Canadian Antiquarian and Numismatic Journal,* 1874–75, pp. 67–73.

Gingras, Larry. "Medals and Tokens of the HBC". *The Beaver,* Summer 1968, Oufit 299, pp. 37–43.

————.*Medals, Tokens and Paper Money of The Hudson's Bay Company*. Published under the auspices of The Canadian Numismatic Research Society, 1975.

————.*Paper Money of The Hudson's Bay Company*. Richmond, British Columbia: 1969.

Goldring, Philip. "Papers on the Labour System of The Hudson's Bay Company, 1821-1900". *Manuscript Report Series No. 362*. Ottawa: Parks Canada, 1979.

Gordon, Daniel M. *Mountain and Prairie: A Journey from Victoria to Winnipeg via the Peace River Pass*. Montreal: Dawson Bros., 1880.

Gourlay, Robert Fleming. *Statistical Account of Upper Canada*. Abridged and with an introduction by S.R. Mealing. Toronto: McClelland and Stewart, 1974.

Gray, Hugh. *Letters from Canada, Written During a Residence There in The Years 1806, 1807, and 1808 ...* London: Printed for Longman, Hurst, Rees and Orme, 1809.

Great Britain. Parliamentary Papers. 1857 *Report from the Select Committee on The Hudson's Bay Company: together with the Proceedings of the Committee, Minutes of Evidence, Appendix and Index*. Shannon, Ireland: Irish University Press Series, Colonies, Canada, 3.

————.1831-32 *Report from the Committee of Secrecy on the Bank of England Charter*. Shannon, Ireland: Irish University Press Series, Monetary Policy, General.

Great Britain. Colonial Office. *Currency laws etc. in Force in the Colonies*. London: G.E. Eyre and W. Spottiswoode, 1882.

Guillet, Edwin Clarence. "Pioneer Banking in Ontario; The Bank of Upper Canada, 1822-1866". *The Canadian Banker*, Volume 55, Winter 1948, pp. 114-32.

Gunn, Donald and Tuttle, Charles. *History of Manitoba from the Earliest Settlement*. Ottawa: 1880.

Gunn, William. *Tables of Exchange on Britain ... above the new par of 24s4d currency per 20s sterling*. Montreal: Armour and Ramsay.

Gwyn, Julian. "British Government Spending and the North American Colonies, 1740-1775". *Journal of Imperial and Commonwealth Studies*, Volume 7, No. 2, January 1980, pp. 74-84.

————."The Impact of British Military Spending on the Colonial American Money Markets, 1760-1783". *Canadian Historical Association*, Historical Papers, 1980, pp. 77-100.

Halifax *British Colonist*.

Halifax *Chronicle*.

Halifax *Journal*.

Halifax *Morning Chronicle*.

Halifax *Nova Scotian*.

Hamelin, Jean. *Economie et Société en Nouvelle-France*. Les Presses Universitaires Laval, 1960.

————."A la recherche d'un cours monétaire canadien, 1760-77". *Revue Historique de l'Amérique Française*, Volume 15, 1961-62, pp. 24-34.

Hammond, Bray. "Banking in Canada Before Confederation, 1792-1867". *Approaches to Canadian Economic History; a Selection of Essays*. Ed. W.T. Easterbrook and M.H. Watkins. Toronto: McLelland and Stewart, 1967.

Hepburn, A. Barton. *A History of Currency in the United States*. New York: Augustus M. Kelley, 1967.

Heriot, George. *Travels Through The Canadas, Containing a Description of the Picturesque Scenery...* London: R. Phillips, 1807.

Hincks, Sir Francis. "Dominion Notes and Currency". *Canadian Antiquarian and Numismatic Journal*, Volume III, No. 2, July 1874, pp. 16-18.

Howard, Clifford S. "Canadian Banks and Banknotes: A Record". *The Canadian Banker*, Volume 57, Winter 1950, pp. 30-66.

Hudson's Bay Company Archives.

Hussey, John A. *Historic Structure Report, Historical Data, Volume II, Fort Vancouver.* Denver: National Parks Service, 1976.

Innis, H.A. and Lower, A.R.M. *Selected Documents in Canadian Economic History, 1783-1885.* Toronto: University of Toronto Press, 1933.

Jamieson, A.B. *Chartered Banking in Canada.* Toronto: Ryerson Press, 1955.

Kelly, Patrick. *The Universal Cambist and Commercial Instructor: being a Full and Accurate Treatise on the Exchanges, Monies, Weights, and Measures of all Trading Nations and Their Colonies...* London: Lackington, 1831.

Keyes, John. "Un Commis des Trésoriers Généraux de la Marine à Québec – Nicolas Lanoullier de Boisclerc". *Revue d'Histoire de l'Amérique Française,* Volume 32, No. 2, Septembre 1978, pp. 181-202.

Laughlin, J. Lawrence. *The History of Bimetallism in the United States.* New York: D. Appleton and Co., 1895.

Leblanc, François. *Traite Historique de Monnaies de France.* Amsterdam: Chez Pierre Mortier, 1692.

Legislative records of the various colonies in addition to those specifically cited.

Lower, Arthur R.M. "Credit and the Constitutional Act". *Canadian Historical Review,* Volume 6, No. 2, June 1925, pp. 123-141.

Lloyd, Samuel Jones (Baron Overstone). *Tracts and Other Publications on Metallic and Paper Currency.* London: Longman and Co., 1858.

Lunn, Alice Jean E. *Economic Development in New France.* Ph.D. thesis, McGill University, 1942.

McCullough, A.B. "Currency Conversion in British North America". *Archivaria,* Volume 16, Summer 1983, pp. 183-94.

———. "Aaron Hart's Treasure: A Sample of Late Eighteenth Coinage in Lower Canada". *The Canadian Numismatic Journal,* Volume 28, No. 1, January 1983, pp. 8-12.

———. "Canadian Sterling Bill of Exchange Rates, 1760-1899". Unpublished paper presented at the 13th Conference on Quantitative Methods in Canadian Economic History, Wilfrid Laurier University, 16-17 March 1984, Table 2.

McCusker, John J. *Money and Exchange in Europe and America, 1660-1775: A Handbook.* Williamsburg: Institute of Early American History and Culture, 1978.

McIvor, R. Craig. *Canadian Monetary, Banking and Financial Development.* Toronto: Macmillan and Co., 1958.

McLachlan, Robert W. "Annals of the Nova Scotian Currency". *Transactions of the Royal Society of Canada,* 1892, Section II, pp. 33-68.

———. *Statistics of the Coinage for Canada and Newfoundland.* 1890.

———. "The Copper Currency of the Canadian Banks, 1837-57". *Transactions of the Royal Society of Canada,* 1903, Section II, pp. 217-72.

———. *The Copper Tokens of Canada.* New York: The American Numismatic Society, 1916.

———. "The Nova Scotia Treasury Notes". *Canadian Antiquarian and Numismatic Journal,* Series 3, Volume 1, No. 2, April 1898, pp. 49-62.

———. "Some Reflections Upon Being Fifty Years a Coin Collector". *Canadian Numismatic Journal,* Volume 6, No. 12, December 1961, pp. 516-18.

Macmechan, Archibald M., ed. *Nova Scotia Archives II, A Calendar of Two Letterbooks and One Commission Book in the Possession of the Government of Nova Scotia.* Halifax: 1900.

———. *Nova Scotia Archives III, Original Minutes of His Majesty's Council at Annapolis Royal, 1720-1739.* Halifax: 1908.

McQuade, Ruth "Halifax Currency in Nova Scotia". *The Canadian Numismatic Journal,* Volume 21, No. 10, November 1976, pp. 399-402.

MacTaggart, John. *Three Years in Canada: An Account of the Actual State of the Country in 1826-7-8.* London: H. Colburn, 1829.

315

Martell, James Stuart. *A Documentary Study of Provincial Finance and Currency, 1812–36.* Bulletin of the Public Archives of Nova Scotia, Volume 2, No. 4, 1941.

Masters, Donald Campbell Charles. "The Establishment of Decimal Currency in Canada". *Canadian Historical Review,* Volume 33, June 1952, pp. 129–47.

Michell, H. "The Gold Standard in the Nineteenth Century". *Canadian Journal of Economics and Political Science,* Volume 17, No. 3, August 1951, pp. 369–376.

Monetary Times.

Montreal *Courier.*

Montreal *Gazette.*

Montreal *Herald.*

Montreal *Transcript.*

Moogk, Peter N. "A Pocketful of Change at Louisbourg". *Canadian Numismatic Journal,* Volume 21, No. 3, March 1976, pp. 97–104.

Moore, Christopher. "The Other Louisbourg: Trade and Merchant Enterprise in Ile Royale, 1713–58". *Histoire Sociale-Social History,* Volume 12, No. 23, May 1979, pp. 79–96.

Moorsom, William Scarth. *Letters From Nova Scotia: Comprising the Sketches of a Young Country.* London: H. Colburn and R. Bentley, 1830.

Nettels, Curtis Puttnam. *Money Supply of the American Colonies Before 1720.* Madison, Wisconsin: 1934.

Neufeld, E.P. *Money and Banking in Canada: Historical Documents and Commentary.* Toronto: McClelland and Stewart Limited, 1964. The Carleton Library No. 17.

———.*The Financial System of Canada: Its Growth and Development.* Toronto: Macmillan, 1972.

New Brunswick. Journal of the Assembly 21 February 1845, p. 140.

———.Journal of the Legislative Council, 1862, pp. 24–30.

Newfoundland *Public Ledger.*

Nova Scotia. Journals of the House of Assembly, 1839, Appendix No. 58, Report of a Select Committee on Currency.

———.Journals of the House of Assembly, 1851–52, Appendix 14.

———.Journals of the Legislative Assembly, 1853, Appendix 25, Copy of a Treasury minute dated June 29th 1852.

Nova Scotia *Royal Gazette.*

Noxon, W.J., ed. *The Diary of Nicholas Garry, Deputy Governor of The Hudson's Bay Company.* Toronto: Canadiana House, 1973.

Nussbaum, Arthur. *A History of the Dollar.* New York: Columbia University Press, 1957.

Officer, Lawrence H. "Dollar-Sterling Mint Parity, Exchange Rates 1791–1834". *Journal of Economic History,* Volume 43, No. 3, September 1983, pp. 579–616.

Ormsby, Margaret A. *British Columbia: A History.* Toronto: Macmillan of Canada, 1958.

Ouellet, Fernand. *Histoire Économique et Sociale du Québec, 1760–1850.* Montreal: Fides, 1966.

Public Archives of Canada (PAC). Annual Report, 1913, Appendix E, *Ordinances Made for the Province of Quebec, by the Governor and Council of the Said Province since the Establishment of Civil Government until 1767,* pp. 45–86.

———.Annual Report, 1914, Appendix C, *Ordinances Made for the Province of Quebec by the Governor and Council of the Said Province from 1768 until 1791 ...*

———.Annual Report, 1918, Appendix B, *Ordinances and Proclamations of the Règne Militaire,* pp. 15–208.

———.MG1, Archives des Colonies, C11A, Correspondence, Volume 47.

———.MG9, A1, New Brunswick Executive Council, Volumes 56–85.

————.MG11, Colonial Office. See correspondence received from all the British North American Colonies, correspondence sent and colonial legislation series. See especially the Miscellaneous series for Blue Books from 1821 on.

————.MG12, Admiralty 106, Navy Board Records, Volumes 2027-2030.

————.MG13, War Office 34, Amherst Papers.

————.MG13, War Office 57, Commissariat Department, In Letters.

————.MG14, Audit Office 3, Accounts, Various, Bundle 120.

————.MG15, Treasury 28, Treasury Board Out-Letters Various.

————.MG15, Treasury 64, Miscellanea, Volumes 101-105, 113, 115.

————.MG19, A2, Ermatinger Papers.

————.MG19, A3, Askin Papers, Volume 61, Account Book.

————.MG19, A5, McTavish, Frobisher and Company, Volumes 1 and 2, Journals of the seigneury of Terrebonne.

————.MG19, B5, Phyn and Ellice.

————.MG19, E7, John Inkster.

————.MG20, Hudson's Bay Company Papers.

————.MG21, Haldimand Papers.

————.MG23, D2, Edward Winslow.

————.MG23, H1, I, John Graves Simcoe, Series 3, Book 11, Public Accounts, U.C.

————.MG23, I 13, Joshua Sharpe Papers, Volume 2.

————.MG23, M3, Newman Hunt and Company.

————.MG24, A12, Dalhousie Papers, Nos 276-286, Reel A-533.

————.MG24, D16, Isaac Buchanan, Volumes 82-87, Accounts; Volumes 88-90, Prices Current.

————.MG28, II, 2a, Bank of Montreal Minute Books.

————.MG29, E67, John Balmer.

————.MG30, D101, Adam Shortt Papers, Volumes 8-10, 40-50, 54 and 56. Notes on banking and currency.

————.MG40, J2, National Maritime Museum, Greenwich, Halifax Dockyard Records.

————.RG1, E1, Minute Books, Quebec and Lower Canada.

————.RG1, E12, Volume 9, Letterbook of Montreal customs officials to the Commissioner of Customs 1832-43.

————.RG1, E15A, Board of Audit of the Provincial Accounts, Quebec and Lower Canada, Volumes 1-48.

————.RG4, A1, "S" Series, Civil Secretary's Correspondence.

————.RG4, C1, Provincial Secretary, Canada East, Numbered Correspondence.

————.RG7, Governor General's Office, G1, Despatches from the Colonial Office.

————.RG7, G8, Records from the Lieutenant Governor's offices.

————.RG8, British Military Records, "C" Series, especially Volumes 102-104, "Command, Money"; Volumes 105-163, "Commissariat"; and Volumes 320-343, "Military Chest".

Paint, Henry M. "Early Banking in Nova Scotia". *The Canadian Banker*, Volume 68, No. 1, Spring 1956, pp. 92-97.

Pargellis, Stanley McRoy. *Military Affairs in North America 1748-65: Selected Documents from the Cumberland Papers in Windsor Castle.* Hamden, Connecticut: Archon Books, 1969.

Patterson, Edward Lloyd Stewart. *Banking Practice and Foreign Exchange.* New York: Alexander Hamilton Institute, 1914.

————.*Canadian Banking.* Toronto: Ryerson, 1932.

————.*Foreign Exchange Arithmetic.* Toronto: Shaw Schools Ltd., 1927.

————.*Notes on Foreign Exchange and a Financial Glossary.* Toronto: Shaw Correspondence School, 1916.

Patterson, Stewart L. "Sterling Exchange". *Journal of the Canadian Bankers Association*, Volume 11, 1903-04, pp. 231-250.

(**Pennington, James**). *The Currency of the British Colonies*. London: Her Majesty's Stationery Office, 1848.

Perkins, Edward J. "Foreign Interest Rates in American Financial Markets: A Revised Series of Dollar-Sterling Exchange Rates, 1835–1900", *Journal of Economic History*, Volume 38, No. 2, June 1978, pp. 392–417.

Petrie, A.E.H. "Documents Relating to Currency, Exchange and Finance in Canada, 1765–1767". *Transactions of the Canadian Numismatic Research Society*, January 1973, pp. 1–25.

Prince Edward Island. Journals of the House of Assembly, 1848. Appendix 1.

———.Journals of the House of Assembly, 1853, Appendix N.

———.Journals of the House of Assembly, 1854, Appendix G.

———.Journals of the House of Assembly, 1872, Appendix X.

———.Journals of the Legislative Council, 1843, Appendix 11.

———.Journals of the Legislative Council, 1846, Appendix 1.

———.Journals of the Legislative Council, 1847, No. 5, Report of the Currency Commission.

———.Journals of the Legislative Council, 1853, Appendix 1 and 17.

Prince Edward Island. Executive Council Minutes. "Prince Edward Island Holey Dollar". *Canadian Numismatic Journal*, Volume 16, No. 4, April 1971, p. 126.

Prince Edward Island *Examiner.*

Prince Edward Island *Times.*

Proulx, Jean-Pierre. *Histoire et naufrage des navires Le Saphire, La Marguerite, Le Murinet et L'Auguste.* Ottawa: Parcs Canada, Travail inédit, v. 337, 1979.

Public Archives of Nova Scotia (PANS). RG1, Volume 20.

Quebec *Gazette.*

Quebec *Mercury.*

Raymond, R. "Valeur Monétaire de la Livre Française". *Mémoires de la Société Généalogique Canadienne Française*, Volume 19, No. 2, Avril-juin 1968, p. 97.

Redish, Angela. "The Economic Crisis of 1837–39 in Upper Canada: Case Study of a Temporary Suspension of Specie Payments". Department of Economics, University of British Columbia, Discussion Paper No. 83-04, March 1983.

———.*The Optimal Supply of Bank Money: Upper Canada's Experience on and off the Specie Standard.* Ph.D. Thesis, Department of Economics, University of Western Ontario, 1982.

———."Why Was Specie Scarce in Colonial Economies? An Analysis of the Canadian Currency, 1796–1820". Department of Economics, University of British Columbia, Discussion Paper No. 83-22.

Reid, Robie Lewis. *The Assay Office and Proposed Mint at New Westminster.* British Columbia: King's Printer, 1926.

Rich, Edwin Ernest, and Johnston, A.M. *London Correspondence Inward from Eden Colville, 1849–52.* London: Hudson's Bay Record Society, 1956.

Ringer, Jim. *Underwater Archaeological Excavation of the Auguste Site, Nova Scotia.* Unpublished manuscript, National Historic Parks and Sites, 1977–78.

Rochefoucault-Liancourt, François, duc de la. *Travels Through the United States of North America, the country of the Iroquois, and Upper Canada, in the Years 1795, 1796 and 1797; with an authentic Account of Lower Canada.* London: R. Phillips, 1799.

Ross, Alexander. *The Red River Settlement: Its Rise, Progress and Present Estate.* London: Smith Elder and Co., 1856.

Ross, Victor W. *A History of the Canadian Bank of Commerce...* 3 Volumes. Toronto: Oxford University Press, 1920.

Rowe, C.F. "The Coins and Currency of Newfoundland". *Book of Newfoundland.* Volume 3. St. John's: Newfoundland Book Publishers (1967) Ltd., 1979, pp. 503-518.

318

Rowley, J.W.H. "Old Currencies in Nova Scotia". *Journal of the Canadian Bankers Association,* Volume II, 1894–95, pp. 413–424.

Ruding, Rogers. *Annals of The Coinage of Britain and its Dependencies, from the Earliest Period... to the end of the Fiftieth Year... of George III.* London: Nicols, Son and Bentley, 1817–19.

St. John's *Newfoundlander.*

Samuelson, Paul A. and Kroos, Herman E. *Documentary History of Banking and Currency in the United States.* 4 Volumes. New York: McGraw Hill and Chelsea House Publications, 1969.

Schull, Joseph, and Gibson, James Douglas. *The Scotiabank Story: A History of the Bank of Nova Scotia, 1832–1982,* Toronto: Macmillan of Canada, 1982.

Shortt, Adam. "Canadian Currency and Exchange Under French Rule". *Journal of the Canadian Bankers Association,* Volume 5, 1897–98, pp. 271–90, 385–401. Volume 6, 1898–99, pp. 1–22, 147–165, 233–47.

———.*Documents Relatifs à la Monnaie, au Change et aux Finances du Canada sous le Régime Français.* 2 volumes. Ottawa: F. Acland, 1925.

———.*Documents Relating to Currency Exchange and Finance in Nova Scotia with Prefatory Documents, 1675–1758.* Ottawa: King's Printer, 1933.

———.The Early History of Canadian Banking". *Journal of the Canadian Bankers Association,* Volume 4, 1896–97, pp. 1–19, 129–44, 235–252, 341–360; Volume 5, 1897–98, pp. 1–21; Volume 7, 1899–1900, pp. 209–226.

———."The History of Canadian Currency, Banking and Exchange". *Journal of the Canadian Bankers Association,* Volume 7, 1899–1900, pp. 209–26, 311–32; Volume 8, 1900–01, pp. 1–15, 146–64, 227–243, 305–26; Volume 9, 1901–02, pp. 1–21, 102–21, 183–202, 271–89; Volume 10, 1902–03, pp. 21–40, 125–45, 211–28, 312–29; Volume 11, 1903–04, pp. 13–30, 106–23, 199–218, 308–327; Volume 12, 1904–05, pp. 14–35, 192–216, 264–282.

———.*The History of Canadian Metallic Currency.* Toronto: Transactions of the Canadian Institute, 1912.

Shortt, Adam, and Doughty, A.G., eds. "Currency and Banking". *Canada and its Provinces: A History of the Canadian People and Their Institutions.* Volume 4. Printed by T.A. Constable at the University of Edinburgh Press for the Publishers Association of Canada, 1913.

Smith, D.B., ed. *The Reminiscences of Doctor John Sebastian Helmecken.* Vancouver: University of British Columbia Press, 1975.

Spearman, James M. *The Colonial Cambist; or Tables of the Assay or Finances, Weight, and Sterling Value of Foreign Coins Circulating, by Authority, in the British Possessions in North America and the West Indies.* London: Parker, Furnival and Parker, 1844.

Spry, Irene M. "The Transition from a Nomadic to a Settled Economy in Western Canada". *Proceedings and Transactions of the Royal Society of Canada,* Fourth Series, Volume 6, June 1968, Section 2, pp. 187–202.

Statutes of the Various Colonies.

Stevenson, James. "The Circulation of Army Bills with some Remarks Upon the War of 1812". *Transactions of the Literary and Historical Society of Quebec.* No. 21, 1891–92, pp. 1–79.

———."The Currency of Canada after the Capitulation". *Transactions of the Literary and Historical Society of Quebec.* (No. 12), 1876–77, pp. 109–134.

———*The Card Currency of Canada During the French Domination.* Quebec: Printed by Middleton and Dawson, 1875.

Stewart, Donald M. "Trade Tokens of Alberta". *Canadian Numismatic Association Journal,* Volume 6, No. 2, February 1961, pp. 63–73.

Stirling, W.E. *Tables For the Conversion of Halifax Currency into Canadian Currency Calculated from 1 to 100 cents and $1 to $1,000,000.* Halifax: Joseph C. Crossill, 1871.

Summer, William Graham. "The Spanish Dollar and the Colonial Shilling". *American Historical Review,* Volume 3, No. 4, July 1898, pp. 607–619.

———.*A History of American Currency with Chapters on the English Bank Restriction and Austrian Paper Money.* New York: H. Holt and Company, 1874.

Taylor, C. James. "The Bank of Upper Canada". Historic Sites and Monuments Board of Canada, November 1979, Agenda Paper.

Trudel, Marcel. *Le Régime Militaire dans le Gouvernement des Trois-Rivières, 1760–1764.* Trois-Rivières: Editions du Bien Public, 1952.

———.*Introduction to New France.* Toronto: Holt, Rinehart and Winston, 1968.

Turk, S. *Some Notes on Foreign Exchange in Canada.* File in the Bank of Canada Library.

Walker, Byron Edmund. *A History of Banking in Canada.* Toronto: 1899. Reprinted from *A History of Banking in All Nations,* Volume 3, ed. by W.G. Summer. Journal of Commerce and Commercial Bulletin: 1899.

Weiss, Roger W. "The Issue of Paper Money in the Colonies, 1720–1774". *Journal of Economic History,* Volume 30, No. 4, 1970, pp. 770–84.

Wiley, R.C. "The Coins of Canada". *Canadian Numismatic Association Journal.* Volume 5, No. 6, June 1960. Continued in Nos. 7, 8, 9, 10, and 11.

———."The Use of Spanish Coins in Canada". *Transactions of the Canadian Numismatic Research Society,* Volume 12, No. 3, July 1976, pp. 62–82.

———."Proclamation Money in Canada". *Canadian Numismatic Journal,* Volume 21, No. 9, October 1976, pp. 371–75.

———."A Canadian Numismatic Dictionary". *Canadian Numismatic Journal,* Volume 16, Nos. 6–7, July-August 1971.

———."French Coins in Canada in 1725". *Canadian Numismatic Journal,* Volume 21, No. 8, September 1976, pp. 310–11.

Zay, E. *Histoire Monétaire des Colonies Françaises: D'après le Documents Officiels avec 278 Figures.* Paris: 1892.

320

Index

Acquits 46, 48-9, 124
Agricultural Bank 98, 99
Alloway and Champion 234
Army bills 83-5
Army sterling 68, 93, 286-87

Baker, I.G., and Company 235
Bank notes 23
Bank notes, American 77-8, 85, 89
Bank notes, controls on 86, 98-9, 113-14, 153, 154, 173, 199, 213-14, 243
Bank notes, denominations 88, 154-55, 172, 239
Bank notes in circulation 98, 114, 115-17, 172, 173, 182-83, 218 See also: Circulation, estimates of
Bank of B.C. 239, 242
Bank of British North America 98, 99, 172, 210, 214, 239, 242
Bank of Canada 86, 88
Bank of England suspension 81, 252-53
Bank of England tokens 189-90, 191, 209, 211
Bank of Montreal 86, 88, 91, 98, 101-02, 112, 113, 223, 234, 235
Bank of New Brunswick 172
Bank of N.S. 152-53, 154-55, 223
Bank of P.E.I. 198
Bank of the People 98, 99
Bank of Upper Canada (Kingston) 86, 88
Bank of Upper Canada (York) 86, 88, 98, 100, 102
Bank tokens 101-02
Banks 78, 85-8, 137, 142, 172-73, 214-15, 234, 242-43, 247 See also: individual banks
Banque du Peuple 98, 99, 101-02
Barter 77, 154, 189, 207, 228, 236
Betts Cove Mining Company 222
Bills of exchange 46-8, 50, 68, 69, 74, 81-3, 92, 128, 146, 165, 191, 208, 230-31, 252-55 See also: Exchange rate
Bons 71-2, 76-7, 100, 142-43, 145, 172, 199, 208-09, 221-22, 247
Bowring Brothers 222
British monetary reform 261
British silver introduced 92-5, 146-49, 170, 209
Brock token 90
Bullion, defined 17

Cambium mintum 18-9
Cambium per litteras 18-9, 20, 251
Canadian money of account 68, 229

Card money 35-40, 45-52, 123, 246
Carswell, S.H. 235
Central Bank of New Brunswick 172, 173
City Bank (N.B.) 172
City Bank of Montreal 98
Circulating medium, composition of 52-3, 71, 75, 101-03, 108, 123, 126, 127-28, 153-55, 163, 175-77, 209, 211, 216, 239, 248
Circulation, estimates of 45, 74, 88-9, 115-17, 133, 158-59, 182-83, 191, 197, 202-04, 214, 233, 244 See also: Bank notes in circulation
Charlotte County Bank 172, 173
Coins: See specific types
Coins, clipped 73
Coins, cutting 71, 131
Coins, debased 17, 73, 79, 91, 101-03, 105, 136, 171, 173-74, 199, 211 See also Merchant's tokens
Coins, defined 17
Coins, importance of 31
Coins, rating of adjusted 30, 32, 33, 40-4, 67-8, 69, 74-6, 78-9, 93, 108, 128-29, 137-38, 148-49, 208-09, 249 See also: Currency legislation; Money of account inflated
Coins, shortage of 21-2, 33, 34, 38, 45, 76-8, 128, 136, 142-43, 164, 166-67, 188, 207, 221, 246
Coins, sources of 32, 34, 40-1, 45, 50, 68-9, 74, 81-3, 124-25, 127-28, 129, 134, 138, 207, 210, 232-33, 235, 238, 246
Coins, sweated 73
Coins, token 17, 208
Coins, post revolutionary French 90-1
Coins, provincial 33, 108-10, 114, 143, 145, 155, 156, 174, 178-79, 199, 201, 208, 215, 220-21, 238
Colonial Bank 112
Commercial Bank (N.B.) 172
Commercial Bank of Newfoundland 214, 222
Commercial Bank of the Midland District 98, 100
Commodity money 33, 188 See also: Made beaver
Connell, J.M. and C. 172
Crown, British 79, 94, 135, 148, 149, 170, 174, 179, 191, 200, 209, 237, 241
Crown, French 67, 71, 75, 79, 91, 103, 128-29, 164, 177, 260 See also: Écu d'argent
Cunard notes 154, 172, 199
Customs currency 93, 147, 287-88

Currency systems: See army sterling; Canadian money of account; customs currency; decimal notation; Halifax currency; monnoye du pays; New England currency; Newfoundland currency; Newfoundland sterling; Northwest currency; Quebec currency; sterling; York currency

Currency legislation 67-8, 74-6, 78-81, 90-2, 95-7, 103-04, 108-10, 114, 130, 135-36, 149-51, 156-57, 164-66, 168-70, 174-78, 189-90, 195-97, 210-12, 215-19, 223, 237-38, See also: Coins, rating of adjusted

Dardenne 126
Decimal notation introduced 103, 108-10, 156-57, 178-79, 200-02, 219-21, 233, 237, 241-42, 249-50
Decimal notation used 106-07, 166, 229
Demarrara tokens 173
Deniers 30, 33
Depreciation of currency 50-1, 84-5, 132-33, 141-42, 192-94, See also: Inflation
Devaluation used to attract coinage 21-2, 108
Discount, defined 20
Dollar 92, 94, 103, 124, 129, 136, 143-44, 164, 170-71, 195-96, 219, 248
Dollar counterstamped 34, 189
Dollar, holey 190-91
Dollar, intrinsic value of 260, 282-85
Dollar, Spanish and Spanish American 34, 68, 74, 94, 126, 130, 150-51, 156, 168-70, 174, 188, 191-92, 201, 208-09, 210-11, 216, 221, 236-37
Dollar, U.S. 78, 105, 108, 151, 168, 169, 174, 200-01, 211, 220, 242
Dominion notes 112-13, 181, 201, 233, 234, 242, 247
Doubloons 137-38, 143-45, 147-49, 156, 165, 168-70, 174, 177, 191, 193, 195-96, 201, 212, 216-17, 219

Eagle 96, 103, 105, 108, 165, 168, 169, 174, 175, 177, 178, 179, 195-96, 200-01, 216-17, 219, 237, 241
Écu d'argent 73, 79, 126 See also: Crown, French; Louis d'argent; Escu blanc
Écu d'or 29, 30, 43 See also: Louis d'or
Ermatinger, Lawrence 82
Escu blanc 30
Exchange rate 83, 85, 133, 134, 138, 144, 147, 166-67, 193, 200, 208, 219, 237, 243-44, 266-81 See also: Bills of exchange; Par
Exchange rate determinants 19, 20-1, 52-5

Farmer's Bank 98, 99
Farmer's Bank of Rustico 199
Fish penny 173
Fitzpatrick, Mr. 199
Five franc piece 90-2, 169-70, 177, 195, 201, 216
Florin 201, 237, 240-41, 242
Forty franc piece 90-1
Forgery 35-6, 84, 102, 145
Forsyth, Richardson and Co. 82

Gordon, Adamson and Company 234
Gore Bank 98
Government notes 77, 107, 131, 133-34 See also: Dominion notes; treasury notes
Grand Portage currency See: North West currency
Greenbacks 111, 233
Guinea 67, 78, 96, 136, 164, 165, 177

Halifax Banking Company 145, 152-53, 154-55, 223
Halifax currency 19, 67, 72, 74-6, 92, 103, 105-06, 130-31, 144, 156, 189, 208-09, 229, 246
Hasyard, James (Henry) 199
Hiaqua 236
Hudson's Bay company notes 230-32, 246
Hoards 49, 51, 67, 163, 189

Inflation 38, 40, 48, 50, 200, 247
International Bank 112

Johannes 68, 73, 78, 164, 165, 169, 177

Lafferty and Smith 235
Legal tender 18
Lester and Co. 82
Liards 30, 33, 126
Lis d'argent 32
Livre of account 29
Louis d'argent 30, 41, 44 See also: Crown, French; Écu d'argent
Louis d'or 30, 41, 43, 67, 126, 165, 170, 177 See also: Écu d'or

Macdonald, Alex 235
Macdonald and Co. 239, 242-43
McArthur and Martin 234
McDonald and Co. 235
McGill, James and Andrew 82
McMicken, A. 234
Made beaver 229-30, 236
Massachusetts currency: See New England currency
Mercantilism 31
Merchant's Bank of Canada 234
Merchant's Bank of P.E.I. 204

Merchant's tokens 89-90, 211, 214, 230, 235, 247 See also: Coins, debased
Mint in B.C. 238
Monetary weights 293
Moidore 73, 78, 165
Money, definitions 17-8
Money of account: See Currency systems
Money of account, inflated 30-1, 246 See also: Monnoye du pays
Money, paper 18, 22 See also: Army bills; Bank notes; Bons; Card money; Dominion notes; Government notes; Treasury notes
Monnoye du pays 30-1, 40, 123, 126, 246 See: Money of account
Municipal notes 100, 171

Napoleon 20 franc piece 90-1, 170, 177, 201
New England currency 126-27, 128, 130
Newfoundland currency 209-10, 218-19
Newfoundland sterling 209-10, 218-19
New France, finances 32, 34-5, 36, 44-5, 48
New York currency 67 See also: York currency
Niagara Suspension Bridge Bank 98, 99
Northwest currency 229
Nova Scotia finances 131

Ontario Bank 234
Ordinances de paiement 45 See also: acquits

Panic of 1837 99-100, 155, 173
Par 19, 105-06, 144, 149-51, 180-81, 188, 193, 197, 247, 249, 289-92
Patagons, Spanish 34
People's Bank (N.B.) 173
Phyn, Ellice and Company 82
Piastre 211
Pistareen 71, 75, 79, 95, 131, 170, 177
Pistolle, French 81, 165
Pistolle, Spanish 29, 34
Premium, defined 20
Province notes. See: Dominion notes; treasury notes; treasury warrants

Quart d'écu 29, 32, 43
Quebec Bank 86, 88, 102
Quebec currency 69-73
Queen Anne's proclamation 70

Reale See: Dollar, Spanish
Recoinage in France 30, 40-4
Reid contracting Company 222
Rents in P.E.I. 195, 197-98
Rutherford, I. and S. 211

Saint Stephen's Bank 172
Shilling 75, 103, 124, 135, 149, 174, 175, 179, 191, 193, 201, 209, 211, 237
Shilling, Spanish 218
Ships – *Auguste* 52
Ships – *Chameau* 45
Silver, market price 261, 297 note 9
Silver/gold price ratio 19, 76, 78, 96, 103, 136, 138, 218
Smith, Benjamin 172
Sol marqué 30, 67, 126
Sovereign 96, 103, 149, 150, 156, 168, 169, 174, 175, 177, 179, 193, 195-96, 200, 209, 211, 212, 215-16, 219, 237, 240-41
Sovereign, Australian 239
Specie, defined 17
Sterling 29, 73, 127, 229, 233, 237, 249
Stiver 173, 211
Summerside Bank 199
Suspension of payments 8, 88 See also: Panic of 1837

"Trade and Navigation" tokens 173
Treasury notes 131-35, 139-42, 145-46, 147, 151-53, 154, 155, 157, 166-68, 172, 188-89, 191-92, 193-95, 198, 201, 212-13, 238-39, 246 See also: Government notes
Treasury warrants 191, 194-95, 198, 200

Union Bank of Newfoundland 214, 222
Union Bank (P.E.I.) 198
U.S. Currency reform 95-6, 107-08
U.S. silver, abundance of 111-12

Wellington token 89-90
Wells, Fargo and Company 239, 242
Westmoreland Bank 173
Williams, G.F. 172

York currency 72, 91-2, 229 See also: New York currency